Writing *Huck Finn*

Writing *Huck Finn*

Mark Twain's Creative Process

Victor A. Doyno

University of Pennsylvania Press

Philadelphia

818.09
TWA
DOY

Mark Twain's previously unpublished words quoted here are © 1991 by Edward J. Willi and
Manufacturers Hanover Trust Company as Trustees of the Mark Twain Foundation, which
reserves all reproduction or dramatization rights in every medium. Quotation is made with the
permission of the University of California Press and Dr. Robert H. Hirst, General Editor of
the Mark Twain Project. Each quotation is identified by an asterisk (*).

Library of Congress Cataloging-in-Publication Data
Doyno, Victor, 1937–
   Writing Huck Finn : Mark Twain's creative process / Victor A. Doyno.
     p.   cm.
   Includes bibliographical references and index.
   ISBN 0-8122-3087-6 (cloth)
   ISBN 0-8122-1448-X (pbk)
   1. Twain, Mark, 1835–1910. Adventures of Huckleberry Finn.   2. Creation (Literary,
artistic, etc.)   I. Title.
PS1305.D69   1991
813'.54—dc20
                                                                      91-25114
                                                                         CIP

This book is dedicated to my wife's family and my family, including those Bohemian, Irish, English, and Italian emigrants who became immigrants. Accordingly, this book also honors the complex processes which make our children individualized Americans.

Contents

THE QUESTION OF UNITY

List of Illustrations

Preface

Why is Mark Twain's *Adventures of Huckleberry Finn* such a fascinating, challenging book? Why do generations of Americans fall in love with this novel? Both scholar-critics and the general public have developed a complex attitude of love, enthusiasm, disappointment, and puzzled respect toward this masterpiece. This study began with curiosity about a beloved—but sometimes disappointing—masterpiece. As I have read the book repeatedly, for over thirty-five years, my understanding has grown. Now friends and civilized enemies who have read pre-publication versions of this book state, happily or grudgingly, that this study "solves" or resolves the ending of *Huck*.

Is it possible to say or think anything new about *Huck*? Yes, if we explore four relatively unstudied resources. The most important changes in understanding occurred for me about twenty years ago when I started to examine closely Twain's famous manuscript version. This portion of the manuscript, now in the Buffalo and Erie County Public Library, corresponds to about 55 percent of the novel and preserves valuable evidence about this era of Twain's best artistic achievement. Prior to 1883, Twain had written much less than half of the book. Then in 1883 and 1884, in a period of extraordinary energy and concentration, he completed the novel. In this relatively short period, he composed more than 23 chapters and, with pen and with pencil, revised the manuscript at least three times before getting it typed. He also revised his last, complex, two-stage typescript before it was set in print. He made, in all, well over 1000 changes; as we can easily imagine, many revisions had several dynamic, interacting effects. Because of a fortunate accident, we have this rich resource which enables us to learn precisely how Twain composed and completed his manuscript, how he conceived and revised at such a high level of achievement. He was, of course, the first reader of his growing novel; we can discover how he wrote and read and re-wrote and re-read *Adventures of Huckleberry Finn*.

The manuscript version—with its cancellations, insertions, and rearrangements—offers us the rare opportunity to look over the author's shoulder while he creates. We can, in effect, learn how *Huck* grew—how the masterpiece developed and matured.

Much scholarly attention has been given to *why* Mark Twain stopped working on *Huck* in 1876. This study explores *how* he completed *Huck* in 1883 and 1884, concentrating on his actual composing processes, in those moments when he was a writer alone in a room with a pen, some paper, and the American language.

Moreover, knowledge of the creative process can increase the sheer pleasure of reading and can add to the fun and beauty of this iridescent text. As the novel changes, glows, and changes again, we can gain knowledge about the speed, care, coherence, and integrity of Twain's artistic imagination.

Because Twain seems to be America's favorite author, his biography has attracted many insightful scholar-critics who have explained connections between his life and his art. But I have come upon three rather neglected but significant resources. One is the unpublished journal Sam Clemens kept of the remarks his young children made as they tried to figure out how the world works. Each parent knows the peculiar combination of innocence, practicality, literalness, and wisdom in a child's comments, such as Susy Clemens's question, "Can God hear me when I whisper?"* Some of these remarks and the familial situations influenced *Huck*.

The file of letters Twain received, now in the Berkeley collection of Mark Twain Papers, helps create a context for knowing what was in his mind in 1883 and 1884. Because he scrawled his reactions on some of the envelopes, for example, "Self-righteous ROT"* or "That lunatic,"* we can document some attitudes.

In addition, full, sympathetic explorations of then-current laws, of Twain's lawsuits, and of his opinions about international copyright cast surprising lights upon the novel. These explorations put the creation of the masterpiece in artistic and economic, as well as familial, political, nationalistic, and literary contexts. Taken cumulatively, these relatively unusual resources contain special information that can be used to reveal some entirely new interpretations.

As in any critical endeavor, this study requires a triangulation of identities: the texts, the critical interpreter, and the ideal readers. I draw primarily upon the well-known final portion of the manuscript, covering about three-fifths of the novel, and the first edition of *Adventures of Huckleberry Finn*. My critical method is primarily genetic, working with sequential close readings of the first, second, and subsequent versions of a passage, drawing upon other corroborative material as needed. With the manuscript as a pre-text, I hope to weave one story of the growth of the text, in a context of aesthetic judgments. Brief stories of the many possible texts Twain wrote, but did not include, will provide occasional sidelights.

Some ideal readers for this study will know *Huck* well and wish to understand it better—or differently. In addition to sharing an intense interest in the novel, some ideal readers will be curious about American cultural myths, about the importance of the book for American literature and society, and about Twain's imagination.

Other ideal readers will be writers—either beginning or experienced—who wish to know precisely, specifically, how Twain created. How did Twain handle characterization? How did he control imagery? What can be learned by watching a genius create? Students of the creative processes will find example after example of how this author shaped with our language. Much information about the creative process can be learned by investigating the major work of a minor author or the minor work of a major author, but even more can be gained by studying the major work of a genius.

Whenever I reveal evidence that Twain canceled a passage, the ideal reader would pause—mentally prolonging the time when Twain could have revised in any one of a hundred ways. There were moments in 1883 and 1884 when Twain read or re-read a passage, pondered, perhaps paused, certainly crossed out, perhaps considered many alternatives before writing the new version—which he sometimes also revised. Too often we who look back in time can easily forget the pauses, the uncertainties, the creative searchings for exactly the right words. Yet in these nuances, in these enchanting details, Twain's artistry lives.

Perhaps three visual analogies may help. Most people who travel to an art museum will look at many paintings for five to fifteen seconds each. But a few people will linger for a while, studying a masterpiece by Brueghel or Bosch, permitting the forms to emerge, perceiving the details and interactions which the average hurrier simply does not see. Or, in another instance, a few people will pause and watch attentively as an artist at an easel attempts to duplicate a landscape or portrait on the wall. Those viewers who linger can continuously compare the original version with the reproduction, learning about each. This critical study is designed for those with the more curious or more investigative temperament, for readers who, if offered a choice between a wide-angle and a close-up lens, will pick the latter, considering the magnification of detail to be revealing.

A third analogy takes this study out of the museum and also emphasizes the temporal aspect of Twain's creative process. Reading this study may be a bit like watching a highly skilled street magician, named Mark Twain, perform his tricks and routines at one-third speed. The observer can catch the preparations, the diversions, the sleight of hand, the dexterity. Moreover, the skill can also later be observed at full speed simply by reading the final, finished text.

By offering a reasonably complex interpretation of this masterpiece, supported by evidence that thoroughly documents the writer's skill, I wish to suggest that Twain's genius can be more fully understood and that, thereby, this vital work can be comprehended.

It may, at first, seem incongruous to read this author carefully, precisely, because Sam Clemens created a pose or mask for Mark Twain as a careless, naive genius, too lazy and too sincere to do anything as difficult or artificial as worry a sentence into shape or correct a mixed metaphor. But this supposed incongruity will fade as we study the manuscript and as our knowledge increases. Because the texture of humor is a fine-spun, delicate material, critical analysis constantly risks seeming, by contrast, gross or obvious. Sensitivity may lapse, and I offer advance apologies. In compensation, we shall have the sheer pleasure of reading splendid passages by Mark Twain, evaluating why some made their way into *Huck* while others did not.

A sense of elemental fair play leads me to caution that this study is neither a variorum edition of the novel nor a collection of all other critical interpretations, although I am certainly deeply indebted to those who have studied Twain and *Huck*. I draw upon their insight and knowledge, hoping to add to it. Although my research has included Clemens's biographical background, the author's working notes, the remarks in his letters, notebooks, and marginalia, as well as his other books and the relevant critical and scholarly studies, our attention will focus primarily on those moments when Twain actually put pen to paper, when he was composing and revising his masterpiece.

This study contains a higher than normal percentage of facts—either newly revealed or previously ignored—about the novel. The facts which form the basis of this study are incontrovertible, inarguable. But to interpret these facts can be the focus of much debate, for instance, "What effect or compound effects did a change create?" I suggest that a full understanding of these facts will support a radically different interpretation of this American masterpiece.

This exploration begins with relatively simple stylistic matters and progresses to more complex thematic issues. From this study will arise a quite new understanding of the novel's meanings, ending, and structure. Much current conventional wisdom declares *Huck* to be a magnificent, flawed work—a splendidly engaging but aesthetically weak novel. This view I oppose; I would suggest that *Huck* is a unified novel with artistic repetitions and with an appropriate and misunderstood but significant ending. I suggest, further, that the people perhaps least likely to understand the ending, because of a limiting bias, could be some literary critics associated with English Departments.

Because *Huck* is so widely read, we find ourselves in a rather anomalous position: the novel has created a community of readers who have experienced its meanings without much shared sense of articulating those meanings—and even less notion about how the novel's meanings interact. Because neither the fun nor the serious meanings could be treated sufficiently in isolation, readers have been satisfied with a vague consensus, sustainable because it is seldom articulated in detail. I offer this study with hopes that subsequent critical discussions will include particular details about how Twain's text grew.

Other reasons for offering this book go beyond devotion to Mark Twain. I wish to present an example of literary criticism which an intelligent reader will find accessible, a book which begins in a clear fashion and which helps the reader explore the heights of literary and cultural understanding. Finally, I hope this study will have a generative effect, encouraging individual readers to begin other intellectual journeys through Twain's world.

*　　*　　*

While this book was in production, during the first few weeks of February, 1991, information gradually surfaced which revealed that the earlier portion of the *Huck* manuscript had been rediscovered. For years scholars had understood the first 45 percent of the manuscript to have been lost. My study began in 1966, dealing with the then-known portion.

During February, March, and April of 1991, it became apparent that indeed Twain had donated the manuscript of the first portion of his novel in July of 1887. But apparently James Fraser Gluck, the gifted, far-sighted collector who requested a Twain manuscript for the library, had at some point taken the first 665-page holograph portion to his home or office—presumably to have it bound as he frequently did with other significant treasures—and simply forgot to return it. This energetic lawyer had health problems and, when his health deteriorated into his final illness, left that portion in his study. After his untimely death at the age of forty five, in 1897, his study was cleared, and the first part of the *Huck* manuscript, clearly labeled, went into one of six trunks where it would remain hidden from scholars' eyes until the cleaning of an attic led to this tremendous find.

This startling rediscovery will ultimately provide a great deal of information about the first part of the novel and about Twain's creative processes in 1875–1882. Many standard views may have to be revised; already we know that Twain did divide the early portion into chapters. But a very preliminary consideration indicates that the newly rediscovered 665 pages represent two distinct, earlier periods of composition (1876 and 1880) and contain absolutely nothing to contradict and much to confirm the findings of this book. Indeed, after difficult and time-consuming legal problems are settled, I shall also probably begin another "intellectual journey" which might be titled, tentatively, "Beginning to Write *Huck Finn*." Some information from the first manuscript portion, henceforth labeled Buffalo Manuscript A, will be included as relevant.

Acknowledgments

I acknowledge, with fond respect and intellectual combativeness, a general debt to former teachers, constant models such as Rudolf Gottfried, and the friends who form an imaginary audience. More specifically, the works of fellow Twainians have had a significant, helpful, formative influence. They have blazed a trail, and we who would understand Twain often place our feet where theirs have been. The late Fred Anderson and Henry Nash Smith, as well as Walter Blair, John Gerber, Lou Budd, Franklin Rogers, Edgar Branch, Sydney Krause, Hamlin Hill, Alan Gribben, Leo Marx, Martha Banta, Horst Kruse, Judith Fetterley, Howard Baetzhold, Robert Hirst, Lawrence Berkove, Robert Regan, Tom Tenney, Jim Cox, and David Sloane have each participated in this exciting revolution in knowledge. Twain has been fortunate to earn the provocative, insightful attention of many superb scholar critics. Walter Blair, in particular, has been informative, gracious, witty, an ideal consultant.

Robert Hirst, Victor Fischer, and Dahlia Armon, resident authorities at the Mark Twain Project in Berkeley, have been especially generous, knowledgeable, helpful resources. I wish to thank them and the Regents of the University of California and my own University for a productive sabbatical. The continuing development in Twain studies will take another giant step as the new edition of *Huck* with the commentary by Walter Blair and Victor Fischer makes a great impact. Mr. Fischer is an unusually skillful reader of Twain's revisions, and I am grateful for his consultations.

Although I happened to begin working with the original manuscript many years ago, I am delighted that the Bruccoli, Budd, Loos's recent two-volume photographic facsimile now places this invaluable resource before the reading public. Today general readers as well as scholars and critics may share the excitement of reading this fascinating material.

The thinking of "new textualist" scholars such as Hershel Parker and Thomas Tanselle has also provided clarity and guidance.

Among the many people who have made my department a special, stimulating place to think, I thank Gale Carrithers, Joe Riddel, Ed Dryden,

Dick Fly, Bob Daly, and Bob Edwards. Many colleagues at Buffalo, including Marcus Klein, Leslie Fiedler, Neil Schmitz, and Fred See, have given constructive, challenging reactions. Lionel S. Lewis, Vicki Hill, and Richard Kopley have also offered helpful commentary. Our faculty, students, and staff—teachers and listeners in rare combinations—have been paradoxically stimulating and supportive.

Several institutions have been generous. Harvard University Press has permitted necessary quotations from the correspondence between Clemens and Howells. The Hartford Twain Memorial and the Elmira Quarry Farm Center for Twain Studies have been very cooperative in assistance with photographs. Steven Mangione photographed the manuscript pages reproduced here. The University of Virginia Library has been helpful about the journal of the children's remarks. This book includes some material I have previously published in earlier form in *Modern Fiction Studies* and in the volume *One Hundred Years of Huckleberry Finn*.

Special mention and great gratitude go to the Mark Twain Project which, under the guidance of Dr. Robert Hirst, actually guards valuable material for the Mark Twain Foundation. I wish to be scrupulous about acknowledging this help and permission to print previously unpublished material; I have noted the protected material by an *. Moreover, as my chapter on copyright indicates, I would emphatically encourage other scholars to be meticulous in respecting such literary rights.

I am also immensely grateful to the Buffalo and Erie County Public Library, which now includes the holdings of the earlier Young Men's Association and Grosvenor libraries. The late Miss Jane D. Van Arsdale and Mr. William H. Loos, Curators of the Rare Book Room, have given great assistance in this study of the manuscript.

For the atmosphere within which I think and work, I thank my family. Finally, I offer gratitude to Sam Clemens and his creation, Mark Twain, not only for imagining this subject matter, in all its complexity, but also in loving respect to the genius who experienced so much, created so well, and learned what he did not plan or wish to know.

Vic Doyno
Buffalo and Berkeley
1966–1991

Introductory

The minute changes made in their compositions by eminent writers are always a matter of both curiosity and instruction to literary men, however trifling and unimportant they may appear to blockheads.

Dr. Johnson

1. Mark Twain in his Quarry Farm, Elmira, study, 1874. Notice the books piled high on the table.

2. A posed family tableau ca. 1884–85.

3. Four views of Twain, 1884, in portraits taken at the same time by Horace L. Bundy, Hartford, Connecticut.

Pray for me — good land! I reckoned if she ~~she~~ knowed me she'd tackle a joke that was more ˄nearer her size. But I let you she done it, just the same — she was just that kind. She had the grit to pray for Judas Iscariot if she took the notion — there warn't no back-down to her, if I knowa girl by the rake of her stern; & I think I do. You may say what you please, but in my opinion that girl had more sand in her than any girl I ever see; in my opinion she was just full

4. Manuscript page 351.

It sounds like flattery, but it ain't no flattery.
352
of sand. ∧ And when it comes
to beauty — and goodness — she
lays over them all. I hain't
ever seen her since that time
that I see her go out at that
door, ∧ like light & comfort a going out of a body's life;
~~turn at the stairs and~~
~~kind of through at kiss back at~~
~~me;~~ no, I hain't ever seen her
since; but I reckon I've
thought of her a many & a
many a million times, & of
her saying she would pray
for me; & if ever I'd a
thought it would do any
good for me to pray for her,
I'm dam'd if I wouldn't
a done it or bust.

5. Manuscript page 352.

1. Taking Our Bearings

Let us imagine that while we were strolling on a hillside high above Elmira, New York, on a windy summer day in 1883, Mark Twain invited us into his octagonal study to look over his shoulder as he composed a part of his novel. The passage we observe involves an emotional farewell scene, including Huck's opinion of an admirable young girl, Miss Mary Jane Wilks, the girl who almost loses her inheritance to the swindling king and duke. She has just offered to pray for Huck. Twain composes Huck's reaction, and the first manuscript version reads:

> Pray for me—good land! I reckoned if she'd a knowed me she'd tackle a job that was nearer her size. But I bet you she done it, just the same—she was just that kind. She had the grit to pray for Judas Iscarott if she took the notion—there warn't no back-down to her, if I know a girl by the rake of her stern; and I think I do. You may say what you please, but in my opinion that girl had more sand in her than any girl I ever see; in my opinion she was just full of sand. And when it comes to beauty—and goodness—she lay over them all. I hain't ever seen her since that time that I see her go out at that door, and turn at the stairs and kinder throw a kiss back at me; no, I hain't ever seen her since; but I reckon I've thought of her a many and a many a million times, and of her saying she would pray for me; and if ever I'd a thought it would do any good for me to pray for her, I'm dum'd if I wouldn't a done it or bust. (MS, 351–52)[1]

Among the many intriguing features of the passage, Huck's voice commands attention; he confides his attitudes easily, charmingly, and his openness and expectation of easy acceptance engages our sympathy as readers.

But Twain revised the passage significantly. Mary Jane's gesture of a *femme fatale*, throwing a kiss from the stair, receives a wavy line of cancellation and a circling line of exclusion. If Twain had allowed this gesture to stand, the novel would have included this explicit hint of sexuality, a topic the book significantly avoids. Part of Huck's innocence depends on his presexual condition. Although the gesture may have been appropriate for the slightly older Mary Jane, its inclusion would complicate the characterization of Huck; he would have to ignore the gesture or respond to it, and either choice would affect both the characterization and the novel. Instead, Twain squeezed in a line above the cancellation so the revised section reads, "I hain't ever seen her since that time that I see her go out at that door, *like light and comfort agoing out of a body's life.*" This simile, combining favorable abstract words and tactile sensation, pays attention only to the deathly emotional impact of separation, and the reader can understand Huck's sorrow. But Twain later decided to drop the addition before the final publication.

Twain also tinkers in the manuscript with a few minor details. The acceptable sentence, "I reckoned if she'd a knowed me she'd tackle a job that was nearer her size," he modified in two ways. Twain changed the folkish "she'd a" to a simple "she." The author gave vitality to Huck's voice by inserting a life-like wordiness in "a job that was *more* nearer her size." Similarly, Twain revised, "she lay over them all" to "lays." These minor changes suggest that Twain gave a respectable amount of meticulous care to his work.

Huck seems to know that it is unusual to praise a girl so much for "grit" or "sand," because abrasiveness is not usually valued in females although determination is. But Huck can praise her independence and strength only from within a young male's verbal system. Twain added, after "full of sand," a sentence declaring that "*It sounds like flattery, but it ain't no flattery.*" Accordingly, Huck's character as narrator attempts to consider everyone's needs, even the reader's need to know how to regard a description.

Similar considerations about sexuality—and about tone and characterization—clearly influenced Twain's revisions for print. Now we have to imagine a later visit—perhaps in 1884—to observe Twain thoroughly revising his typescript of the same passage for print, making many changes. He modified the opening phrase, "Pray for me—good land!" by dropping "good land." Perhaps this very mild oath would give Huck too polite, too coy, a tone of voice. Huck's voice had first used a slang phrase, "back-down," and then, perhaps, the author's mind shifted to the girl's figure. Huck's voice had momentarily hit an inappropriate tone, a complex adult tone more suitable to an experienced Mississippi riverboat pilot evaluating the physical form of a female's rear angles than to Huck's pre-sexual naturalness: "there warn't no back-down to her, if I know a girl by the rake of her stern; and I think I do." But this masculine evaluative boasting was dropped, and Twain restores Huck's innocent voice, as he simply praises, "there warn't no back-down to her, I judge." The boy's earlier extreme enthusiasm becomes somewhat tempered by the moderate tone of "I judge"; several other emotional matters are toned down. Most revisions create several overlapping, interactive effects, affecting, for example, tone, characterization, and description.

Huck's innocence is also preserved by a suppression of some intricate satire on religion. The passage opens with Mary Jane's offer to pray for Huck, and he concludes, in the manuscript version, by saying, "if ever I'd a thought it would do any good for me to pray for her, I'm dum'd if I wouldn't a done it or bust." This slang phrasing for, "I'm damned if I wouldn't have prayed for her" carries a witty involution that disappeared when Twain shifted the word choice for print to "blamed." Once more Huck seems younger, and the adult author's potential for satiric sharpness remains concealed.

Later in 1884, Twain read the proofs of his novel, and he must have approved this final version of the passage:

> Pray for me! I reckoned if she knowed me she'd take a job that was more nearer her size. But I bet she done it, just the same—she was just that kind. She had the grit to pray for Judus if she took the notion—there warn't no backdown to her, I judge. You may say what you want to, but in my opinion she had more sand in her than any girl I ever see; in my opinion she was just full of sand. It sounds like flattery, but it ain't no flattery. And when it comes to beauty—and goodness too—she lays over them all. I hain't ever seen her since that time that I see her go out of that door; no, I hain't ever seen her since, but I reckon I've thought of her a many and a many a million times, and of her saying she would pray for me; and if ever I'd a thought it would do any good for me to pray for *her*, blamed if I wouldn't a done it or bust. (245)

Purchasers of the first edition, and of all subsequent editions, can read a final, smooth version, enjoying Huck's relatively consistent, somewhat laconic tone.

This brief consideration of the growth and development of one passage can serve as an introductory indication of what can be perceived by the use of genetic criticism, by, in effect, going back in time to look over Twain's shoulder as the novel grew. Although we shall never again have to be quite this concerned with minute matters, one can observe the values of focused textual interpretation, the labor and value of specific understanding, and the dynamic, interacting, compounding effects of revisions. Themes, motifs, meanings can emerge, and emphasis can shift. Moreover, the passages that are not changed can be understood as being, at first, provisional, tentative, conditional, subject to revision, but gradually confirmed, affirmed, as they survive through at least four authorial re-readings. The unchanged passages are never really final until turned over to the printer. And Twain also made some changes even after the printer had the novel.

Genetic Criticism

Genetic criticism concentrates upon, but is not limited to, the observable changes in the texts between the earliest available draft and the final, usually printed, form. The primary subject matter includes, if available, jottings and notes, exploratory or discovery drafts, manuscripts, cancellations, insertions, revisions, rearrangements, copy sheets, proof sheets, galley revisions, and the final text. The creative process can be studied by analyzing what Twain actually wrote—even if the words or thoughts were, in the heat of composition, canceled instantly or changed later, after time, in the cool precision of re-reading. For example, one instance of Twain's quick self-critical judgment occurs when Huck explains how the king plans to repeat a swindle:

> and the king he went ashore, and told us all to stay hid whilst he went up to town and smelt around to see if anyone had ⟨hear⟩ got any wind of the Burning Shame there yet. (MS, 428)

A split-second before completing the word "heard" Twain changed his word choice to be consistent with the emphasis upon the sense of smell. His artistic imagination, then, was rapid enough to censor mixed sense imagery in mid-word. But the significance of this olfactory imagery decreased when, in print, he renamed the swindle, "The Royal Nonesuch." Genetic criticism suggests that once an author has committed a word or series of words to paper, revision by cancellation, substitution, or insertion involves a mental process amenable to study. In some cases, a word or a phrase may only flash or flicker on the page for one to ten seconds before the pen cancels it; in other cases a word or phrase may endure through several revisionary readings only to be cut at the last minute. The author chooses between versions, mentally rejecting one and putting another in its place. What are the intellectual and artistic effects?

   In some cases genetic criticism can reveal an author's original intentions or the meanings an author staked out in the early plans. But often the writer discovers, creates, and connects while writing. In many cases genetic criticism can increase our knowledge of how the author's mind was working while creating art and, perhaps, artistic ambiguity. Although it is usually difficult or impossible to know an author's original intentions or intended meanings from the final text alone, and although one or two revisions are seldom enough evidence for a new interpretation, a pattern of revisions may provide a sufficient basis for inferences. In this case, we have a more than ample body of evidence. Indeed, I hope that other scholar-critics who master this material may see other constellations of meaning in Twain's creative process.

Usually I shall present first the earliest surviving manuscript version, then describe the growth into the final printed version. The very few illegible cancellations will appear as an appropriate number of bracketed Xs. Textual notations present cancellations in angle brackets ⟨ ⟩, and insertions appear in *boldface italics*. Thus a change that was immediately corrected in manuscript running sequence would be noted as, "whilst he went up to town and smelt around to see if anybody had ⟨hear⟩ got any wind of the Burning Shame." But if the passage was revised later, with a cancellation and insertion, usually above the line, as would occur with a caret, it would, hypothetically, be noted as ". . . to see if anybody had ⟨heard⟩ *got any wind* of the Burning Shame." MS indicates the placement in the manuscript; quotations from the first American edition are noted simply by page number.

Because numerous critical controversies sweep across the literary landscape, it may be helpful to stake out a position, indicating some advantages, limitations, and presumptions of genetic criticism. Perhaps the best place to start is with the status or authority of texts. Some critics, often using a romantic or inspirational mind set, contend that when an author writes and/or revises, he or she has either no intentions or intentions that cannot be determined. Proponents of this view will be able constantly to decide on a case-by-case basis whether Twain's revisions appear random or meaningless. It is not necessary for a genetic critic to prove that *all* changes are meaningful, only that some reward study. Once the sequence of verbal expression, e.g., from first to fifth version, is agreed upon, the critic may decide to remain willfully ignorant of the information or the hermeneutic effort—the battle for understanding—can begin. Of course, not all changes are improvements, and the genetic scholar-critic must evaluate constantly.

Another rival critical group would contend that there is only one perfect form of a text, the form the text possesses on the day that it appears at the printer's office. Or, in contrast, others would reify the form the author would have approved if he or she were an ideal, consistent, perfectly attentive proofreader with no financial, practical, or commercial limitations upon the text. According to these positions, all earlier versions were just failed attempts to find the one perfect form, and the author brands his or her intentions and meanings on the work all at once on one day, usually the moment when the manuscript passes to the printer. However, a genetic critic would respond that the intentions and meanings change and develop as the artist writes; the lines written in the morning influence, guide, shape, restrict, or discover possibilities for the lines written in the afternoon. The first draft and each succeeding state of the text earn only a provisional status, open to revision through draft after draft as the author recursively creates, discovers, discards, blots, suppresses, refines, and confirms meanings and phrases, finding his or her fiction and form. This provisional status continues until the author, sometimes reluctantly, sometimes exultantly, sometimes with relief, disgust, or detachment, releases the work. Certainly the post-transfer decisions are often more affected by business, audience, or marketing pressures. A case in point involves Twain's late decision to drop the raftsman passage (see Appendix).

Other contemporary critics would contend that the particular form or wording of a text does not matter, that words are relatively unimportant or almost all meaningless, creations of a largely or totally historically-determined—or alternately subjectivist—universe. Although I am certainly cognizant of the effect of the observer upon the interpretation, I nevertheless oppose those contemporary critics who would deny that the specific words of a text matter. While recognizing the massive importance of Twain's and every critic's subjectivity, I suggest that the particular text of a novel carries great significance. We wish to read Twain's *Huck*, not a garbled text. As better texts become available, our levels of understanding will improve.

Certain limitations complicate genetic criticism. At first a reader may feel overwhelmed by the sheer number of changes; then one faces the difficulty of determining sequences; and finally one confronts the critical task of figuring out the meanings and interactions of the changes. For example, a change in olfactory imagery or phrasing may emphasize a pattern, raising the importance or even modifying the meaning of another passage which had been written earlier. Selection of good examples necessarily means that many merely interesting examples must be omitted.

It would be a mistake to regard genetic criticism as simply "new criticism" with a temporal dimension. In the effort to understand, a genetic critic should also include biographical, psychological, cultural, and publication information; because the creative processes can draw upon many sources, the genetic critic cannot automatically exclude any source of information. Recent works by Hershel Parker and G. Thomas Tanselle provide an intellectual framework.

The language usually applied to this form of criticism contains several biases, usually implying that the work of art improves as the artist expends more time on it. Some language is vegetative, e.g., "seed," "flower," "blossom," and "prune"; some language is organic, containing connotations of vitality, "grow," "evolve," "develop," "devolution," or "lick the cub into shape." Some phrasing is spatial, "assemble," "balance," and "mosaic." Other language frames include cooking: "blend," "brew," "season," or "concoct"; chemistry or pharmacy appears in "titration" and "filter." Many phrases from the visual arts seem appropriate: "patina," "glossy enamel," or "veneer." Classical studies call upon "palimpsest." Many terms, of course, could draw upon several fields: "contribute," "add," "adjust," "alter," "strengthen," "suppress," or "weaken," and "improve." Most of the terms, like "revise" (literally *re-see*) smuggle in an interpretive bias, frequently leading the reader to consider all changes for the better, as if artist and work inevitably march toward perfection. But the best genetic criticism is fully participatory, with the temporal sequences continually held to open-minded, sharp-minded, comparative aesthetic judgments. The alert reader must constantly ask: "What is the effect of the change?" and "Is the later version better?" In this process of frequent questioning, most readers develop a greater understanding of their own aesthetic standards.

Part of the appeal of genetic criticism can involve a spurious appeal of scientism. By studying inks and watermarks and by using ultra-violet light to read through heavy cancellations, we can amass a consoling—or staggering—number of facts. But after the information has been assembled, the critical inquiry still depends upon interpretation of the material. Alternative explanations and inferences can be welcomed, weighed, and tested for coherence, contradiction, probability, and explanatory power. Although a genetic critic may sometimes be tempted to believe that he or she can describe the creative process exactly, we must realize that the proposed reasons, explanations, and comparative aesthetic judgments may be possible, probable, or convincing, but not all are certain. The possibility always exists, theoretically, that Twain may have made any one individual change not for a discernible or knowable reason, but by whim, by unconscious impulse, by automatic "taste," because of impatience or indigestion, or by mere chance. But the consideration of many revisions reveals patterns of meaning and intention. A thorough study of the manuscript leads to the conviction that the vast majority of the changes reflect Twain's deliberate, palpable, impressive artistry.[2]

Twain's creative processes were recursive. He would write first draft pages, relatively exploratory, "discovery" drafts, finding out where his story was going. Of course, these pages or sections would sometimes receive both development and error-correction types of changes as Twain would repeatedly re-see, re-hear, or catch errors. Sometimes he would copy over a sheet that had presumably become so heavily revised that it was no longer clearly legible. And sometimes these copy sheets would remain relatively clean, but some intended copy sheets would themselves also become subject to extensive revision. Moreover, at every stage, Twain was polishing phrasing and correcting errors. Because the manuscript preserves both early discovery draft sheets and later copy sheets, both with and without revisions, we can observe different stages. Such a diversity of activity leads to many possibilities.

Because the material is reasonably complex—well over a thousand changes with many interacting effects—several schemes of organization and presentation are possible. Apparently the simplest method would be a page-by-page, line-by-line retelling or narrative. Although such an approach might approximate the writer's experience of simultaneity among multiple processes, with constantly shifting concentration, this method would lead to a baffling plethora, putting important and unimportant changes of all types in the narrative order of the novel. Another method would first narrate the first draft as a whole, including only the running sequence cancellations and substitutions. Then the revisions in pen and in pencil could be considered, followed by the changes between the final manuscript state and the printed version. This method would, in my judgment, provide an unrealistic and quite repetitive story because Twain could easily, for a hypothetical example, revise page 250 once or twice before composing page 450. Moreover, most readers can focus attention upon only a limited number of topics at a time.

But the evidence does fall quite naturally into groupings. Accordingly, I have used an analytical framework, paying attention first to stylistic matters, such as tone, characterization, and imagery, before proceeding to several new thematic issues. This progression is inductive. But this organizational method should not be taken to mean that Twain's creative process made him do all revisions concerning, say, characterization or humor in only one portion of the manuscript or all at one time. The amount of evidence about stylistic matters should encourage sensitive, open-minded readers to take quite seriously several surprising theories advanced about the thematic issues.

Twain on the Writing Process

Certainly it makes sense to be aware of what Twain himself wrote about his methods of composition. Although framers of criticism usually regard the remarks of an author about his work with cautious skepticism, in this case Twain's comments have a particularly revealing use of similes and metaphors. In 1890, in response to a question about his methods of composition, Twain replied:

> Your inquiry has set me thinking, but, so far, my thought fails to materialise. I mean that, upon consideration, I am not sure that I have methods in composition. I do suppose I have—I suppose I must have—but they somehow refuse to take shape in my mind; their details refuse to separate and submit to classification and description; they remain a jumble—visible, like the fragments of glass when you look in at the wrong end of a kaleidoscope, but still a jumble. If I could turn the whole thing around and look in at the other end, why then the figures would flash into form out of the chaos, and I shouldn't have any more trouble. But my head isn't right for that to-day, apparently. It might have been, maybe, if I had slept last night. (Bainton, ed., *The Art of Authorship*, 85)

We notice that Twain approaches this complex topic with his usual blend of self-deprecation and precise images. Just as the pier-glass passage in *Middlemarch*, Chapter 27, reveals George Eliot's epistemology and aesthetic, the kaleidoscope simile reveals Twain's and, consequently, deserves explication.

In 1816, Sir David Brewster invented this device, which became a popular form of home entertainment. In a kaleidoscope, at one end of a tube fragments of brightly colored glass move within a circle, drawn by gravity and overlapping one another in a seemingly infinite variety. Such is the view from the outside, from "the wrong end" of the kaleidoscope. However, viewed from the proper end, through the inside, one sees only a portion of the glass fragments. Moreover, the portion of the fragments which does appear is multiplied by three mirrors set lengthwise in the tube at about a sixty-degree angle to one another, forming a triangular tunnel of vision. The reflection repeats the form of the exposed portion most effectively when the device is held up to a light source for examination. The selection of a portion, the constantly changing shapes and overlaps as the fragments move, and the precision and clarity of the multiple reflections make the kaleidoscope a stunning embodiment of the Greek word roots: to see beautiful forms (*kalos*, beautiful, *eidos*, form, *scope*, watcher). A similar device, the teleidoscope, uses a clear lens to fragment and multiply images of actual scenes or people. The appeal of the instruments involves the variety and beauty of the images, combined with immediate changes and multiple reflections of the forms.

Although Twain claims difficulty in thinking abstractly about his method of composition, his brilliant kaleidoscope comparison explains a great deal. By studying his revisions, we can, in fact, look through the correct end of the kaleidoscope. Since one revision may affect, for example, tone, characterization, imagery, and thematic emphasis, the concept of transparent overlap seems helpful. A shift in one of the fragments may dynamically alter the appearance of the whole; for instance, when a yellow fragment falls from behind a blue fragment to a position in front of a red one, a green portion vanishes and an orange section appears. Moreover, the analogy has for our purposes another application: just as a few distinctive glass fragments may be recognizable and their familiarity appreciated in different configurations, several significant portions of the manuscript do deserve repeated examination in different contexts. Because Twain revised several times, with different effects, a manuscript passage may be observed more than once.

But the challenge of understanding the creative process apparently appealed to Twain. As he continues, we notice the primary importance of reading and the shift to a more regularized, mechanical, architectural comparison for his house of fictions:

> However, let us try guessing. Let us guess that whenever we read a sentence and like it, we unconsciously store it away in our model-chamber; and it goes with a myriad of its fellows to the building, brick by brick, of the eventual edifice which we call our style. And let us guess that whenever we run across other forms—bricks—whose colour, or some other defect, offends us, we unconsciously reject these, and so no one ever finds them in our edifice.

He recognizes the role of the unconscious, thinking of the process as automatic with little explicit self-involvement.

Yet Twain understood that work and some individual choices occur:

> If I have subjected myself to any training processes, and no doubt I have, it must have been in this unconscious or half-conscious fashion. I think it unlikely that deliberate and consciously methodical training is usual with the craft. I think it likely that the training most in use is of this unconscious sort, and is guided and governed and made by-and-by unconsciously systematic, by an automatically-working taste—a taste which selects and rejects without asking you for any help, and patiently and steadily improves itself without troubling you to approve or applaud. Yes, and likely enough when the structure is at last pretty well up, and attracts attention, *you* feel complimented, whereas you didn't build it, and didn't even consciously superintend.

The contrast between "patiently and steadily" improving and the "unconscious" permits some deflection of criticism, some personal protection, if the artistic choices meet criticism. The writer's ego will accept "attention" but maintains psychic distance.

Twain's mind characteristically becomes more concrete as he builds to a magnificent example of a stylistic-thematic embodiment, a long, involved, clear sentence:

> Yes; one notices, for instance, that long, involved sentences confuse him, and that he is obliged to re-read them to get the sense. Unconsciously, then, he rejects that brick. Unconsciously he accustoms himself to writing short sentences as a rule. At times he may indulge himself with a long one, but he will make sure that there are no folds in it, no vaguenesses, no parenthetical interruptions of its view as a whole; when he is done with it, it won't be a sea-serpent, with half of its arches under the water, it will be a torchlight procession.

Precise, vivid images can be either inanimate or animate; the creative process is not one thing. Parts may be in a dynamic kaleidoscope or may be mechanical bricks; imagined connections in a sea-serpent may be brought to the surface, exposed to the light in a celebratory ordering.

His casual voice returns in the final paragraph with an attitude of apology and self-deprecation, using a comic tone to conceal a concluding evasion:

> Well, also he will notice in the course of time, as his reading goes on, that the difference between the *almost right word* and the *right* word is really a large matter—'tis the difference between the lightning-bug and the lightning. After that, of course, that exceedingly important brick, the *exact* word—however, this is running into an essay, and I beg pardon. So I seem to have arrived at this: doubtless I have methods, but they begot themselves, in which case I am only their proprietor, not their father. (Bainton, ed., 85–88)

Twain casually reveals his own ability to discriminate between some word that, like a lightning bug, only lives and illuminates and the right word that can, with sudden, awe-inspiring power and frightening precision, hit. Even in this casual reply, his word choice and metaphoric ability crackle. The concluding complexity of inorganic bricks and an organic method which begat itself permits Twain to offer opposing opinions, while the "proprietor" denies paternity in the process of a graceful withdrawal.

Although we will probably never completely solve the mystery of what Twain knew with conscious intelligence and what he knew only subconsciously, what he intended and what he created accidentally, we do have the valuable evidence of how he worked. Certainly much of his "automatically working taste" can be traced back to his days as a typesetter, as a reader, as an aspiring young journalist. In all likelihood, Twain's mind needed to work only half-consciously to make many error corrections or "polishings" which would demand full concentration from a less gifted writer. And although Twain himself probably might be surprised by and perhaps could not explain some of his own changes, we can rely upon his stunningly appropriate image of the kaleidoscope.[3]

Inside Mark Twain's Mind: 1875–1884

In order to build a factual foundation for this reassessment of *Huck*, it is necessary to re-examine some documents from the 1875–1884 period. These materials reveal four areas of Twain's early interests: the accurate rendition of children's voices and points of view, children's misunderstandings of literature, the stages of a child's development, and the topic—of crucial importance to an author—of national and international copyright protection.

The beginnings of the long project that would become *Adventures of Huckleberry Finn* combined technical and personal concerns. When Twain completed *The Adventures of Tom Sawyer*, his attention was drawn, almost irresistibly, to the character Huck. This unschooled lad, a person outside normal social definition, fascinated Twain. Huck had begun to live and, in fact, almost takes over the ending of Tom's novel—because his personality possesses more vitality than Tom's.

Two letters which surround, oddly enough, July 4, 1875, indicate *Huck*'s conception at the completion of *Tom*. In the first letter, William Dean Howells, writing as an *Atlantic* editor in pursuit of a publication, explores with Twain possibilities, both aesthetic and financial, for the book we know as *Tom*. Howells probably urged that the story continue into Tom's adulthood:

> You must be thinking well of the notion of giving us that story. I really feel very much interested in your making that your chief work; you wont have such another chance; don't waste it on a *boy*, and don't hurry the writing for the sake of making a book. Take your time, and deliberately advertise it by Atlantic publication. Mr Houghton has his back up, and says he would like to catch any newspaper copying it. (July 3, 1875, *Twain-Howells Letters*, Vol. 1, 90–91)

Indeed, Twain would take a great deal of time to create his chief work, but it was too late for the well-intentioned advice to apply to *Tom*. Significantly, the problem of piratical publication appears early.

Twain's reply reveals his great concern with the technical matter of point of view and with the literary model for a rogue biographical picaresque fiction:

My Dear Howells:

I have finished the story & didn't take the chap beyond boyhood. I believe it would be fatal to do it in any shape but autobiographically—like Gil Blas. I perhaps made a mistake in not writing it in the first person. If I went on, now, & took him into manhood, he would just be like all the one-horse men in literature & the reader would conceive a hearty contempt for him. It is *not* a boy's book, at all. It will only be read by adults. It is only written for adults.

Moreover, the book is plenty long enough, as it stands. It is about 900 pages of MS., & may be 1000 when I shall have finished "working up" vague places; so it would make from 130 to 150 pages of the Atlantic—about what the Foregone Conclusion made, isn't it?

I would dearly like to see it in the Atlantic, but I doubt if it would pay the publishers to buy the privilege, or me to sell it. Bret Harte has sold his novel (same size as mine, I should say) to Scribner's Monthly for $6,500 (publication to begin in September, I think,) & he gets a royalty of 7 1/2 percent from Bliss in book form afterward. He gets a royalty of ten percent on it in England (issued in serial numbers) & the same royalty on it in book form afterward, & is to receive an advance payment of five hundred pounds the day the first No. of the serial appears. If I could do as well, here & there, with mine, it might possibly pay me, but I seriously doubt it—though it is likely I could do better in England than Bret, who is not widely known there.

You see I take a vile, mercenary view of things—but then my household expenses are something almost ghastly.

By & by I shall take a boy of twelve & run him on through life (in the first person) but not Tom Sawyer—he would not be a good character for it.

I wish you would promise to read the MS of Tom Sawyer some time, & see if you don't really decide that I am right in closing with him as a boy—& point out the most glaring defects for me. It is a tremendous favor to ask, & I expect you to refuse, & would be ashamed to expect you to do otherwise. But the thing has been so many months in my mind that it seems a relief to snake it out. I don't know any other person whose judgment I could venture to take fully & entirely. Don't hesitate about saying no, for I know how your time is taxed, & I would have honest need to blush if you said yes.

Osgood & I are "going for" the puppy Gill on infringement of trademark. To win one or two suits of this kind will set literary folks on a firmer bottom. The New York Tribune doesn't own the world—I wish Osgood would sue it for stealing Holmes's poem. Wouldn't it be gorgeous to sue Whitlaw Read for *petty larceny*? I will promise to go into court & swear I think him capable of stealing pea-nuts from a blind-pedlar. (July 5, 1875, *Twain-Howells Letters*, Vol. I, 91–92)

This well-known letter indicates an extraordinary amount about the craftsman behind the pose. Twain's evaluative thinking about problems of point of view and narrative voice while completing *Tom* would shape *Huck*. He realized the crucial importance of the narrator, explicitly rejecting Tom as unsuitable. Twain's mind typically repeats the appeal of the first-person narrator. His citation of a literary model, Le Sage's *The Adventures of Gil Blas*, places the conception within a recognized genre. But Twain's attitude toward *Gil Blas* changed through several clearly documented positions. Earlier, on December 27, 1869, Clemens had written Olivia that he was not marking the book for her, saying that she need not read it because, "It would sadly offend your delicacy." But later in his career, after completing *Huck*, when Brander Matthews commented about the similarity between *Gil Blas* and *Huck*, Twain assured Matthews that he had not read *Gil Blas*. Matthews's comment, "I knew he was not a bookish man," is utterly mistaken.

Again, the issue of piratical publication, infringement of trademark, and, by implication, lack of authorial protection appears as a recurrent concern. Any reader who believes Clemens's persona of Mark Twain may be surprised that an unsophisticated bumpkin could be so precise about point of view and about finances, or could be so engaging as he requests technical, editorial help. As the editors of the *Mark Twain-Howells Letters* point out, the letter contains "the germ of *Huckleberry Finn*. It is significant that the technical problem of point-of-view was present to Twain from the first" (Vol. I, 93).

Then on July 6, 1875, Howells replied encouragingly, "Perhaps you'll do Boy No. 2 for us." In another letter (September 11, 1875), Howells mentions a series of letters on the problem of international copyright by Charles Reade republished in Whitelaw Reid's New York *Tribune* in June–September. Thus Twain's mind could connect literary theft, international copyright, Whitelaw Reid (a name Twain misspells as "Read") and Charles Reade. Because Twain was repeatedly victimized—robbed really—by pirated editions, these related issues crop up frequently. Twain and Howells were planning a campaign to improve the situation for authors, e.g., letters of September 14 and 18, 1875. Twain did not yet know that pirated editions of *Tom* printed in Canada would rob him of about $5,000 before and while the first American edition went on sale. Thereafter the Canadian editions continued to sell in the U.S. at substantially lower prices than the authorized edition.

After the Clemens family visited the Howells, Twain learned what the Howells' seven-year-old son John, nicknamed Bua or Booah, thought about Homer. Twain seemed interested in what must have been the boy's unsophisticated, naive, probably literalist, almost certainly honest bit of literary criticism because he wrote Howells:

> Booah's idea of the wasteful magnificence of the Greeks is delicious! Pity but you could ingeniously draw him out, on the whole subject, & thus build an article upon A Boy's Comments Upon Homer.
> I've got another rattling good character for my novel! That great work is mulling itself into shape gradually. (October 4, 1875, *Twain-Howells Letters*, Vol. 1, 105)

Although the dominant scholarly opinion is that Twain did not begin *Huck* until 1876, it is possible that Twain's mind was busy in a pre-composition stage ("writing it in the first person" and "Boy No. 2"). An extensive cancel in this same letter probably refers to some novel in human terms, and it could refer to a boy's development. It is significant that Twain apparently knew and was thinking about stages of progressive development. The cancelled portion includes:

> Those [?] graded foetuses one sees in bottles of alcohol in anatomical [?] museums. . . . I can look back over my row of bottles, now, & discover that it has already developed from a rather inferior frog into a perceptible though libelous suggestion of a child. I hope to add a bottle a day, now, right along. (October 4, 1875, *Twain-Howells Letters*, Vol. 1, 105)

While the identity of the novel cannot be made incontrovertibly, it is significant that it deals with matters that occur in *Huck*. If the cancel refers to some early form resembling *Huck*, the phrase "libelous suggestion of a child" would make some sense; moreover, the portion after the cancel, which informs Howells that "(All of the above ruthlessly condemned by the Head Chief of the Clemens tribe)," could be interpreted to mean that the new character might be a Finn-type boy, probably not Olivia Clemens's kind of character. Or perhaps Olivia objected to the whole cancel, with the graphic description of foetuses. But aside from these speculations, it is of great consequence that a child's view of literature and Twain's familiarity with stages of child development appear in close proximity.

Apparently Howells kept a journal of comments made by his child because Twain wrote, on August 9, 1876, from Quarry Farm, that:

> I am infringing on your patent—I started a record of our children's sayings, last night. (*Twain-Howells Letters*, Vol. 1, 143)

His handwritten journal survives but is unpublished. "A Record of Small Foolishnesses," contains over eighty separate incidents, spanning the period from August 8, 1876 to 1885, presenting both Clemens's analysis of his children's personalities, his reflections on child rearing, and many precious anecdotes indicative of childish combinations of honesty, naivete, and inexperience. Sensitive parents can easily recognize the bittersweet quality of a child's remarks; the child's understanding of the world may be consistent and intelligent, but utterly innocent, causing gross misperceptions which, by their naive nature, are memorable to the adult's ear. But these misperceptions may convey an implicit criticism of the deceptions or skewed values in the adults' shared world, a world that adults seldom question because they have become familiarized or habituated to the society. Close study of this "Record" reveals that these attitudes, situations, and phrases influenced *Adventures of Huckleberry Finn* and other writings.

In the same letter, Twain told Howells about his creative involvements:

> The double-barreled novel lies torpid. I found I could not go on with it. The chapters I had written were still too new & familiar to me. I may take it up next winter, but cannot tell yet. I waited & waited, to see if my interest in it would not revive, but gave it up a month ago & began another boy's book—more to be at work than anything else. I have written 400 pages on it—therefore it is very nearly half done. It is Huck Finn's Autobiography. I like it only tolerably well, as far as I have got, & may possibly pigeonhole or burn the manuscript when it is done. (Aug. 9, 1876, *Twain-Howells Letters*, Vol. 1, 144)

Both the unwarranted optimism about completion and the ambivalence about the manuscript's fate seem characteristic, but the letter clearly announces the choice of the first-person point of view and Huck's identity as narrator. Although the information in the rediscovered manuscript portion may reveal a new sequence of interpretations, scholarly opinion currently believes that Twain continued the work at two separate periods, 1879 or 1880, and 1883–1884. His famous comparison of the well of inspiration which needed time to fill up aptly represents the temporal dimension. By the end of 1876 he had probably completed what would become Chapters I through XVI (including the famous Raftsman passage) but excluding the adventure on the *Walter Scott* and the following debate on King Sollermun and the French language (half of XII, XIII, and XIV). Probably at that point Huck had apologized to Jim, changing the possibilities for the novel, and the raft was run over by the steamer.

In 1880 he probably resumed the story, creating the story of the Grangerford-Shepherdson feud (Chapters XVII–XVIII). Then sometime between 1880 and 1883, possibly in 1882, he created the king and duke, the two unprincipled adult con-men (at least part of XIX, XX, and XXI).[4]

Accordingly, in May of 1883 he had a manuscript of about 50,000 words. Twain would complete about 70,000 words and revise the novel extensively in a period of high energy and in an atmosphere of artistic exhilaration. On July 20, 1883, Twain wrote to Howells, probably primarily about what we would call the discovery or exploratory draft stage of composition:

> I haven't piled up MS so in years as I have done since we came here to the farm three weeks & a half ago. Why, it's like old times, to step straight into the study, damp from the breakfast table, & sail right in & sail right on, the whole day long, without thought of running short of stuff or words. I wrote 4000 words to-day & I touch 3000 & upwards pretty often, & don't fall below 2600 on any working day. And when I get fagged out, I lie abed a couple of days & read and smoke, & then go it again for 6 or 7 days. I have finished one small book, & am away along in a big one that I half-finished two or three years ago. I expect to complete it in a month or six weeks or two months more. And *I* shall *like* it, whether anybody else does or not. It's a kind of companion to Tom Sawyer. There's a raft episode from it in second or third chapter of Life on the Mississippi. (*Twain-Howells Letters*, Vol. 1, 435)

Although the optimism about finishing is both vague and unrealistic, the tone is exuberant and infectious!

The book was created in a supportive, loving familial context.[5] Although no critic has yet made a case for communal authorship of *Adventures of Huckleberry Finn*, a large number of people could have influenced the text in a variety of ways. We know that Clemens's wife, Olivia, his children, his good friend William Dean Howells, his nephew-in-law and business agent Charles Webster, the Elmira typist Harry M. Clarke, and two compositors had the opportunity to affect the text.

The standard view of family participation in the process is captured by Susy Clemens's word, "expergation." Her biography of her father has the following explanation:

> Ever since papa and mamma were married papa has written his books and then taken them to mamma in manuscript and she has expergated them. Papa read "Huckleberry Finn" to us in manuscript just before it came out, and then he would leave parts of it with mamma to expergate, while he went off up to the study to work, and sometimes Clara and I would be sitting with mamma while she was looking the manuscript over and I remember so well, with what pangs of regret we used to see her turn down the leaves of the pages which meant, that some delightfully dreadful part must be scratched out. And I remember one part pertickularly which was perfectly fascinating it was dreadful, that Clara and I used to delight in, and oh with what despare we saw mamma turn down the leaf on which it was written, we thought the book would be almost spoiled without it. But after it was published we changed our minds. We gradually came to feel as mamma did. (*Papa*, 188–89)

The possibility arises, and Walter Blair agrees, that Susy confused the manuscript and the proofs ("just before it came out"). But there is, characteristically, a more complex explanation in Twain's memory. Perhaps Twain was, in his later comments, fabricating to maintain his dignity and independence. But his explanations present the kind of trickery Clemens enjoyed:

> I remember the special case mentioned by Susy, and can see the group yet—two-thirds of it pleading for the life of the culprit sentence that was so fascinatingly dreadful, and the other third of it patiently explaining why the court could not grant the prayer of the pleaders; but I do not remember what the condemned phrase was. It had much company, and they all went to the gallows; but it is possible that that especially dreadful one which gave those little people so much delight was cunningly devised and put into the book for just that function, and not with any hope or expectation that it would get by the expergator alive. It is possible, for I had that custom, and have it yet. (*Papa*, 189–90)

Although the comment concedes that a good many passages went "to the gallows" it appears that the teasing and the ultimate result was within the author's control. In the *Autobiography*, Twain's explanation seems similar:

> The children always helped their mother to edit my books in manuscript. She would sit on the porch at the farm and read aloud, with her pencil in her hand, and the children would keep an alert and suspicious eye upon her right along, for the belief was well grounded in them that whenever she came across a particularly satisfactory passage she would strike it out. Their suspicions were well founded. The passages which were so satisfactory to them always had an element of strength in them which sorely needed modification or expurgation, and was always sure to get it at their mother's hand. For my own entertainment, and to enjoy the protests of the children, I often abused my editor's innocent confidence. I often interlarded remarks of a studied and felicitously atrocious character purposely to achieve the children's delight and see the pencil do its fatal work. I often joined my supplications to the children's for mercy, and strung the argument out and pretended to be in earnest. They were deceived, and so was their mother. It was three against one, and most unfair. But it was very delightful, and I could not resist the temptation. Now and then we gained the victory and there was much rejoicing. Then I privately struck the passage out myself. It had served its purpose. It had furnished three of us with good entertainment, and in being removed from the book by me it was only suffering the fate originally intended for it. (*Autobiography*, Vol. 1, 89–90)

Yet we know that Twain did bend the truth in his *Autobiography*. Although the psychological interaction is beyond exact reconstruction, there is only minimal evidence in the manuscript of familial censorship. Neither Victor Fischer nor I have found evidence of Livy's handwriting in the later portion of the manuscript.

On August 22, 1883, Twain was still quite enthusiastic:

> My Dear Howells—
> How odd it seems, to sit down to write a letter with the feeling that you've got *time* to do it. But I'm done work, for this season, & so have got time. I've done two seasons' work in one, & haven't anything left to do, now, but revise. I've written eight or nine hundred MS pages in such a brief space of time that I mustn't name the number of days; *I* shouldn't believe it myself, & ⟨therefore⟩ of course couldn't expect you to. I used to restrict myself to 4 & 5 hours a day & 5 days in the week; but this time I've wrought from breakfast till 5.15 p.m. six days in the week; & once or twice I smouched a Sunday when the boss wasn't looking. Nothing is half so good as literature hooked on Sunday on the sly. (*Twain-Howells Letters*, Vol. 1, 438)

Livy also commented on this unusually good attitude:

> We are having a delightful time here. Mr. Clemens is at work—and I never saw him in better working condition, or with more enthusiasm for his work. (Salsbury, ed., *Susy and Mark Twain*, 168)

The influence of William Dean Howells was considerable. I believe that Howells queried passages and offered helpful suggestions; we know that Howells had the manuscript typed and edited it and, as well, assisted with proofreading. Letters document that Twain relied on his friend's judgment, taste, and proofreading ability (see, for examples *Twain-Howells Letters*, 122, 124, 129, 493–500). Twain gave Howells *carte blanche* in making corrections on *Huck* and expressed great gratitude for the help. Yet Twain apparently exercised professional care—albeit exasperated or accompanied by cursing—while handling his proofs. He wrote to Howells on June 28, 1884:

> My days are given up to cursings—both loud & deep—for I am reading the H. Finn proofs. They don't make a very great many mistakes; but those that do occur are of a nature to make a man curse his teeth loose. (*Twain-Howells Letters*, Vol. 2, 493)

Walter Blair writes that "despite the groaning, the author depended upon Howells to read only a small portion of the page proofs and read the rest himself, finishing up by the end of August [1884]" (*Mark Twain and Huck Finn*, 360).[6]

Two brief letters, from the end of that summer, to Charles Webster reveal both Twain's care and temper:

> Aug 11 [1884]
>
> Dear Charley—
>
> Most of the proof was clean & beautiful, & a pleasure to read; but the rest of it was read by that blind idiot whom I have cursed so much, & is a disgraceful mess.
>
> Send me slips from where the frauds arrive & *sit down to supper* in Miss Mary's house, up to slip No. 73.
>
> Send me also slips from No. 75 up to 81.
>
> And insist that the rest of the proofs be *better read*.
>
> Yrs.
>
> S L C
>
> (Webster, ed., *Mark Twain Business Man*, 272)

Twain's casual but angry charge that the proofreading had been done by "that blind idiot," with the implication that Webster also hired sighted idiots, must have irritated Webster. But Twain certainly seems quite careful. Just three days later he wrote:

> Dear Charley—
> The missing galleys are the ones I sent to Howells, no doubt. In that case I don't need to re-read them.
> If all the proofs had been as well read as the first 2 or 3 chapters were, I should not have needed to see the revises at all. On the contrary it was the worst & silliest proof-reading I have ever seen. It was never read by copy at all—not a single galley of it. . . .
>
> Yrs
> S L C
> (Webster, ed., *Mark Twain Business Man*, 272)

Apparently his workman-like attitude toward his texts remained at least through August 14, 1884.[7]

I have concluded that Twain approved the changes, either idly or with full concentration. I consider Twain responsible for the text, although probably not responsible for the titles of the illustrations or the running titles. For the sake of alertness, I suggest that modern readers continuously judge whether the changes within the manuscript are similar to or different from those which occur between the revised manuscript and the printed text. I have concluded, as stated, that the artistic and thematic achievements of the finished novel belong to Mark Twain.

A Glance Forward

> I have noticed, in such literary experiences as I have had, that one of the most taking things to do is to conceal your meanings when you are *trying* to conceal it. Whereas, if you go at literature with a free conscience and nothing to conceal, you can turn out a book, every time, that the very elect can't understand.
> Colonel Sellers in Twain's *The American Claimant*,
> Chapter V

Let us look forward—downstream so to speak—over the intellectual journey of this study, using a telescope or teleidoscope to become aware of distant prospects we shall later examine closely.

We shall explore how *Huck* grew, how the novel developed to completion. After this preliminary information, we shall begin *in medias res* simply because the main available manuscript portion begins that way, picking up the story in the midst of the Bricksville mob's attempt to lynch Colonel Sherburn. As we proceed through the novel, an interpretation of the beginning, middle, and end will develop. Because the middle portion suffers from neglect by critics and because the ending enjoys extraordinary critical attention, this exploration will restore some balance. Although this study does not catalogue all the revisions, it does offer a selective presentation of some revisions which supports an interpretation of Twain as a deliberate artist with particular, discernible meanings.

The admittedly reductive distinction between stylistic and thematic chapters permits a progression. The stylistic chapters present a partial taxonomy of the interactions of literary devices in the creative process, and readers who are novelists or short story writers have found the information about this craftsmanship particularly helpful. Literary scholars and critics, on the other hand, have found that the detailed demonstration of Twain's artistry leads them to take even more seriously the achievement of the novel and to weigh more heavily the thematic revisions. This methodology begins in a formalistic fashion and reserves several surprises for the historical, economic, psychological, structuralist, and deconstructive critics.

This sequential attention to different elements in various portions of the manuscript compelled omission of some valuable material. "If I'd a knowed what a trouble it was" to analyze Twain's creative process, I might have tried to delegate the task to a dozen computers. But the wealth of evidence remains available for use by other scholars proposing other theories.

Adventures of Huckleberry Finn presents many "stories," some already recognized, such as the conflict between river and shore, or Huck's search for a father, or the picaresque criticisms of society, or the effort to free a slave, or the struggle for ethical action in an apparently amoral society. Without in the least denying the importance of these interpretations, I wish to emphasize another story, another *agon*, which unifies the novel: the narrative of a minimally literate boy in conflict with a society which defines itself and exercises control *through books*. In a way, Huck's experience is one we all can share; all who grow up in a literate society feel, at various times, controlled by people who have read books—perhaps special books or certain books. In his effort to achieve personal freedom, Huck has been controlled by books read by Miss Watson and the Widow Douglas (the Bible and spelling books), Tom Sawyer (at first "pirate books and robber books"), and a great many others. Repeatedly someone asserts situational dominance over Huck by assuming the power of books or the power of greater literacy. Huck attempts to come to terms with this power by reading, but he frequently finds the books in conflict with reality, even while he lives through parodies of books. But repeatedly impressed by the power of books, he attempts accommodation. He even wrote a book, compiling his *Adventures* while waiting for Tom's wound to heal. But Huck finally—with metafictional comments—rejects the process of writing.

Issues of literacy, literary deception, literary copyright, and national independence, as well as issues of ethical development, shape the novel. Obviously the effort to help free Jim is crucial; similarly important is Huck's effort to free himself from Tom Sawyer's delusional respect for bookish authorities. In a larger sense, by the end of the novel the liberation from European stratification, pretensions, and literature opens possibilities for American literature.

A parallel story involves the person Sam Clemens using the persona Mark Twain to write a story that will win acceptance by his audience while attempting to determine the limits or truth of fiction. What was happening in 1883 and 1884 while Twain wrote and revised? Twain was developing his verbal artistry and, paradoxically, developing a complex, ultimately negative attitude about literature. He assumed his place in the tradition while also demonstrating the limits of the traditional. This undermining of literature as a way of knowing was probably not part of his original intention in 1876, but by the time the novel concluded, the qualification became comprehensive, ranging from the use of a barely literate narrator to a final—widely misunderstood—reflexive parody of adventure literature.

The normal expectations of genre become unstable; the title *Adventures of Huckleberry Finn* creates expectations for adventure, escape, memoir, or confessional literature. But the readers actually find the form transformed into a letter. Similarly, "Adventures" appears as a word with favorable connotations at the beginning of the novel, but the word and the title gradually acquire negative connotations.

We shall observe a number of intra-textual battles, struggles between one version and another, each claiming at one moment a place in *Huck*. Analogously, as shall become clear, an inter-textual battle happens as Twain discovers his place and national stance within the context of world literature.

The complex unity of the novel indicates, of course, the nature of the writer's imagination. I shall speak of Sam Clemens, meaning the historical figure (b. 1835, d. 1910); I shall speak of Mark Twain, meaning the timeless literary artist and persona created by Sam Clemens. Clemens/Twain was fascinated by twins, duplication, and duplicity. Any artist who deals with representation duplicates some form of reality; and within the world of the novel, duplications are obviously doublings, repetitions, and variations of one another as well as of "reality."

As a youth, Sam Clemens accepted slavery unquestioningly, but as an adult he paid University education fees for two black students as reparations. Yet Mark Twain drew upon Sam Clemens's youth, creating a powerless lad who lived outside the boundaries of conventional society, a boy who felt the pressures of society but nevertheless tried to help free a slave and free himself. The adult Sam Clemens can be thought of as, in effect, retrospectively testing out alternatives, engaging in imaginative self-transformation. What was it like for a child or young man to have opposed slavery? Tom Blankenship, a child in Hannibal, served Twain's imagination as a partial model for Huck, and this child's older brother, Bence Blankenship, apparently did actually smuggle food to a runaway slave on Sny Island, despite the possibility of a $50 reward (Blair, 109). Could Sam, as a child, have opposed the evils of slavery? Could a child have succeeded? What were the influences of the society upon the values of a developing adolescent?

One basic idea of this critical study may be presented boldly at the outset and reinforced, I hope, in the following pages. Twain's creative imagination is extraordinarily repetitive, creating a book which resembles an intra-textual echo chamber. An idea, topic, problem, or situation will be brought up and developed, often to re-appear in a matching but contrary form. At some fairly deep level of consciousness, Clemens/Twain perceived or constructed reality in this paradoxical fashion, seldom letting one view of reality stand uncorrected or unmodified by a contrasting vision. If Henry James would characteristically control the tone, word choice, and nuances of qualification in a precise and quite subtle fashion, Twain, on the other hand, would usually present a topic or situation two or three times, creating the qualifications or moral judgment by artistic juxtapositions or by variations of the details. The intellectual style seems to be additive, paratactic, rather than delicately qualified. Twain seldom builds a fictional world by minute Jamesian discrimination or systematic subordination; instead he creates a universe of plenitude, vivid particularity, continuous flow, and fascinating repetition. This mental habit of Twain's has been widely recognized with Blair calling it "motif with variations," and Baldanza naming it "repetition with variation."

Such a mental mode seems appropriate for a comparatively uneducated, perhaps insecure, self-taught, non-systematic, but enthusiastic and highly sensitive thinker. Such a mental habit also fits a parodist; the artistic imagination need not create entirely new material because it can replicate material by stylistic variation. The habit, however, of repeating and parodying other literature or one's own material could potentially lead the novelist into a reflexive or destructive, artistically introverted situation.

Two brief but well-known incidents serve as illustrative examples. At one point in the novel, Huck becomes a part of the Grangerford household. This family is feuding with the Shepherdsons, but toward the end of the episode Sophia Grangerford elopes with Harney Shepherdson. During the ensuing chase and general slaughter, Huck watches as his friend Buck is killed by men on horseback. Most readers would agree that the action provokes strong emotions of sorrow. Yet this entire situation recurs in fragmentary form, with the significant variation of a comic tone, two and three chapters later when two con men attempt to stage parts of *Romeo and Juliet* and *Richard III*. The allusions to feuds, elopement, and battle scenes repeat important elements in the Grangerford episode, but with a shift in tonality. Frequently in *Huck* Twain treats a topic first in a serious and then in a comic or parodic fashion.

Similarly, the passage about Boggs presents an abusive drunkard riding into town, shouting, and finally being shot in a pitiable fashion. But in the very next chapter, Huck goes to a circus where another drunkard shouts at the crowd and seemingly risks his life trying to ride a circus horse. This scene, however, also becomes comic in tone; to the crowd's amusement, the drunk reveals himself to be a deceptively splendid rider, capable of wonderful tricks.

In a way, this critical endeavor could be an analogue of this revelation, proving that apparent sloppiness conceals artistic skill. Such a view of Twain results from cumulative study. The first revelation of a hitherto unrecognized correspondence may be merely interesting. By the fifteenth or thirtieth, the reader may be persuaded that Clemens's/Twain's mind indeed possessed this peculiar talent for self-travesty. The repetitions can lead to structural cycles. For example, this study concludes by exploring the possibility that Jim's imprisonment on the Phelpses' farm represents a little-known post-Civil War repetition of slave status which was legally but immorally inflicted on Black people.

Actually, as Twain was writing and revising the last three-fifths of *Huck*, he was polishing his style and improving his novel as a deliberate literary craftsman. He was also working out, in fictional form, conflicts about human nature, individualism, freedom, slavery, religion, morality, literacy, nationalism, copyright law, and literature. These debates result in the implicit attitude which in his later years became his explicit, scathing pessimism. These conflicts and his habits of repetition, parody, and self-parody contributed to the self-qualifications of his fiction. The ending of the novel can be understood as a dramatization of the negative possibility of literature as a truth-telling medium.

Just as we must be aware that a distinction between stylistic and thematic concerns is reductive, I acknowledge the critical commonplace that a certain historical situation is necessary to illuminate some aspects of a text. In the 1990s we can see some ideas in the artistic text that readers in 1920 or 1940 simply could not see. Yet it is comforting to recognize that the wonderful, complex evidence of the manuscript and its textual revisions remains extant, permitting readers to discover how a genius creates, how *Huck* grew.

Notes

1. "MS" always indicates the original manuscript portion already available in the Buffalo and Erie County Library. The recently discovered portion will be cited as "MS. A." In all quotations from the manuscript, contractions are silently expanded. Similarly, signs such as "+" for "and" are given in verbal form. Line endings are not preserved in my transcriptions.

Readers who cannot visit the Buffalo manuscript can consult Lou Budd's two-volume edition, *Adventures of Huckleberry Finn (Tom Sawyer's Comrade): A Facsimile of the Manuscript*. In addition, the appendices of the new Mark Twain Project *Works and Papers of Mark Twain, Adventures of Huckleberry Finn* (Berkeley, CA, 1988) edited by Walter Blair and Victor Fischer assist the reader in reconstructing the manuscript version. This new California edition of *Huck* (cited hereafter as *Huck*, 1988) provides a wealth of relevant information and sets the new standard. A facsimile of the first edition is readily available in Hamlin Hill and Walter Blair's edition, *The Art of Huckleberry Finn*.

2. A brief introduction to some very helpful biographical and critical studies can be found in the Bibliography.

3. Readers wishing to learn more of Twain's statements about his creative process may consult "Notes on Those Extraordinary Twins," his commentary on the writing of *Pudd'nhead Wilson*, which is usually published with the novel.

4. Although Walter Blair's detailed explanation of the composition, as given above, seems convincing and is widely accepted, it should be noted that Sherwood Cummings argued intriguingly in 1989 in *Mark Twain and Science* that the Mis-

sissippi trip influenced this portion. The recent rediscovery of the first 665 pages of manuscript may cast a new light on this entire topic.

5. It is perhaps unusual in literary studies to state theories which fail for a lack of evidence, but it may save other investigators some trouble to know that two personal difficulties in the author's life apparently did not influence the book. Sam Clemens's aging mother was declining in health and suffering visual delusions. Sam's stock investments were also declining, causing margin calls. Neither of these personal difficulties seems to have affected the composition of the novel.

6. Further detailed information about this period of proofreading and book making can be found in Blair's *Mark Twain and Huck Finn*, Chapter 25, and essay and in the new California edition's Textual Introduction.

7. More information about the text appears in essays by Allison Ensor in *American Literature* and by John C. Gerber in *Proof.* Victor Fischer's Textual Introduction in the California *Huck*, 1988 (432–514) is a model of concise, detailed information.

Stylistics

In them circumstances ⟨he could always throw⟩ *it warn't no trouble to him to throw* in an amount of style that was suitable.

Huck Finn Manuscript, page originally
numbered 507, renumbered 500

500

~~what~~ lays over the yaller fever, for interest, when he does come. Tom was over the stile & starting for the house; the wagon was spinning up the road for the village, & we was all bunched ~~in~~ the front door. Tom had his store clothes on, ~~& an audience~~ — & that was always nuts for Tom ~~Sawyer.~~ In them cir cum-stances, ~~it warn't no trouble to him to throw~~ ~~he could always throw~~ in an ~~amount of~~ style that was suitable. He warn't a boy to meeky along up that yard like a sheep; no, he come c'am & important, like the ram.

6. Manuscript p. 500. Printed version appears on p. 35 of this volume.

233

the King says —

"Can any of you gentle-
men tell me where Mr. Peter
Wilks lives?" they give a glance
at one another, & nodded their
heads, as much as to say,
"What did I tell you?" Then
one of them says, kind of soft
& gentle:

"I'm sorry, sir, but the
best we can do is to tell you
where he did live, yesterday
evening."

went all to smash, &

Sudden as winking,
The derned old cretur fell
up against the man, & put his chin
on his shoulder, & cried down

7. Manuscript p. 233.

mouth off once too often, &
was in a mighty close place.
I asked her to let me think, a
minute; & she set there, mighty
impatient & excited & beautiful,
but looking kinder happy &
eased-up, like a person that's had a tooth pulled out.
So I went to studying it out.
I says to myself, I reckon
a body that up & tells the truth
when he is in a tight place,
is taking considerable
many risks, though I ain't
had no experience, & can't
say for certain; but it looks
so to me, anyway; & yet here's
a case where I'm blamed if it
don't look to me like the truth is

8. Manuscript p. 329.

2. Precisely the Right Tone of Voice

> . . . the difference between the *almost right word* and the *right* word is really a large matter—'tis the difference between the lightning-bug and the lightning.

Are we justified in discussing Mark Twain as a careful and precise artist? We can explore this basic question by studying parts of his creative process, such as tonality, characterization, or imagery, and by then examining how these stylistic achievements interact with his creation of the novel's meanings.

If we accept the persona of Mark Twain at face value, we conceive him as an unschooled hick, a surprisingly lucky lout, a naive native genius too careless by temperament to bother about details and too casual to do anything so difficult as revise a sentence. If Sam Clemens had such a personality, he would have been an unusual typesetter; hence the pose was contrary to at least a part of Sam Clemens's personality. But such a pose created a uniquely valuable effect: it helped put the relatively unschooled writer from Hannibal, Missouri beyond nitpicking or sophisticated criticism and potential humiliation by the literary establishment. The American literary world has been—and still is—peculiarly supportive of such a character. Many American teachers, literary critics, and ordinary citizens appear more sympathetic to democratic mixtures of illiteracy and sincerity than their British or French counterparts. Moreover, the popular traditions of regional writing permit a supposedly unsophisticated person to speak with authenticity, frequently unaware of the humor, in a dead-pan fashion.

The choice of an almost illiterate narrator to tell the tale or to write the letter we know as *Adventures of Huckleberry Finn* slants several issues of major importance. As shall become clear, Twain's exploration of the value of fiction is affected by his choice of a narrative consciousness. Moreover, Huck's fictional background creates a comparatively rare situation: the onset of Huck's literacy is delayed until an age of great growth in moral decision-making ability.

The aesthetic advantages of creating a definite point of view are enormous—as any historian of fiction can testify. Twain's earlier short popular works often had definite narrators, such as the unsuspecting stranger in "The Notorious Jumping Frog of Calaveras County" or Aunt Rachel in "A True Story," but many longer works, such as *Innocents Abroad* and *Roughing It*, had an inconsistent first-person narration which combined voices of naivete and of experience.[1] With *Huck Finn* Twain accepted the apparent limitation of one definable point of view—that of a young boy—and thereby created an immense freedom and aid for himself as a novelist. The opening page of the newly discovered manuscript reveals that Twain wrote at the top of the page:

> Huck*leberry* Finn
> Reported by
> Mark Twain
>
> (MS.A, unnumbered page)*

Henceforth, Twain's lively (and relatively easily distractible) attention can be focused: What would a twelve- to fourteen-year-old boy notice? and How would this youth tell about the incident? The boy's ways of seeing and of saying make possible a uniquely vivid characterization of the storyteller-participant. But, as shall become clear, Twain occasionally had difficulty staying within his chosen point of view.

The related question is, "Why choose Huck?" If Tom Sawyer's personality would be—as Twain intuited—wrong, why would Huck's character be right for such a narration? Within the world of his fiction, Huck represented a polar opposite to Tom. Huck is a strong presence in *Tom Sawyer*, but his personality is not fully defined. Moreover, Huck had, to some extent, begun to live and command more of the author's interest toward the end of *Tom*. Huck would change considerably from the boy described in Chapter VI of *Tom Sawyer*. Huck's uneducated status created several advantages: he could live freely as a twelve- to fourteen-year-old, yet he could see and comment innocently as a somewhat younger person because he had not yet been fully socialized by a normal family or by much time in school. He could be a young Gil Blas, a naive, enthusiastic, good-hearted person adrift in a corrupt world. He could wander in the picaresque style, usually outside society's structures, occasionally incorporated but nevertheless at heart a transient. Huck's unique blend of innocence, practicality, spiritedness, and literalness create a disarmingly appealing, lifelike character. And these attributes carry thematic importance and may coincide with or reflect parts of a putative national character. Twain's achievement involves the use of Huck's voice, full of freshness and eagerness, as a wistfully striking contrast to the world's bleak reality.[2] The contrast resembles that operative in a tall tale when a deadpan or naive narrator does not seem aware of his outrageously funny statements. Twain can have Huck utilize both types of contrast.

Twain possessed a sensitive ear for capturing precisely a child's voice. He and Howells apparently agreed that John Habberton's book *Helen's Babies* did not capture a child's speech accurately (*Twain-Howells Letters*, 165). Clemens did himself try in his "A Record of Small Foolishnesses" to preserve speech, to stop time and capture, as if in amber, a moment: "Susie began to talk a little when she was a year old. If an article pleased her she said, 'Like it—awnt (want) it—hab (have) it—take it' and took it unless somebody got in ahead and prevented"*[3] ("A Record," 3). Another incident from the journal reveals both the author's fidelity in recording the speech and the power given to Susie to name her newborn sister. When Clara was

> one hour and 4 minutes old, she was shown to Susie. She looked like a velvet-headed grub worm squirming in a blanket—but no matter, Susie admired. She said, in her imperfect way, "Dat bay (baby) got boofu' hair"—so Clara has been commonly called "Bay" to this day, but will take up her right name in time.* ("A Record," 4)

And the child's second nickname, Ben, was given to Clara by her younger sister, Jean. Apparently the children's speech was taken quite seriously by the attentive parents.

Susie also imitated her father's drawl, asking her English nurse, Lizzy Wills, "Lizzie, can you talk like papa?"* and demonstrating his "drawling manner of speaking."* ("A Record," 5). Susie was quite sensitive to tone of voice and once, after her mother reprimanded her in front of visitors, Susie complained with injured dignity, "But you didn't speak to me right, Mamma"* ("A Record," 27–28). Similarly, when Sam Clemens had read a passage twice to Clara but the child still did not understand, Susie explained to her father, "You read it so 'stinctly that 'fused Bay"* ("A Record," 26–27).

Such sensitivity to tone, inflection, and pronunciation was an important part of Sam Clemens/Mark Twain's personality. Moreover, he had a wordsmith's fascination with a child's literalism and enthusiasm. Once Clara learned with surprise that it was her father's birthday, but she did not have a present for him. She responded to the situation by running upstairs and giving him one of her toys. But soon afterwards Susie criticized Clara for playing with the toy, and Clara replied, "I gave it to him for his birthday,"* meaning she did not give it to him forever ("A Record," 32). Towards the end of *Adventures of Huckleberry Finn*, Huck praises the sermons of Uncle Silas Phelps saying,

> He was the innocentest best old soul I ever see. But it warn't surprising; because he warn't only just a farmer, he was a preacher, too, and had a little one-horse log church down back of the plantation, which he built it himself at his own expense, for a church and school house, and never charged nothing for his preaching. (MS, 497–98)

Mark Twain inserted, before the next sentence, "*and it was worth it, too.*" He captures the tone of childish enthusiasm, the explicit but entirely ironic financial approval which undercuts the praise. Such tonal complexity depends, at least in part, on the author's familiarity with the speech habits of real children. (Of course, this enthusiastic approval/criticism has obvious thematic importance.) Part of the pleasure of reading and re-reading *Huck* lies in the ability to hear tones of voice imaginatively, to listen eloquently, with full human sympathy.

Huck's voice greets us in a special way, and Twain labored over this boy's exact tone. At first Huck sounded proper, saying, "You will not know about me . . . ,"* but that was changed to, "You ⟨will⟩ *do* not know about me. . . ." *Not until Twain had again canceled and revised did Huck's friendly, vernacular way of talking live on the page:

> You ⟨will⟩ ⟨*do* not⟩ *don't* know about me, without you have read a book by the name of "The Adventures of Tom Sawyer," but that ain't no matter. That book was made by Mr. Mark Twain, and he told the truth, mainly. There was things which he stretched, but mainly he told the truth. (MS.A, unnumbered first page)*

Huck continued:

> That is nothing. I never seen anybody but lied, one time or another, without it was Aunt Polly, or the widow, or maybe Mary. Aunt Polly—Tom's Aunt Polly, she is—and Mary, and the Widow Douglas, is all told about in that book—which is mostly a true book; with some stretchers, as I said before. (17)

He speaks to us directly and individually. Much seems to be dependent upon our knowledge derived from another book, but Huck dismisses our ignorance of the book as nothing. The boy's thought process is quite repetitious. Truth is an issue, yet "truth" is made syntactically equal to "nothing." Twain's artistry captures Huck's dialect; the lad uses "without" to mean "unless" and "but" to have two meanings, and we easily understand. Huck as narrator assumes our familiarity and interest in his memoirs, although the language has some defamiliarizing function. As we rapidly assimilate information, we are expected to agree with Huck's opinions and generalizations. He uses series of thoughts and a self-interrupting style, as if he is thinking aloud. Because he interrupts himself for clarification or for qualification, he seems open-minded, as if he is not enshrining his own statements. Because we hear the thought process, not the final product of the thought-to-language development, we tend to trust the thinking as honest. Yet we should realize that in his rush of statements we find little subordination, and that he verifies his remarks mostly by repetition. Huck seems uncomplicated; his ordinary level of diction clearly announces significant topics, mentioning a "book" four times, "truth" three times, and lying or "stretchers" three times. Yet the qualifications Huck includes, "mainly" and "mostly," indicate that he sees exceptions as well as generalizations. The speaking voice seems frank and enthusiastic, eager and uncomplicated.

The second paragraph of *Huck* presents a summary, from Huck's point of view, of the conclusion of *Tom Sawyer*. There may be other books which similarly insist upon their special status and origin as books, but they must be rare.

Huck becomes specific about his situation, and we learn more of his "style":

> The widow she cried over me, and called me a poor lost lamb, and she called me a lot of other names, too, but she never meant no harm by it. She put me in them new clothes again, and I couldn't do nothing but sweat and sweat, and feel all cramped up. Well, then, the old thing commenced again. The widow rung a bell for supper, and you had to come to time. When you got to the table you couldn't go right to eating, but you had to wait for the widow to tuck down her head and grumble a little over the victuals, though there warn't really anything the matter with them. That is, nothing only everything was cooked by itself. In a barrel of odds and ends it is different; things get mixed up, and the juice kind of swaps around, and the things go better. (18)

Huck's way of talking includes pleonasm, as in saying "The widow she." He seems to be relatively unresponsive to the traditional cliches of religion such as "poor lost lamb." In fact, he may at one point have been ignorant of the biblical allusions, and we may ponder with amusement his possible puzzlement when the widow called him a "lamb" since he knows himself as a boy. His literalist explanation of the ritual of grace as grumbling over the food reveals that he sees what is actually happening—but he misreads the frown of concentration for dissatisfaction—without reference to superstructures or abstract systems. He knows, as a street child would, whether a person intends harm or kindness, and he sees beneath the words. Huck does not appreciate restrictions or need boundaries. He keeps letting the reader share his situation by phrases such as "You had to come to time," and the process creates a sympathetic identification of reader with narrator. Because Huck sounds confident and trustworthy, the reader enters Huck's world confident that a mixed condition is better.

With this information in mind, let us turn to the manuscript to listen and observe how Twain shaped his narrator's tone of voice. After Colonel Sherburn has shot Boggs, a mob decides to lynch the killer and tears down his fence. Huck describes the situation as the Colonel appears:

> Sherburn never said a word—just stood there, looking down. It seemed to me that the stillness was as awful, now, as the racket was before; and somehow it was more creepy and uncomfortable. Sherburn run his eye slow along the crowd; and wherever his eye struck, the people tried a little to outgaze him, but couldn't; they dropped their eyes and looked ⟨sickish⟩ ⟨and⟩ sneaky. Then pretty soon Sherburn sort of laughed; not the kind of laugh you hear at the circus, but the kind that's fitten for a funeral—the kind that makes you feel crawly. (MS, 162–63)

The voice is recognizably Huck's, but it sounds a bit too formal, a bit too measured, and the expression seems distant. Twain's revision went through at least two stages: in the manuscript he dropped "sickish and," leaving the townspeople looking furtive, but not ill. A fair amount of the revision within the manuscript is of this sort, dropping acceptable phrases. Later, when revising the book for print more significant changes were made. Twain dropped the adequate, formal second sentence; perhaps the sentence was a shade too balanced, too structured, too literary a tone for Huck. The revised way of saying it seems simple and direct: "The stillness was awful creepy and uncomfortable." The temporal comparison disappeared, but the functional words have been extracted and put in a simple asymmetrical form.

Twain changed Huck's way of describing the laugh. "Not the kind of laugh you hear at the circus, but the kind that's fitten for a funeral—the kind that makes you feel crawly" became "not the pleasant kind, but the kind that makes you feel like when you are eating bread that's got sand in it"

(190). The loss of the polar contrasts seems, at first, regrettable. Perhaps Twain thought the circus reference too artificial a foreshadowing of the immediately following incident at the circus; at any rate, the new version, "not the pleasant kind," seems functional but unexceptional. The circus-funeral contrast is suppressed and, instead, Twain has Huck speak not of opposite situations but of concrete, tactile reality: "bread that's got sand in it." Moreover, the reader is not told about feeling "crawly," but is given a vivid image of personal muscular discomfort. As a result of such revisions, Huck speaks with a tone of voice which sounds lively but without apparent literary polish.

Although Twain usually revised Huck's speech toward vividness, occasionally he had trouble with his narrator's voice. Infrequently the authorial voice pushes through Huck's, using inappropriate or literary language. For example, Huck originally said "The king was saying—in the middle of a sentence" (MS, 256). Clearly Huck would be unlikely to say "sentence" in this context, and the printed version reads, " . . . in the middle of something he'd started in on—" (217). A similar but even more authorial and emphatic voice once broke through Huck's explanation to Jim about the morality of kings. Huck has had only enough exposure to literature to confuse the Scherazade demand for stories with Henry VIII beheading his wives:

> ⟨'Fetch⟩ '*Ring* up Fair Rosamun'. Fair Rosamun answers the bell. Next morning, 'Chop off her head'—and next thing you see is the Chief of police with it in ⟨a basket⟩ a rag. ⟨Ole⟩ And he made every one of them tell him a tale every night; and he kept that up till he had hogged a thousand and one tales that way, and then he got out a copyright, and published them all in a book, and called it Domesday Book—*which was a good name, and stated the case*. Of course most any publisher would do that, but you wouldn't think a king would. (MS, 199–200)

Clearly, Clemens/Twain's own negative attitude toward publishers seethes through the voice of the boy. Although both the bloody description and the "copyright-publisher" segments were canceled, this thematically important issue will re-surface later in the composition. The changes hypostatically delete evidence that there was a Mark Twain angry about greedy, larcenous publishers behind Huck's voice and thereby keep a more believable narrative tone. The limitation of narration in *Huck* places the voice under the restriction of being a consistent character, and Twain usually succeeds in creating the child's tone. We must, however, be continuously sensitive to the possibility of overlap of authorial and narrator's voices, since both are planners, relaters, and commentators.

All the revisions in the novel are, in a way, revisions of Huck's voice, with the possible exception of changes in other characters' speech (although purists could theoretically argue that even these changes are examples of Huck's scrupulous retelling, in dialect, of his experiences). The revisions of other voices permit little doubt about the precision of Twain's artistry.

Variations in tonality are most easily seen in dialogue because the contrast between two characters frequently permeates their language. Accordingly, let us examine two dialogues involving the king, one comparatively private, the other quite public. After these detailed examples, we shall not have to be quite so particular again. The first situation occurs as the king, the aging confidence man, senses a possible swindle and attempts to get more information. This section leads into the important Wilks episode. When first composing this section, at the discovery draft stage, Twain probably did not know where his incident would lead. When Huck and the king pick up a country bumpkin in their canoe, the king begins casually:

> "Where you bound, young man?"
> "For the steamboat; going to Orleans."
> "Git aboard," says the king. "Hold on a minute, my servant'll help you with them bags. Jump out and help the gentleman, Adolphus" . . . (MS, 218)

Twain gives the king more words than needed and thereby characterizes him as loquacious by inserting the pleonasm, "Where you bound *for*, young man?" The growth from manuscript to printed text included several polishing changes, dropping the final "e" from "Where," and twice changing "help" to "he'p." As a result, the king's tone becomes that of a wordy, bossy master of limited pronunciation. The country bumpkin, on the other hand, seems at first unimportant and received no attention in this portion.

But after the local youth implies that a chance exists for a mistaken identity, the king begins to seek more information. Apparently Twain became intrigued by the tricks the king and duke could pull on the Wilks family. The author's handwriting and the omission of short, necessary words may indicate that he composed this next section at an unusually rapid rate. Perhaps his haste came from excitement at the chance to link the con men, the king and duke (false royalty) and sanctimonious religion (the false Reverend Elexander Blodgett and later the false Reverend Harvey Wilks) with his favorite plot devices of mistaken identity, deafness, duplicate brothers, and duplicity.

The king senses a chance for money and desires information, saying:

> ". . . I'm ⟨just⟩ *jest* as able to be sorry for Mr. Wilks for not arriving in time, all the same, if he*'s* ⟨has⟩ missed anything by it,—which I hope *he* hasn't."

The country jake replies:

> "Well, he don't miss any property by it, because he'll get that, all right; but he's missed seeing his brother Peter die—which he mayn't mind, nobody *can* tell as to that—" (MS, 220)

Some revisions are required by sense, probably because Twain, in his excitement, skipped ordinary, necessary words like *he* and *can*. And Twain also works to keep the king's informal dialect voice.

At this point in the manuscript Twain may have become more concerned with the country fellow as a storyteller, the key informant for the king's possible plot. The bumpkin at first says:

> . . . He left a letter behind, for Harvey, and said he had told in it where his money was and how he wanted the rest of the property divided up so that George's gals would be all right—for George didn't leave anything. (MS, 223)

Clearly this passage sounds like straightforward, tedious yet proper, prose. Twain revised "where his money was *hid*," making explicit a possible future plot complication.[4] He later changed, for print, the ordinary "gals" to "g'yirls," thereby creating the voice of a rural dialect, and developed the speaker's characterization by canceling "anything" and using a double negative, "didn't leave nothing."

The king continues to pump for information, "Why do you reckon Harvey don't come? Where does he live?" But Twain canceled the final letter from "Where," carefully, consistently, maintaining the king's dialect (206).

Furthermore, we can observe Twain experimenting with the precise sounds for the voices. In the top margin of MS, 227, he jotted "young fel'r" and "wid'r," oral versions, but then canceled these spellings. Similarly Twain adjusts the country bumpkin's "I was afraid" to ". . . afeard." Many revisions, in fact, shift away from proper diction toward regional, colloquial pronunciation. "Yellow boys," meaning gold pieces, occurs twice, and both are changed to "yeller boys"; "foreign" becomes "furrin." Many changes of this sort provide compelling evidence of the attention Twain lavished on minor details, putting the sounds of local color and the dialect on paper, as he had for many years.[5]

The voice of the king also received a great deal of attention in another, more public scene. Twain seems to have been intrigued enough to lavish care upon the creation of the personality of this aging confidence man.[6] When the king impersonates the bereaved Rev. Harvey Wilks, he must have the right tone of voice as he manipulates the crowd while he dramatically debates in public with the iron-jawed Dr. Robinson, who attempts but fails to unmask the impostor. The king ingratiates himself with the townspeople by making the correct invitations, saying:

> "—they being partickler friends of *the* diseased. That's why they're invited here this evenin'; but to-morrer we want all to come—everybody; for he respected everybody, he liked everybody, and so it's fitten that his funeral orgies should be public." (MS, 256–57)

Many readers have not perceived how cleverly Twain has constructed this paragraph, beginning and ending with the king's outrageous malapropisms which characterize him as ignorant. Most readers catch the mistake of "orgies," but the opening error of the king's usual "diseased" for "deceased" is scarcely observed. Hence the readers duplicate the Doctor's situation, perceiving error, but not the full extent of the error.

The king repeats "orgies" several times and receives a corrective note from the duke, but continues:

> "I use the word orgies, not because it's the common term, because it ain't— obsequies is the common term—but because it's the right term." (MS, 258)

Twain revised this passage in an enormously subtle way; the modified manuscript version reads: "obsequies *bein'* the common term—but because *orgies is* the right term." The insertion of "*bein'*" subordinates the correct phrase, makes it more parenthetical, more under the breath, as if less time has elapsed in the saying. On the other hand, the change from the less definite "it's the right term" to "*orgies is* the right term" shifts the definite verb to assert boldly the grotesquely incorrect word. The entire paragraph becomes paradoxically more subtle and more bold. The king's voice seems to be absolutely in command of the situation as he explains:

> "Obsequies ain't used in England no more, now—it's gone out. We say orgies, now, in England. Orgies is better, because it means the thing you are after, more exact. It's a word that's made up out of the Greek orgo, outside, open, abroad; and the Hebrew jeesum, to plant, cover up: hence inter. So, as you see, funeral orgies is an open or public funeral." (MS, 258–59)

Twain's later change in the printed version from "out of" to "out'n" and from "or" to "er" simply improves the dialect and thus gives greater emphasis to the humorous incongruity between pedantic-sounding derivations and wildly non-standard usage. The king's tone of voice—imperious and imperative—conveys his pretentious, ignorant arrogance.

All of this minute attention to the king's language prepares for the stark contrast of the Doctor's speech denouncing the king as a fraud. After Doctor Robinson laughs at the king's speech and refuses the impostor's hand, he criticizes the king's imitation of an Englishman. The Doctor then turns to the girls and says:

> "I was your father's friend, and I'm your friend; and I warn you as a friend, and an honest one, that wants to protect you and keep you out of harm and trouble, to turn your backs on that scoundrel, and have nothing to do with him, the ignorant hog, with his putrid and idiotic Greek and Hebrew as he calls it. He is the thinnest of thin imposters. . . ." (MS, 262)

Twain moderated the Doctor's contempt in the printed version by changing "the ignorant hog" comparison to "the ignorant tramp" and by omitting the malodorous "putrid"; as a result the description is less pungent but the Doctor is more dignified in tone. The meaningless intensive, "thinnest of thin imposters," becomes simply "the thinnest kind of an impostor." The Doctor states that the rascal:

> "has come here with a lot of empty names and facts which he has picked up somewhere, and you weakly take them for proofs, and are assisted in deceiving yourselves by these thoughtless unreasoning friends here, who ought to know better." (MS, 262–63)

The Doctor's language becomes less elevated, less polysyllabic, and his tone less melodramatic as "weakly" disappears and as "assisted in deceiving yourselves" becomes "helped to fool yourselves." The Doctor's characterization of the townspeople changes somewhat by changing "thoughtless unreasoning" to the more ordinary word "foolish" (218). The Doctor, in obvious contrast to the king, seems less pretentious in his word choice.

Originally, the Doctor's impassioned pleas had been melodramatic in tone:

> "Mary Jane Wilks, you know me for your friend, and your honest and unselfish friend. Now listen to me: cast this paltry villain out—I beg you, I beseech you to do it. Will you?" (MS, 263)

While preparing for the printed version, Twain dropped the repetition of "honest" as a self-characterization. The phrase "cast this paltry villain out" sounds so melodramatic that a standard gesture, a pose, and a tableau spring immediately to mind; the printed "turn this pitiful rascal out" seems slightly less melodramatic, but more contemptuous. "I beseech you" was dropped, but the request, in printed form, gains some emphasis because "beg" became italicized. The Doctor's voice becomes more genuine, less pedantic, and the contrast between the pretentious rascal and the correct, blunt, honest country doctor is heard more clearly in the finished text. Such attention to voice and tone contributes both to the sense of realistic conflict and to the allocation of sympathy among the characters.

Just how important the imagination of the human voice was to Twain in those actual moments of composition cannot be over-emphasized. A case in point occurs quite a bit later in the novel, after the boys have engineered Jim's escape, when Huck talks to Jim, and Jim answers. The unrevised, first manuscript version reads:

> "<u>Now</u>, old Jim, you're a free man <u>again</u>, and I bet you you won't ever be a slave any more."
> "En a mighty good job it was, too, Huck. It was planned beautiful, en it was <u>done</u> beautiful; en ⟨day⟩ dey ain't <u>nobody</u> kin git up a plan dat's mo' mixed up ⟨XXX an' fine⟩ den what dat one wuz." (MS, 707)

This fascinating revision occurs when Twain works on Jim's voice. At this point in the novel, after the chase and shooting on the Phelps's farm, Jim has been silent for a considerable time, and Twain therefore had not 'heard' Jim speak in his imagination for quite a while. The change of "day" to "dey" occurred in the process of the original composition, and thereafter Twain makes no apparent dialect changes in the rest of the speech, because then he was 'hearing' Jim. But once Jim's voice was 'heard' accurately, Twain had to go back in his manuscript to change the earlier "was" to "wuz" and " 'uz", precisely capturing Jim's speech.

One of Huck's remarks about Tom Sawyer may serve as an emblem of Twain's actual practice. The original version read:

> In them circumstances he could always throw in an amount of style that was suitable. (MS, 500)

But Twain crossed out "he could always throw" and wrote in above the cancellation so that the revised version reads:

In them circumstances *it warn't no trouble to him to throw* in an amount of style that was suitable.

The revision presents a brilliantly paradoxical metafictional statement. Although there is little substantive difference between the versions, Twain has himself taken the trouble to create a revision which emphasizes the ease of appropriate style. Genetic criticism reveals that effort was exerted to create a sense of effortlessness. A full understanding of Twain's precision in tonality prepares us to understand the larger, overlapping but more substantive topics, such as characterization.

Notes

1. See, for example, Franklin R. Rogers's *Mark Twain's Burlesque Patterns* (esp. 26–94) for one treatment of the evolution of narrators' personalities.

2. Among the many studies of Twain which explore the role of innocence, Tony Tanner's *The Reign of Wonder: Naivety and Reality in American Literature* and William C. Spengemann's *Mark Twain and the Backwoods Angel: The Matter of Innocence in the Works of Samuel L. Clemens* deserve special mention.

3. Precisely this pronunciation is recalled by Twain when he wrote in *Pudd'nhead Wilson* about Roxy's child "Tom" who is brought up as a pampered, willful child: "He would call for anything and everything he saw, simply saying, "Awnt it!" (want it) which was a command. When it was brought, he said in a frenzy, and motioning it away with his hands, "Don't awnt it! don't awnt it!" and the moment it was gone he set up frantic yells of "Awnt it! awnt it! awnt it!" and Roxy had to give wings to her heels . . ." (39).

4. This section of the novel, like several others where an episode is beginning, needed many clarifying revisions. Twain had to change the temporal scheme to allow sufficient time for a transatlantic message and for the Wilks brothers' voyage. And Twain also revised for simple clarity; the king inquires, "Did they send them word?" and Twain canceled "they" and substituted "anybody" (MS, 206).

5. It was occasionally difficult for Twain to capture some of the voices and phrasing accurately. For example, later in the episode Twain first had the king say, "Good land, duke, lemme hug you! It's the most gorj'" but then Twain struck out "gorj'" and wrote in "gorgue," clearly an alternative method of spelling, then crossed out "gorgue" and substituted "gorjis," an apparently acceptable version of "gorgeous" (MS, 251). However, by the time the novel appears in print the word has become "dazzling." Perhaps "gorjis" seemed too hard to recognize, and the change to "dazzling" is an example of revision of voice toward clarity and readability. Throughout the novel Twain was concerned with voice, tone, and dialect. He even tinkered with the voice of the very minor character Sister Hotchkiss, working on the short words to get her dialect precisely to his liking by changing "heard" to "hearn" (MS, 723). See also David Carkeet's "The Dialects in *Huckleberry Finn*" for an

intelligent analysis of the evidence. See also Twain's comments about revising "A True Story" in the letter to Howells of 20 September 1874.

6. The king's character has, of course, certain traits required both of a novelist and of Huck, including fluency, fabulating skill, deceptiveness, and the ability to make a rapid, shrewd analysis of character. It is worth mentioning that Twain was later called, ironically enough, "the King" by Miss Lyon, his secretary from 1902 to 1907; Livy's nickname for her husband was "Youth."

3. Characterization

How could Twain create such a variety of lively, fascinating characters? The fictional world of *Huckleberry Finn* contains numerous memorable people, ranging across the spectrum from saints to sinners. Most of those who populate this world share an important trait, a mental ability central to this novel: almost all employ duplicity. Only a few are accidentally deceptive; most deceive deliberately.

Let a short catalogue of the relatively moral, minor female characters serve as illustration. Miss Watson deceives Jim about her intention to sell him, Mrs. Judith Loftus tricks Huck when she gets him to throw a lead bar in order to penetrate his disguise, and Sophia Grangerford deceives Huck in order to get him to carry a message which starts the elopement and the massacre. Similarly, Mary Jane Wilks helps to fool the king and duke, and Aunt Sally Phelps enjoys deceiving her husband about the arrival of their expected guest. This level of duplicity among these comparatively moral and truthful folks reveals the peculiar instability of the novel's world.

Even Jim withholds from Huck until the novel's end the knowledge that Pap Finn is dead, thus assuring that Huck will not return North and thereby abandon the escaped slave in a vulnerable situation. If we add to these deceptions the countless deceits created by the king and duke as well as the immoral and moral tricks played by Tom and Huck, we realize that we are exploring a universe of pervasive duplicity.

Twain revised skillfully to characterize these people. The writer may alter many variables; a minimal list would include the character's physical description, speech, and action, as well as other people's descriptions, speech, and actions regarding the first person. And, of course, the context, emphasis, and cumulative interactions also affect our perception of each characterization. Within the Wilks episode, our attention will range from the minor to the major characters and from those who deserve the readers' sympathy to those who command our contempt.

Let us begin with a quite minor character, the genuine brother of Peter Wilks, a man who arrives from England too late to see his brother alive and instead finds two rogues trying to steal his estate. At one point in the ensuing conflict, both the fraudulent and the recently arrived brothers describe what was tattooed on the dead man's breast. After the king has bluffed, the real brother has his turn:

> "Good!" says the old gentleman. "Now what you did see on his breast—or what you could a seen, anyway, for they're there—was a *small dim* P, and B, (*which is an initial he dropped when he was young,*) and a W, with dashes between them, so P-B-W-." (MS, 395)

Several points may be made about this revision. Twain effectively developed the man's speech by creating a self-interrupting style. The insertion "*small dim*" provides more concrete detail, and the second insertion adds a temporal dimension as the brother parenthetically remembers intimate details which the befuddled townspeople cannot know. Accordingly, the newly arrived brothers seem more alone as well as more credible. These precise details add to the suspense and create a marked contrast between the king's simple bluff and the brother's touching memories. Twain drew upon the literary tradition of identification by skin marking, which ranges back to the *Odyssey*, partially to increase plot complications and also to help create a vital personality.

Upon occasion, a minor character may have come to life but, for novelistic reasons, be doomed to suffer a polite form of euthanasia, becoming less vivid through the revision process. For example, Twain apparently decided to de-characterize Joanna Wilks. In the manuscript version the passage reads:

> "Well, it's jest perfectly awful, I think," says the hairlip. "I'll go to uncle ⟨Harney⟩ Harvey and _____." (MS, 359)

The unfortunate girl briefly came alive by using two absolute adverbs, one mispronounced, the other inappropriate. Twain may have even tried, momentarily, to present her speech impediment in her pronunciation of the uncle's name, or it may have been a momentary authorial confusion with the name of Harney Shepherdson. The printed version, however, has lost much of its color and individuality; the adverbs have disappeared, and the passage is straightforward: "Well, it's awful, I think," says the hare-lip. "I'll go to Uncle Harvey and . . . " (247). The revision transforms this minor character into a less vivid, less individualized character. The change reduces the child's function in the novel so that she serves only as a counterpoint to her more fully developed sister, revealing that Huck can lie dexterously to Joanna while he cannot easily lie to Mary Jane.

Indeed, Mary Jane Wilks functions as an exemplary angel-woman of Twain's imagination. She serves as a contrast to Emmeline Grangerford, who could write pathetic sentimental poetry on any mournful occasion. Mary Jane reacts to the death of her uncle and to the resulting altered circumstances with dignity and honesty; she reacts to her deception by the king and duke with intelligence and force. Exactly how Twain created her character deserves close examination. In the manuscript, when Huck reveals the deception by her "uncles," Twain first wrote:

> It jolted her up, like everything, of course; but I ⟨had⟩ was over the shoal water, now, so I warbled right along, and told her every blame thing, from where we first struck that young fool going up to the steamboat, plumb through to where she flung herself onto the king's breast at the front door and he kissed her sixteen or seventeen times—and then up she jumps, with her face afire like sunset, and says: (MS, 333–34)

Twain inserted another description after "warbled right along": "—*her eyes a-blazing higher and higher all the time*." This description adds gradations of spunk to the qualities of the deceived girl, and the fire imagery prepares for the concluding sunset comparison. The text leads the alert reader to infer that Mary Jane's personality is energetic, principled, coherent, and consistent.

Further in the manuscript, when she reassures Huck, a similar revision occurs. Mary Jane tells Huck, "O, come, stop blaming yourself—it's too bad to do it, *and I won't allow it*—You couldn't help it; it wasn't your fault." (MS, 347–48) This insertion establishes a more commanding personality, an attitude of dominance both quaint and admirable in the recently orphaned adolescent girl.

Mary Jane is also elaborately characterized when Huck thinks of the farewell scene, the passage cited in the first chapter. Such characterization is reciprocal; as Huck describes her he also characterizes himself.

Huck's presentation of himself—the core of the novel—conveys a complex balancing of attitudes. Motherless child of a homeless, violent, alcoholic, Irish father, Huck has certain predictable personality traits such as an imagination of disaster, a desire to keep everyone happy, a need to maintain control, a great ability to mediate, and a highly developed ability to observe and infer about moods and intentions. As a neglected, abandoned, abused child, he has developed both a necessary independence and a surprisingly resilient self-esteem. Like many children of alcoholics, Huck has almost no knowledge of what is normal; this part of his personality contributes to his frequent innocent tones, his open-eyed wonderment, such as when he describes the homes of the Widow Douglas and the Grangerfords. Huck's famous ability to tell lies is a necessary survival trait. His trip down-river offers a perfect example of what children of alcoholics call "the geographic cure," flight from an impossible situation. Huck usually controls his emotions, fearful of extremes.[1] In addition, Huck is highly responsible, self-accusatory, and quite able to see a situation or conflict from many points of view. He probably is also too deferential to authority, and he probably has a hard time distinguishing between legitimate and illegitimate authority. He may handle some moral questions too simply, with his own survival or avoidance of harm as primary considerations. A full understanding of Huck's characterization can develop by considering first the general modifications, then the revisions about Huck's kindliness in a moral crisis and, finally, his cleverness in deceptions, a personality trait which he shares with the king and duke.

As has been noted, Twain modified some of Huck's statements because they were too rough, too adult, or too colloquial for his character (e.g., "If I know a girl by the rake of her stern; and I think I do"). Twain revised to achieve the proper amount of impropriety, the correct degree of incorrectness. For example, after Huck has taken the Wilks's money from the king and duke and hurriedly placed it in Peter Wilks's coffin, the boy says that he didn't want to be "catched with six thousand dollars in my hands that nobody hadn't hired me to take care of. Not any of the pie for me, says I" (MS, 300). The last sentence—a colorful, mock-polite refusal—Twain replaced with a more ordinary, sensible conclusion, "I don't wish to be mixed up in no such business as that, I says to myself" (231). Similarly, when the boy explains his plan to Mary Jane, he says, "And if it just so happens that I miss fire, and don't get away, but get took up, along with them" (MS, 338). The phrase "miss fire" apparently likened Huck to a gun or an explosive, and Twain decided to omit this inappropriate comparison in print.

Some modifications in Huck's characterization certainly emphasize his highly developed social intelligence. Huck seems to know exactly what to say in certain conversations to win over his listener. For example, when Mary Jane Wilks reacts to his revelation about her 'uncles' with indignation: ". . . we'll have them tarred and feathered, and flung in the river!" Huck originally replies, "Do you mean, before you go to Mr. Lothrop's, or—" (MS, 334). This first manuscript version has Huck's disagreement stated openly, bluntly. Twain, however, inserted in the manuscript at the beginning of Huck's reply, "*Exackly. But.*" Huck agrees with the indignation, recognizing Mary Jane's need for vengeful language and continues with his plan by asking the same question in a doubting rather than a confrontive tone. The third stage, the printed version, sounds a more vague, concessive, and questioning tone: "Cert'nly. But do you mean, *before* you go to Mr. Lothrop's, or—" (241). Similarly, later, after Huck's plan is well formulated, he again runs into some unexpected difficulties with Mary Jane:

> "'Deed <u>that</u> ain't the ticket, Miss Mary Jane," I says, "by no manner of means. I <u>want</u> you to go <u>before</u> breakfast."
> "Why?"
> "Now what did you reckon . . ." (MS, 343)

By dropping "I want you to" and "Now," Twain softened Huck's response considerably. The revised sentence at first seems less effective because the possible reference to time ("Now") in the passage had been appropriate, but the tone of "Now what do you reckon" may seem somewhat heavy and scornful compared with Huck's more gentle, more considerate revised attitude: "'Deed, *that* ain't the ticket, Miss Mary Jane," I says, "by no manner of means; go *before* breakfast" (243). Huck's tone of voice characterizes him as a polite planner who respects his helper.

In a closely related passage, when explaining how to prove the king's and duke's misdeeds, Huck advises Mary Jane to send up to Bricksville and say that they "got the boys that played the Burning Shame, and ask for some witnesses—⟨You'll have the⟩. Why, you'll have that en-tire town down here before you can wink, *Miss Mary* ⟨*Jane*⟩. And they'll come a-bilin', too, you hear <u>me</u>" (MS, 341). Huck's voice, at first, hits a wrong tone, speaking of "the boys" with adult male familiarity. In print, the word "boys" was revised to "men," a change that lessens the chance that the frauds could be regarded merely as mischievous pranksters and instead increases the distance between Huck and the "men." The peremptory "you hear <u>me</u>" was also dropped before print. Modifications of tonality interact with characterization.

Twain complicated Huck's personality by attention to his ethical attitudes or moral sense. Indeed, part of the fascination Huck has exercised over generations of readers comes from his peculiar combination of good-heartedness with cleverness—and his joining innocence with accurate observation. Once when Huck is compelled by the king to put on his better clothes, he says "I done it, but it was because I had to, it wasn't because I wanted to." This original version makes Huck's situation similar to Jim's because both are forced to do the king's bidding, Jim as a slave, and Huck almost as a slave. But in the revised text's phrasing, "I done it, of course," Huck seems more free and adventuresome because his temperament appears comparatively flexible.

Huck's personality is further developed by his joking or confiding to the reader. In the manuscript Huck had said, "So then I lit out—for bed, I said—which was another stretcher. When I got by myself, I took a think" (MS, 283). In revising this section, Twain made Huck's deception more deliberate, his thinking more active: "So then I lit out—for bed, I said, meaning some time or another. When I got by myself, I went to thinking the thing over" (225). The lie of the first version becomes a deliberately imprecise, misleading truth in the second; consequently we come to trust Huck's ability to think in the second version.

Most readers, however, are fascinated not by Huck's intellectual development but by his elemental decency, his good-heartedness. This trait Twain created with some care. When Joanna Wilks questioned Huck about his life as a servant in England, she suspected he was lying. Huck managed to cover some of the lies, leading her to say that she'd believe some of what he said. The manuscript continues:

> So I let it stand at that. It was getting off tolerable easy, and I didn't want to crowd her.
> I went to bed, then, pretty soon, but didn't go to sleep. It laid kinder heavy on my conscience to see them girls getting robbed, because it seemed— (MS, 278)

In the second paragraph, Huck speaks—uncharacteristically—in a rather abstract fashion, and we can speculate that "because it seemed" would have led to more such thinking on the next page. But Twain canceled the second paragraph.[2] Then he canceled the first paragraph and continued the sequence by having each of the other sisters sail in and bawl out Joanna for making Huck feel ashamed.[3] This change results in Huck making his decision to attempt to steal the money back. But his decision grows out of his concrete reactions to the admirable personality of each girl rather than from his own abstract reasoning. The manuscript describes the second sister's action:

> and if you'll believe me, she did give Hair-Lip hark from the tomb! Says I to myself, And this is <u>another</u> one that I'm letting him rob! (MS, 281)

In an unusual revision, Twain inserted a paragraph sign between the two sentences, in effect making "Says I to myself . . ." a one-sentence paragraph with great emphasis. Instead of talking to his readers about his conscience, Huck simply talks to himself, responding to the girls' personalities. This kind of revision presents Huck as a sympathetic, intuitively decent character.

Once Huck has decided to tell Mary Jane about the fraud, he tells her somewhat roughly, somewhat sarcastically in the first version:

> "Don't you holler. Just set still, and take it like a major. I got to tell the truth, and it ain't got no resemblance to pie, neither, so don't you be disappointed." (MS, 332)

But in print, Huck's words become less sarcastic and hence more sympathetic. Twain drops the inappropriate military reference, but Huck instead advises her to "take it like a man." Perhaps the tone resembles that of an adolescent toward a chum, oblivious to sexuality, urging acceptance of adulthood. Twain also omitted the sardonic comparison to "pie." In the final printed version, Huck's tone sounds more considerate:

> "Don't you holler. Just set still, and take it like a man. I got to tell the truth, and you want to brace up, Miss Mary, because it's a bad kind, and going to be hard to take, but there ain't no help for it." (240)

The third sentence makes the obligation to tell the truth and to accept the truth mutual. The final tone sounds polite to "Miss Mary," honest and empathic.

Huck's ability to share Mary Jane's emotions also affects another passage. While trying to avoid telling her that the bag of gold can be found lying on her dead uncle's stomach, Huck says:

> Blame it, I didn't want to set her to thinking about her troubles again, and her poor old dead uncle; and I couldn't seem to frame my mouth to tell her what would make her see that corpse laying in the coffin with that bag of money on his stomach. (MS, 348)

In the printed version, Twain dropped the mild anger, "Blame it," and the explicit mention of "her poor old dead uncle." Huck's difficulty with his mouth is changed slightly, from the static "frame" to a more active phrasing, "I couldn't seem to get my mouth to tell her. . ." (244). Huck seems to be more separated from his mouth, as if his control over the organ that gives disturbing information has suddenly vanished.

Although he seems quite sensitive to the emotions of others, Huck usually says very little about his own deep emotions. After he gives Mary Jane a note telling where he put the money he says, in the first version, "It kinder made my eyes water a little, to remember her crying there all by herself in the night" (MS, 349–50). In print, Twain canceled "kinder," and the emotion, although still understated, becomes less vague in the mere laconic description of effects, "made my eyes water" (245). Huck is crying for her, with her, and, as one orphan touched by the plight of another, perhaps he cries a bit for himself as well. The emotion, characteristically, is understated, as it had been at the end of the Grangerford feud: "I cried a little when I was covering up Buck's face, for he was mighty good to me."

Although Huck is usually relatively reticent about his powerful, decent emotions, he often can be explicit and ironic about another side of his personality. When he is with the king and duke, his duplicitous traits dominate. This doubleness forms a salient part of Huck's characterization just as it represents a significant factor in Twain's fiction. The boy's cleverness can be dramatized, but he should not appear too similar to the scheming swindlers or else his character would suffer contamination. Let us pick up the narrative after Huck has decided to try to steal the money back from the king and duke. While looking for the money in their bedroom, Huck gets trapped. The manuscript version states:

> But I see I couldn't do nothing without a candle, and I dasn't light one, of course. So ⟨I was going to leave, then, and have a think, but I didn't get the chance.⟩ I heard their ⟨voices⟩ *footsteps* a-coming, and was going to skip under the bed; and I reached for it. . . . (MS, 286)

Twain changed "voices" to "*footsteps*," a fairly unimportant modification permitting the impostors to keep up the pretense of the duke as an inarticulate deaf man until they enter the privacy of the room. The more interesting change involves the cancellation of the portion in brackets. The words seem unexceptional, and one speculates that it is actually Twain who attempted to figure out what to do next with the plot. At any rate, Twain canceled the portion, and then, on the reverse of MS, 286, Twain composed a passage to be inserted:

> *I judged I'd got to do the other thing—lay for them, and eavesdrop. About that time,*

This alteration obviously puts Huck in much more control at the beginning of the episode. It is worth emphasizing that in the completed novel this episode duplicates the earlier situation on the *Walter Scott*, when Huck also heard villains with loot plotting how to end their venture, but this time Huck has planned the eavesdropping.[4]

Although Huck had been an innocent thrill-seeker on the *Walter Scott*, he functions as a skillful thinker in the Wilks episode. But the skill of his thinking resembles that of the thieves, and this similarity forced several cancellations. At one point in the manuscript Huck says:

> I judged they hadn't come up for nothing but to talk a little business, and wouldn't stay long; it wouldn't be quite the thing for them to jump the wake so early. (MS, 286–87)

The passage has Huck thinking as the king and duke *should* be plotting; the passage was canceled and instead, in the next paragraph, only the king states directly the need to return to the grieving people downstairs. Perhaps Twain realized that, momentarily, Huck was identifying too closely with the rascals.

Similarly, on MS, 289, Huck was:

> reckoning we would give that wake the slip, late in the night, some time, and pack off down the river with the swag. So was the duke; but when he mentioned it, the king rips. . . .

Twain canceled the passage and only the duke states the opinions; it is apparent that Twain had to limit the intellectual similarity of Huck and the thieves. By taking the thoughts away from Huck and giving them only to the swindlers, Twain keeps Huck comparatively innocent.

Although this kind of differentiation limited Huck, Twain endowed him with the ability to be cleverly ironic. After the men discuss their plans, while Huck eavesdrops, they re-hide the gold, thinking that:

> . . . it warn't in no danger of getting stole, now.
> Which was a mistake. I had it out of there before they was half-way downstairs. (MS, 294)

The manuscript version is abrupt and forceful. But in the printed version Twain amended the section to read:

> . . . it warn't in no danger of getting stole, now.
> But I knowed better. I had it out of there before they was half-way down stairs. (229)

Since Huck's putative ignorance has been a repeated motif (e.g., earlier "Don't know nothing" and "Perfect saphead" passages), the revised version seems particularly satisfying. Huck's superior knowledge, in this deceptive universe, earns additional respect because of the ironic expression.

Similarly, his canniness and social intelligence permit him to predict and exploit the thieves' thinking. After the scoundrels discover that the gold is missing, they cross-examine Huck about their room:

> The duke says:
> "Have you seen anybody else go in there?"
> "No, your grace, not as I remember, I believe."
> "Stop and think."
> I studied a while, and then says:
> "Well, I've seen the niggers go in there several times."
> "What? all of them?"
> "No—at least not all at once. That is, I don't think I ever seen them all go <u>in</u> at once; and I believe I never see them all come <u>out</u> at once but just one time." (MS, 318–19)

After "I studied a while," Twain wrote in a caret and inserted "***and I see my chance***;". This change makes Huck much more calculating. He utilizes perfectly the opportunity to stop and think in order to create his misleading reply. By pretending to be an unknowing and cooperative absolute literalist, Huck encourages the king and duke to look down upon his thinking ability and therefore to accept all his information as true, since the speaker must be too simple to be deceptive. Huck gradually feeds them minimal literal answers to their questions, letting them project their own trickery on the slaves. On the reverse of the manuscript page, Twain wrote in an insertion to follow "Well, I've seen the niggers go in there several times":

> ***Both of them give a little jump; and looked like they hadn't ever expected it, and then like they <u>had</u>. Then the duke says:***

Huck closely interprets their reactions, and it provides comedy to observe the frauds deceive themselves with Huck's help.

Once the thieves are committed to this line of thinking, Twain allows Huck to become more blatantly ironic in revision. Huck explains:

> "so, I see***n***, easy enough, that they'd shoved in there to do up your ***majesty's*** room, or something, sposing you was up; and found you <u>warn't</u> up, so ***they*** was hoping to slide out of the way of trouble ⟨before⟩ without waking you up, if they hadn't already waked you ***up***." (MS, 320)

The situation creates complex irony because Huck, as the servant, explains the actions of other servants while he himself slides "out of the way of trouble." The king and duke think themselves clever investigators while they dupe themselves. As if to emphasize Huck's mock subservience, Twain modified "to do up your room" to "to do up your *majesty's* room." The insertion recalls the king's false dominance and stresses Huck's and Twain's contempt for the conned, pretentious thief.

Huck's character blends cleverness with compassion, even for the king. After the escape from the mob, when the king and duke return once more to the raft, they argue about the loss of the money, and the duke starts to choke the king. The original version reads:

> The king begun to gurgle, and *then* he gasps out:
> "'Nough!—I own up!"
> So the duke took his hands off, and says: (MS, 419–20)

The moment, of course, had frightened Huck, and for the printed version Twain inserted right after the confession:

> I was very glad to hear him say that, it made me feel much more easier than what I was feeling before. (264)

Huck had felt fear both that his own involvement in the theft would be discovered and that the aged king would be injured. Characteristically, the boy's relief is a double emotion.

The similarity and difference between Huck and the rascals is also developed by creating parallel contexts, using the structural resemblance between the opening of the Wilks and Phelps episodes to establish differences in character.[5] At the beginning of the Wilks episode, the king had learned about the situation by pumping a local youth for information. Likewise, after Huck discovers that Jim has vanished from the raft, he shrewdly pumps a country boy for information and learns that the king has sold his chance on Jim for forty dollars. Huck pretends that he had been endangered by the runaway slave and questions the country boy. In the two cases the king and Huck lie, learn of the situation and gather names, then go into town, claim loss, and cry deceptively. The king tries to steal property; Huck tells the duke he wishes to regain his own property, but he actually wishes to restore Jim's freedom.[6] Twain's imagination presents the pattern in duplicate, revealing that Huck can be as deceptive as the king and that Huck can duplicate the pattern for unselfish reasons with himself in control.

Although each scene is presented realistically, the doubling technique qualifies the "reality" of the novel. The similarity of the two actions emphasizes the importance of the difference of intent between the king and Huck.

Huck's final confrontation with the duke offers a masterpiece of mutual deception, partially enriched by revision. When Huck happens upon the duke in town, the villain demands ten cents from Huck. The manuscript reads:

> I had money, so I give him ten cents, but begged him to spend it for something to eat, and give me some, because I said it was all the money I had, and I hadn't had nothing to eat since yesterday. (MS, 453–54)

Twain modified the printed text to read "I had considerable money" (274), perhaps to give Huck more financial freedom; certainly the revision makes Huck seem smarter, trickier than the duke.

The most extensive manuscript revision in this transitional section has the same effect. When Huck is inquiring about "his" slave, the duke makes him promise not to tell about the Burning Shame ruse in exchange for information about Jim. Huck relates:

> So I promised, and he says:
> The man that bought him is named Abram Foster—

But Twain first inserted a caret after "says," indicating that he planned a short insertion, then canceled that caret and made another caret with the word "OVER," indicating that he immediately wished more space to develop the insertion we find on the reverse of MS, 457:

> *"A farmer by the name of Silas Ph—" and then he stopped. You see, he started to tell me the truth; but when he stopped, that way, and begun to study and think, again, I reckoned he was changing his mind. And so he was. He wouldn't trust me; he wanted to make sure of having me out of the way the whole three days. So pretty soon he says:*

Huck is not at all deceived, but can follow the duke's thinking almost second by second. We notice, as a mere curiosity at this point, that the novelistic process resembles the deceptive process. Repeatedly we shall notice a relationship between the deception of Twain's characters and the character of Twain's deceptions. Huck manipulates the duke into sending him away immediately: "That was the order I wanted, and that was the one I played for. I wanted to be left free to work my plans" (MS, 458). Twain's skill in effectively revising to make the good-hearted Huck a cannier perceiver commands respect.

Although the king and duke have much less complex characters, Twain had to use similar skills to individualize each of these rapscallions to increase the distance between his villains. Their characterizations are developments of clear traits, with occasional modulation for novelistic reasons. For example, at the beginning of the Wilks episode, the king describes the situation as follows: "Alas, alas, our poor brother—⟨!"⟩ *gone, and we never got to see him; oh, it is too hard!*" (MS, 234). The king's comment is ironic because he had never seen Mr. Wilks; he speaks to articulate the situation, thereby putting himself in command, claiming the relationship, and concealing his deception in a moment of bathos. Twain apparently wished to emphasize the sanctimoniousness and exaggeration of the king by revising the printed text to read, "oh, it's too, *too* hard!" (210). The king's echoic verbal fluency and verbose duplicity receive a touch more emphasis.

The king's hypocrisy depends upon the townspeoples' credulity, of course; Twain apparently wished to place the blame fairly. Accordingly, he modified the manuscript passage, "The king he visited around, in the evening, and sweetened everybody up, and made himself ever so popular;" (MS, 311), to read in print, "and made himself ever so friendly;" (234), thus shifting the emphasis from the opinion of the people to the false acting of the king.

Twain's contempt for the two thieves consistently softens in the revision process. As a detailed study will reveal, the bestial imagery describing them decreases. And the terms of disgust are slightly modified. For example:

> then the king he shoved in and got off some of his usual rot, and at last the job was through, (MS, 308)

became slightly reworded in the final version by changing "rot" to "rubbage" (233). Although both men are scoundrels, the king's talkative hypocrisy and ignorant colloquialisms seem different from the duke's pretensions to learning and culture as revealed in his Shakespeare plays.

The initial characterization of the duke presents a man both physically threatening and verbally vivid. One type of revision seems designed to make the duke appear as a slightly less lively rural personality. For example, when the thieves each believe the other has stolen the money, the manuscript version has the duke say:

> "It makes me feel right down ridicklous to think I was soft enough to believe that rubbage." (MS, 420–21)

but Twain changed to a more conventional "It makes me feel ridiculous. . ." (264). Moreover the same kind of change occurs as the duke curses the king:

> "Cuss you, I can see, now, why you was so anxious to make up the deffersit—you wanted to get what money I'd got out of the Burning Shame and one thing or another, and scoop it all, you unsatisfiable, tunnel-bellied old sewer!" (MS, 421)

Twain dropped the concluding rude, splendidly accurate smelly characterization of the king from the printed version, and the duke sounds, unfortunately, much less vivid and angry.

The duke's potential for violence also decreased: "Do you reckon that nigger'll blow on us? ⟨I'd⟩ *We'd* kill him if he done that!" (MS, 454) is changed so the threat in print is "We'd skin him . . ." (274), a more vague rural expression which contributes to the general softening and raising of the duke's diction and characterization. When the duke suspects Huck, he originally said, "Blamed if I think I'd trust you. By George, if you was to blow on us—" (MS, 455). Twain crossed out the exclamation in manuscript and wrote in, "*Why*," turning the vehemence into a bland phrase which would not be criticized. Nevertheless, Huck perceives the duke as a definite threat. The manuscript states, "I never see the duke look so wicked out of his eyes before. I went on a-whimpering. . ." (MS, 455–56). But Twain revised out the threatening "wicked" and replaced it with a word without ethical implications but with only a vague visual meaning, "*ugly*." Although we may regret that the revision moves the characterization of the duke away from vividness toward blandness, he does function as a subordinate figure of evil.

The care and artistic insight Twain used in his revisionary process should help destroy the idea that he was a careless, hasty genius. On the contrary, he developed a whole spectrum of characters—from the very good, through the complex Huck, to the very evil—with the detailed precision needed for memorable fiction. Moreover, Twain made all types of revisions at the different stages. Because of the overlapping effects of the changes, the kaleidoscope image seems appropriate.

Notes

1. Sympathetic readers from non-alcoholic homes may re-read, slowly, the last six paragraphs of Chapter VI, when Huck's father gets the D.T.s and attempts to kill

Huck. The child's final words, after training a gun on the passed-out father, are probably the most emotional but understated in the book: "And how slow and still the time did drag along."

2. Huck apparently has no moral difficulty telling unimportant lies about his life as a valet in England to Joanna, but his conscience is quite troubled about the king and duke robbing the girls. It is possible that Twain relied upon the word "kinder" or "kinda" when Huck tried to figure out a moral dilemma; the word choice seems amazingly apt, for it both creates a vagueness and mentions Huck's main criterion for problem solving, being kind.

3. The importance of shame and guilt is explored in "Christianity in Conflict with Morality" (Chapter 8).

4. Since the *Walter Scott* episode was a manuscript insertion, it is impossible to prove which overhearing episode was written first. But as shall become clear, I believe that the overhearing aboard the *Walter Scott* was written after some version of the Wilks episode was composed.

5. A contrast exists between Huck, with his many false names, and the king and duke whose real names are non-existent.

6. In each case, blacks are sent away (the Wilkses' slaves and Jim), and in each case a white youth who knows the truth (Mary Jane and Huck) is sent four miles "right out into the country back here" or "forty mile back here in the country," with instructions to move quickly and not talk. In the first case, Huck wants to prevent Mary Jane Wilks from revealing her knowledge of the frauds; in the second case, the duke wants to prevent Huck from revealing anything about the Burning Shame (Royal Nonesuch) show.

4. Humor

> I value humor highly, and am constitutionally fond of it, but I should not like it as a steady diet. For its own best interests, humor should take its outings in grave company; its cheerful dress gets heightened color from the proximity of sober hues. For me to edit a comic magazine would be an incongruity and out of character, for of the twenty-three books I have written eighteen do not deal in humor as their chiefest feature, but are half and half admixtures of fun and seriousness. I think I have seldom deliberately set out to be humorous, but have nearly always allowed the humor to drop in or stay out, according to its fancy.
>
> Letter to S.S. McClure about a possible editorship of
> a magazine. Quoted by A.B. Paine, *Mark Twain,*
> *A Biography*, II, 1100

Although Twain casually claimed that he "allowed the humor to drop in or stay out according to its fancy," the evidence contradicts him. The humor which we treasure apparently came rather easily to Twain, but effort was needed to fit the comedic imagination to the aesthetic requirements of the novel.[1] Twain's additions and deletions cast a revealing light on this fictional achievement. He revised his humor to differentiate characters and deepen characterization. In addition, Twain's humorous talent certainly affected plot and thematic issues. The integration of the humor in the novel was not effortless, but often the result of careful revision.

One relatively simple use of humor involves the differentiation of characters. There were times, in the early stages of the writing of the Wilks episode, when several different characters were not clearly distinguished. For example, when the king and duke were searching for some new swindle, Twain originally has Huck say:

> They couldn't hit on any project that suited, exactly; so at last the duke said he reckoned he would lay off an hour or two and see if he couldn't put up something for the benefit of the Arkansas village; and the king allowed he would drop over to 'tother village, without any plan, but just trust in Providence to direct him the profitable way—meaning the devil, I reckon. (MS, 213–14)

Since both schemers use similar irony, their personalities are momentarily blurred. But the duke will ultimately become a less gifted fraud; accordingly after "the duke said he would lay off" Twain inserted "*and work his brains*," comically making his mental processes more labored than the king's. At a later stage of revision, the duke's phrase, "put up something for the benefit of the Arkansas village," becomes simply "put up something on the Arkansaw village" in the printed text (204). This finished statement about the duke effectively attributes less irony to him, presenting him as a less gifted, more mechanical fraud. In this case, Twain moved away from irony, subordinating the possibilities of humor to the novelist's need to distinguish between his characters.

Of course, many revisions involving humor either create or integrate larger issues, such as plot developments, situations, or thematic lines. A major plot development, for example, probably grew from Twain's desire to continue a humorous situation and prolong the satire on religion. The humorous possibilities of the entire Wilks episode increase substantially with a revision which Twain made in the manuscript version. The king is posing as the Reverend Elexander Blodgett and is pumping the rural lad for information about the Wilks situation in order to steal from the heirs. The lad says about the legitimate heir:

> "O, he lives in England—Sheffield—hasn't ever been in this country. He hasn't had any too much time—and besides he mightn't a got the letter at all, you know." (MS, 223–24)

Twain, in accord with the speaker's parenthetical style, revised in, after Sheffield "—*preaches there*—," a decision of great importance. Twain had the king posing as the Reverend Blodgett for four pages of manuscript and may have liked the situation of the greedy scoundrel posing as a minister. The revision permits Twain to develop a similar imposture at great length, having the king impersonate another minister and act both grieved and sanctimonious. Twain's satire against ministers and conventional religion could thus be enormously extended. Furthermore, the new role which the king must play of a fluent, cliche-spouting minister will provide for dramatic contrast with the duke's role as the deaf, inarticulate brother.

Later in the manuscript, we find a related passage in a summary paragraph describing Harvey Wilks's work as a dissenting minister. Twain added humor to Huck's voice by simply adding a syllable, creating the comic, unsophisticated mistake, "a dissent*er*ing minister" (MS, 227).[2] Such a revision seems, at first, like an unimportant change, but a careful reader may understand something about how Twain's imagination worked by remembering that the Wilks episode ends bizarrely with disinterring a corpse. The second claimant, the real brother, is indeed both a dissenter and a disinterer, for his appearance leads to a disagreement and an exhumation. When we understand the close interaction in the creative process of verbal wit, thematic concerns, and plot convolutions, we can feel the pulse of Twain's creative abilities.

As the novel grew through revision, the king became a more intelligent and more ironic character. Toward the end of his conversation with the rural jake, the king has determined that there is enough money to attempt to steal and has gathered a mass of other information which he will be able to use to support his false claim upon the Wilks's inheritance. Twain probably relished the humor of the situation because he expanded it by adding a passage on the back of MS, 228. The king concludes his dialogue with the country bumpkin:

> *"When did you say he died?"*
> *"I didn't say; but it was last night."*
> *"Funeral to-morrow, likely?"*
> *"Yes, ⟨a⟩'bout the middle of the day."*
> *"Well, it's all terrible sad; but we've all got to go, one time or another. So what we want to do is to be prepared; then we are all right."*
> *"Yes, sir, it's the best way. ⟨X⟩Ma used to always say that."*

When the pumping for information concludes, the king practices this bit of synthetic emotion, in keeping with his ministerial pose and in preparation for his later imposture. The king thinks he is now well "prepared" for his fraud, but he will not ultimately be right or all right. The cliche of the informant's reply continues the difference in characterization between the naive rural lad and the clever king, who is now confident enough to be ironic.

Several gradations of humor occur, ranging from the fairly complex covert humor, which occurs when the king conceals from the townspeople and Huck reveals to the readers, to the overt comedy which occurs as the king entertains the townspeople. The covert humor is more complex; the king's verbal facility and sense of superiority permit Twain to create many involuted humorous touches. One is delicately grotesque. When the king has mistakenly called the funeral obsequies "orgies," the duke slips him a note reading, "obsequies, you old fool." After the king reads the note he says:

> "Poor William, his heart's always right." (MS, 257)

Twain first underlined "always," then crossed out the underlining, reducing the emphasis, and, probably at about the same time, inserted "*afflicted as he is*," and underlined "heart," making a more explicit ironic contrast because it is really the exact opposite of the duke's qualities. The resulting final version:

> "Poor William, afflicted as he is, his *heart's* aluz right." (217)

is a savagely comic misstatement. Although the duke's ears are exceedingly sensitive, his emotionally and ethically undeveloped heart is quite afflicted.

The king's overt humor appeals to the townspeople and, accordingly, may seem somewhat heavy-handed to modern readers. After Doctor Robinson has denounced the frauds and failed to convince the townspeople or the orphaned girls to spurn the impostors, he says:

> "All right, I wash <u>my</u> hands of the matter. But I warn you all that a time's coming when you're going to be sick whenever you think of this day"—and away he went.
> "All right;" says the king, kinder mocking him, "we'll try and git 'em to ⟨throw⟩ send for you"—which made them all laugh, and they said it was a prime good hit. (MS, 264–65)

The joke developed and improved gradually. Twain probably first had in mind some phrasing like "throw the business your way," but immediately decided to let the king's phrasing remain less callous. Instead the humorist revised the warning to "you're going to *feel* sick and changed the king's reply to "All right, *doctor*." These revisions build an obvious preparation for the king's crude joke. The effect upon the novel of the finished joke is that the king has a brief victory over the doctor, and the townspeople seem more easily duped by the king's non-subtle humor.

Satire on religion required great sensitivity, and several revisions actually toned down or softened the humor. Some of these revisions are unfortunate from the modern point of view, but the originals probably would have been regarded by parts of Twain's first audience as too strong a satire or as a satire on an inappropriate target. For example, after the impostors have cried over Peter Wilks's coffin:

> every woman, nearly, went up to the girls, without saying a word, and kissed them, solemn, on the forehead, and then put their hand on their head, and looked up towards the throne, with the tears running down, and ⟨then let go⟩ then busted out and went off sobbing and swabbing, and give the next ⟨heifer⟩ *woman* a show. I never see anything so disgusting. (MS, 240–41)

The satire on religion is considerably altered by revising the manuscript's "throne," a reference to the seat of God, to the printed text's general word choice, "sky." The revised version keeps the satire on the women striking a melodramatic pose, in the manner of Emmeline Grangerford, but omits a religious focus for the satire. Similarly, Twain's original comparison of the women to heifers presented them as being large, dumb, and easily led.[3] "**Woman**" was clearly much less offensive. In general, Twain's revisions of humor in the Wilks episode frequently involve toning down potential offenses for novelistic considerations.

The original version of the king's coffin-side oration was a tour-de-force of religious cliches, which Huck quoted directly at unusual length:

> "Friends—good friends of the diseased and ourn to, I trust—it's indeed a sore trial to lose him, and a sore trial to miss seeing of him alive, after the wearisome long journey of four thousand mile; but it's a trial that's sweetened and sanctified to us by this dear sympathy and these holy tears; and so, out of our hearts we thank you, for out of our mouths we cannot, words being too weak and cold. May you find sech friends and sech sympathy yourselves, when your own time of trial comes, and may the affliction be softened to you as ourn is to-day, by the soothing ba'm of earthly love and the healing of heavenly grace. Amen." (MS, 241–42)

But in re-hearing this passage Twain shifts the entire section to indirect discourse and adds at least a cup of liquid diction, thereby incorporating Huck's sarcastic attitude:

> Well, by-and-by the king he gets up and comes forward a little, and works himself up and slobbers out a speech, all full of tears and flapdoddle about its being a sore trial for him and his poor brother to lose the diseased, and to miss seeing diseased alive, after the long journey of four thousand mile, but its a trial that's sweetened and sanctified to us by this dear sympathy and these holy tears, and so he thanks them out of his heart and out of his brother's heart, because out of their mouths they can't, words being too weak and cold, and all that kind of rot and slush, till it was just sickening; and then he blubbers out a pious goody-goody Amen, and turns himself loose and goes to crying fit to bust. (212–13)

By having Huck's derogatory opinion frame the passage, Twain manages to give less emphasis to humorous criticism of the highly conventional language of religion and more attention to the king's hypocritically moist manipulation of his subject and his audience.[4] Accordingly, the king's ability to rain and drizzle triteness so facilely reflects only indirectly on religion and the townspeople's willing acceptance of cliches.[5] The intervention of Huck's consciousness, with his explicit criticism of the king, prevents the reader from developing any sympathy. In this case, the comedy of disgust can reach a philosophic power. If one wished to set a difficult task for a humorous novelist, it could be: create a criticism of a sacrosanct subject, but have the criticism come from the mouth of an unsympathetic character, reported by a sympathetic character. With his revision, Twain creates such an complicated achievement.

The religious service to bury Mr. Wilks could, of course, be a dismal part of the novel.[6] The people are burying both a loved, decent man and the hidden gold. But Twain's presentation of Huck's views brightens the tone in a remarkable way. After the people have filed past the coffin, while the family is sobbing, Huck observes:

> There warn't no other sound but the scraping of feet on the floor, *and blowing noses.*

But then Twain added to the paragraph, on the back of MS, 302:

> *—because people always blows them more at a funeral than they do at other places except church.*

The scene is lightened by Huck's quasi-philosophic comment; the entire range of human behavior is momentarily summoned and compared. A deft hit links human discomfort and church behavior, but the innocent observation seems objective; hence, whatever emotion the scene deserves occurs in the context of a bittersweet smile.

Huck's description of the remainder of the ceremony seems subtly comic:

> They had borrowed a melodeum; and when everything was ready, a young woman sat down and pumped up its sufferings and everybody ⟨joined⟩ jined in and sung. (MS, 304)

Twain inserted after "a melodeum," "*a sick one,*" which correlated with the idea of the instrument as having "sufferings." But "sufferings" may have been uncomfortably close to the family's real grief. Perhaps in order to lessen the parallel, the printed version relates that the young woman "set down and worked it, and it was pretty skreeky and colicky, and everybody joined in and sung" (232). Twain transformed the idea of "sufferings" into an audible, minor, non-threatening irritant. The sick "melodeum" is literally a flawed "song to God," used to ridicule mechanical and human imperfection, sanctimoniousness, and hypocrisy while modified to protect valid human feelings in a religious service conducted by a king-minister impostor.

Another effect of Twain's revision involves the creation of tonal vitality, the constant possibility of surprising but not random shifts in tone. Much of the humorous development involves the unexpected. As the Wilks situation begins, when the king explains the situation to the duke:

> he tried to talk like an Englishman; and he done it pretty well, too, *for a slouch*. (MS, 230)

Huck's obvious sarcasm breaks up the predictable rhythm of the sentence by inserting the insulting stinger at the end. Huck's speech frequently has such irregularity, verve, and freshness.

This tonal vitality occurs often, adding to the constant pleasure of reading. At one point Huck describes the king's efforts to ingratiate himself with the townspeople in an obvious attempt to suppress suspicion. As the king works the crowd, "he blatted along, and managed to inquire about pretty much everybody in town, by name" (MS, 245). Twain apparently decided to adjust the level of the townspeople in the final text by amending to "pretty much everybody and dog in town, by his name" (213), immediately creating, in Huck's additive, non-discriminative style, both a comic diminution of the townspeople and a sarcastic, positive, but humorously incongruous, appraisal of the king's memory.

Twain's humor was also frequently spontaneous and subtle, and occasionally intricate. The quickness of his verbal wit is aptly demonstrated by a simple revision in the flow of original composition. When the townspeople are trying to decide between the king and duke and the newly arrived brothers, the Doctor says:

> "Come along, Hines; come along, the rest of you. We'll take these fellows to the tavern and ⟨confront⟩ affront 'em with the t'other couple." (MS, 379)

Twain's cleverness creates a minor change, made immediately in the heat of composition; although "confront" would be perfectly satisfactory, "affront" is a brilliant malapropism, implying insult. Twain's comic skills include the quickness to seize an ordinary phrase and spin it in mid-sentence, converting conventional serviceable language into something new. We do not know, with certainty, whether the "mistake" is Huck's or the Doctor's, but with the malapropism in the final version, this local authority figure gets a minor, human flaw.

This same attention to minute verbal detail and to restraint in the interests of the novel itself appears throughout the creative processes. Several brief examples from the later part of the novel are simply too enjoyable to omit. The portions of the manuscript which deal with Huck's arrival at the Phelps's farm, his surprising identification by Aunt Sally as Tom Sawyer, his meeting with Tom, and Tom's teasing of Aunt Sally with a false identity and kissing her received much revision. Pages were renumbered, many pages were dropped, and several pages needed recopying.

One minor problem involved Huck's "baggage." He had to leave the farm, supposedly to fetch his baggage but actually to alert Tom. After the boys do talk, Huck returns, not with relatively light baggage, but with Tom's trunk. A manuscript page originally numbered 504 and later renumbered 497 reveals that Huck was once welcomed back by a sarcastically humorous Uncle Silas:

> When we got home and ⟨took⟩ *fetched* the trunk ⟨out⟩ *in*, uncle Silas *chuckles and* says:
> "So that's your carpet bag, is it? You're too modest, Tom; don't let it strike in, it might kill you."

But this characterization of Uncle Silas presented him as ironic, and Twain omitted it, apparently preferring to keep the humorous emphasis upon Silas as an innocent, bumbling incompetent. (Twain also had other, thematic reasons to drop any association of Huck with a "carpet bag.")

Further into the episode, we find a large gap, where after reading a copy page numbered 510 we turn to 511 only to find directions to "Skip to page 517." Under a cancel we can read on the top of manuscript page 517 what must be an indication of the early, crude, abrupt version of Tom's joke:

> "Oh, nothing," says Tom, "only it's just all a joke which we hatched up: I ain't no William Thompson, I'm Sid Sawyer!"
> Then there was <u>another</u> hugging match, you bet you; and gaily times after it.

The passage reveals that at one time Tom lacked his polish, his tonal control over the joke. Most readers who end up despising Tom would probably be glad that Twain took the trouble to change Tom from being mechanical to being somewhat witty in his jokes, as he is in the final version.

But the core of the humor in the Phelps episode remains Huck's characterization and his tone. After Tom claims Sid's identity, the Phelps family has a feast. As we read the paragraph it is helpful to think of Sam Clemens's happy memories about the Quarles farm. Moreover, it may also be helpful to keep in mind Twain's joking about the value of Silas Phelps's sermons: "And never charged nothing for his preaching, *and it was worth it, too.*" (MS, 498):

> We had dinner out in that broad open passage between the house and the kitchen; and there was things enough on that table for seven families—and all hot, too; none of your blamed meat that's laid in a cubboard in a damp cellar all night and tastes like a hunk of your old cold grandfather *in the morning*. Uncle Silas he asked a pretty long blessing over it, but it was worth it; and it didn't cool it a bit, neither, *the ⟨X⟩ way I've seen them kind of interruptions do, lots of times.* (MS, 517–18)

For the final version Twain toned down the crudity of the humor. "Blamed meat" became "flabby tough meat." More importantly, what "tastes like a hunk of your old cold grandfather" became an almost equally disgusting, but less familial and more reflexive phrase, "tastes like a hunk of your old cold cannibal" (289). Readers who have just imaginatively attended the Wilks funeral may be less offended, and Twain probably enjoyed the involuted humor of asking readers to imagine how a "cannibal" might taste.

Occasionally Twain's verbal facility led him to an extreme of artifice, even in Huck's language, which one associates with intricate, allusive Renaissance rhetorical witcraft. For example, at one point Tom and Huck are hiding in the cellar when Silas Phelps comes downstairs to fix the rat holes:

> Then we heard steps on the stairs, and blowed out our light, and hid; and lo and beholes, here comes the old man, with a candle in one hand and a bundle of stuff in t'other, looking as absent-minded as year before last. (MS, 622)

The phrase "lo and beholes" mocks the dignified religious phrase, 'lo and behold,' and seems elaborately ingenious because all the people are in a cellar and concerned about filling rat-holes. But it would affect Huck's characterization. The phrase was omitted in the printed version, and few critics—if any—would mourn its loss.

The boys' antics on the Phelps farm include many humorous incidents, but several passages involving snakes may conclude this exploration of the range and delicacy of Twain's revisions. At one point the boys gather a collection of snakes, but when they return to their sack:

there warn't a blamed snake up there, when we went back—we didn't half tie the sack, and they worked out, somehow, and left. But it didn't matter, much, because they was still on the premises. So we judged we could get some of them again. (MS, 669)

On the manuscript page Twain inserted after "on the premises *somewheres*." This revision presents Huck's naive point of view and concern that the snakes will still be available, while emphasizing the indefiniteness of their locations. Of course, such a situation will drive Aunt Sally to distraction. The phrase "But it didn't matter, much," was blatantly ironic, because the pause entirely reverses the meaning of the words and is thus wrong for Huck's voice. Twain canceled the first comma, and Huck therefore seems comically oblivious to the confusion which shall occur.

The phrase "blamed snakes" appears in print as "blessed snakes." This change in adjectives transforms the phrasing from mild anger to mild affection expressed by a word with religious connotations, used sarcastically. For a time, a confusing Edenic allusion was possible in the manuscript version when the snakes "generally fell in your plate," but that was changed to "*generly landed* in your plate" (MS, 670). However Uncle Silas's wish that "there hadn't ever been no snakes created" was allowed to remain. These revisions indicate that Twain had an excellent sense of pacing and the ability to develop authorial irony while subordinating that of the narrator and eliminating potentially distracting allusions.

Much of the humor, of course, depends on Huck's own voice, on his own blend of naivete and enthusiasm. Huck regards Aunt Sally's reaction to a house full of snakes with deadpan wonder:

Why, after every last snake had been gone clear ⟨of⟩ out of the house for as much as *a* week, aunt Sally warn't over *it* yet; she warn't near over it; when she was setting thinking about something, you could touch her on the back of her neck with a feather and she would jump *right* out of her stockings. It was very curious. (MS, 672)

The cancelled "of" may indicate that the passage was composed rapidly; corroboration exists in the evidence that Twain omitted several small words and had to insert them later for sense, such as "for as much as *a* week" and "over *it* yet." The entire passage is a splendid combination of partial information and innocent surprise. We are not told why the boys would deliberately touch her on the back of the neck with a feather, nor how her phenomenal reaction was first discovered, nor what the boys' attitude was. All this teasing provocation is unstated, and the reader's imagination must supply the details. The description of the poor woman's reaction to this continued torment by the boys was changed to read "she would jump *right* out of her stockings." This increased exaggeration makes the calm statement of wonderment, "It was very curious," much more humorous.[7]

Twain's creation of humor retains some mystery; but we now realize that many factors contribute dynamically to the difficult, delicate achievement, including the character's voice, the pacing of the statement, and the elements of incongruity. In addition to creating the comedy, which only *seems* effortless, Twain concentrated enough to integrate his humor smoothly into the structure of his novel, revealing characters and embodying themes, avoiding some inadvertent cruelties and omitting some excesses, creating for generations of readers the pleasures and joys of a masterpiece.

Notes

1. A large amount of information about American humor and Mark Twain's own embodiment of it is available in Walter Blair's *Native American Humor*, Bernard DeVoto's *Mark Twain's America*, Constance Rourke's *American Humor*, and Kenneth Lynn's *Mark Twain and Southwestern Humor*. Walter Blair and Hamlin Hill's *America's Humor: From Poor Richard to Doonesbury* emphasizes the literary precedents for the humor in *Huck* in Chapters 29 and 31. David E. E. Sloane's *Mark Twain as a Literary Comedian* provides a comprehensive view of authorial development, with Chapter 8 concentrating on *Huck*.

2. It is impossible to determine whether "preaches there" was put in before or after the "dissenting minister" passage. A similar revision occurs later in the novel when Twain wrote about the undertaker's "softly soothing ways," but in print the adjective became an active compound, "soothering," and the undertaker remains continuously busy in our memories.

3. In 1869 Twain had used similar bovine diction, "psalm singing cattle," in a letter to Joseph Goodman.

4. The passage has received the attention of several scholars, including Delancey Ferguson, *Mark Twain: Man and Legend*, 221–22; Henry Nash Smith, *Mark Twain: The Development of a Writer*, 121–22; Janet Holmgren McKay, 41–50.

5. In Note A-11 Twain suggested several topics to be put into the story, including "A wake". Although the extended arrival scene does not actually constitute a wake, it comes close. We are not told of any other formal ritual before the funeral. Twain's working notes are reproduced in Blair and Fischer's edition of *Huck*, 1988, 711–764.

6. Sam Clemens/Mark Twain knew how interested and curious children would be about the description of a funeral. An entry for March and April 1883 follows:

During these months and part or all of February, Patrick's seven children had a rough time of it, with the dire scarlet fever. Two of them escaped very narrowly. Clara Spaulding arrived on a visit, and Susie gave her a full and animated account of these momentous and marvelous things. Aunt Clara said:

"Why, considering how very very low these two were, it seems next to miraculous that they got well. But they <u>did</u> get well?"

"Yes—both of them." Then, after a pause—pensively: "<u>It was a great disappointment to us.</u>"

Aunt Clara was astounded—in fact pretty nearly paralyzed; but she didn't [X] "let on"—only said—

"Why?"

"Well, you know, aunt Clara"—another pause—grave deliberation, to get her thought into form—"Well, you see, aunt Clara, we've never had any experience of a funeral."

"Oh, I see. But you—you didn't want the children to die?"

"Well, no—not that, exactly. But—in case they did die—well,—they—we—well, you know, we've never had a funeral."

"Still, it was scarlet fever, and you wouldn't have been allowed to attend it."

"No—I suppose Mamma wouldn't have let us. But then, you know, we could have observed it."

It was the eclat of the thing—the pomp, and solemnity and commotion. That is what Susie was after. ("A Record," 97–98)

7. Fischer and Blair (*Huck*, 1988, 726, fn1) present information about Note A6 that explains how young Sam Clemens used snakes to upset his Aunt Patsy Quarles. The following incident from July, 1882 in his own household may also have influenced the creation of the incidents. The resemblance of situations seems obvious:

Elsewhere I have spoken of Susie's proclivity for large words. The other day Bay crept behind Clara Spaulding's chair and nearly succeeded in touching her cheek with a wet little wee turtle. Clara S. gave a slight scream, and Susie (who was watching,) was racked and torn with laughter—and said: "Aunt Clara, if it had actually touched your cheek ⟨xxx⟩ I should have been transformed!" [meant transported—with glee.] ("A Record," 62)

5. Description and Imagery

"Why, Mars Tom! You said yo'own self, dat a letter—"

"Do you want to drive me crazy? Keep still. I only used it as a metaphor."

That word kind of bricked us up for a minute. Then Jim says, ruther timid, because he see Tom was getting pretty tetchy—

"Mars Tom, what is a metaphor?"

"A metaphor's a—well, it's a—a metaphor's an illustration." He see that *that* didn't git home; so he tried again. "When I say birds of a feather flocks together, it's a metaphorical way of saying—"

"But dey *don't*, Mars Tom. No, sir, "deed dey don't. Dey ain't no feathers dat's more alike den a bluebird en a jaybird, but ef you waits tell you catches *dem* birds a-flockin' together, you'll—"

"Oh, *give* us a rest. You can't get the simplest little thing through your thick skull. Now, don't bother me any more."

Tom Sawyer Abroad, Chapter V

Several historical changes have affected how readers now respond to figurative language. Many nineteenth-century readers responded with great pleasure to Twain's lengthy descriptions of landscapes and storms, valuing their vividness and pictorial quality. But the availability of photography, cinema, and television now provides the modern reader, effortlessly, with great visual detail and range. Accordingly, the modern reader may need some patience and historical imagination to savor what the earlier readers valued. Another difference involves the ability to appreciate patterns of indicative or iterative imagery. For example, recent generations of readers trained in "new criticism" may recognize patterns of animal imagery to which Twain's first readers would probably be oblivious. But Twain's verbal artistry can withstand intense scrutiny under varying aesthetic standards.

Twain usually exerts control over descriptive language in three ways. He revises for consistency of sense imagery; he usually revises to emphasize concrete sense impressions; and he frequently changes the language to adapt to the world of the novel. Twain manages to create for Huck a descriptive language that sounds fresh, vital, and truthful.

His ability to make the sense impressions reinforce one another seems quite subtle. For example, at the beginning of the Wilks episode, the scheming king hails a large riverboat as part of his preparation for a falsely impressive arrival in town. The manuscript reads:

> and when they found we only wanted to go four or five mile, they was mad, and give us a cussing, and said they wouldn't land us. But the king was c'am. He says: (MS, 231–32)

Into this aural passage, Twain placed one word to create "they was *booming* mad. . . ." This addition makes the sound description more consistently vivid and provides a contrast between the angry steamboatmen and the calm, deliberate king, who is in control of the situation.

Then, after arriving in town, the king inquires where Peter Wilks lives. One of the townsmen replies:

> "I'm sorry, sir, but the best we can do is to tell you where he did live, yesterday evening."
> The derned old cretur fell up against him, and put his chin on his shoulder, and cried down his back. . . . (MS, 233–34)

Twain attempted, momentarily, to modify the passage by changing the up-down directional aspect. He wrote in "*kerflummuxed*," a word he tried repeatedly to apply to the king. But then Twain decided to describe the action more directly by substituting "*went all to smash.*" Twain also created a superb additional ironic simile which speeds up the entire description:

> *Sudden as winking*, the derned old cretur <*kerflummuxed and*> *went all to smash, and* fell up against <him> *the man*, . . .

This revision clarifies possible vagueness in an economical, visual/tactile way; it implies that the king had planned for a performance of this type, and, of course, the simile combines speed and deception, as when a wink is used to convey collusion. By the time the passage reached print a slight fine-tuning for politeness occurred as "derned" became "ornery." This minor change also reveals Twain's habitual changing of words which assert to words which dramatize. In this case the explicit condemnation of "derned" vanishes into a word which justifies the attitude.

Twain frequently modified simple descriptions toward concrete language. While the king and duke are discussing, in the midst of their fraud, their plans for escape, the king originally says, "after we disappear" (MS,

290). But Twain changed this fairly straightforward word choice, in print, to "after we've slid" (228). The new verb presents the planned, elusive deception with an accurate and fresh tactile slang image.

Changes in description or imagery, of course, have an effect upon the tonality of a passage. Huck's explanation to Mary Jane Wilks about the fraud seems fairly serious in tone in the first version:

> I asked her to let me think, a minute; and she set there, mighty impatient and excited and beautiful, but looking kinder happy. So I went to studying it out. I says to myself, <a> I reckon <that> a body that tells the truth <,> when he is in a tight place, is taking considerable many risks; though I ain't had no experience, and can't say for certain; . . . (MS, 329)

A minor change lightened the tone; Twain used a non-standard verb "ups" that conveys irregular or surprising action as a young boy would express it: "a body that *ups and* tells the truth." But the best aesthetic improvement occurs as Twain creates an additional concrete description of Mary Jane. Twain inserted another tactile, almost muscular or kinesthetic, simile, picturing her as "*eased-up, like a person that's had a tooth pulled out*." The addition precisely conveys relief from pain and anxiety. Moreover, the ordinariness of the description makes Mary Jane a more familiar, hence less threatening, person to whom to tell the truth. The informality of the changed version fits Huck's voice. By the time the passage reached print it read:

> and she set there, very impatient and excited, and handsome, but looking kind of happy and eased-up, like a person that's had a tooth pulled out. (240)

The shift from "beautiful" to "handsome" resembles other de-sexualizing changes that keep Huck's point of view appropriate to a prepubescent youth. "Handsome" creates an implication of admiration for a pal. These revisions present an example of the kaleidoscopic interrelationship of characterization, speaking voice, and concrete description. In context, these changes also lighten the tone of the passage so as to make Huck's moral-philosophical questioning seem attractive rather than conniving or cunning.

Another category of change involves revision necessary—or desirable—to make a description fit more smoothly into the world of the novel. Usually these changes begin with a satisfactory or vivid phrase. They seem inexplicable except as evidence that Twain possessed a keen awareness of how his language could possibly conflict with its immediate context or with the thematic requirements of the novel itself. Even simple repetition was liable for revision. When the king and duke are faced by the genuine brothers, Huck says, "I reckoned they'd turn pale. But no, sir, nary a pale did <u>they</u> pale" (MS, 370). Although the final word is an unusual use of language, Twain finally revised it to read, "nary a pale did *they* turn" (250), a more balanced but much more conventional phrasing.

Other changes clarified potentially confusing phrasing. For example, when the frauds confront the newly arrived brothers, the duke "just went a goo-gooing around, happy and content, like a jug that's googling out buttermilk" (MS, 370). Since the jug is emptying, "content" could possibly cause confusion with the *contents of the container*. Twain revised the section to read "happy and satisfied" in print. This version presents, in context, an effective contrast, for shortly thereafter Twain wrote, "as for the king, he just gazed and gazed down sorrowful on them newcomers." Thus the sorrowful king and the satisfied duke act to embody the opposite extremes, giving the pair of villains a wide range of possible attitudes.

When the townspeople begin to question the rival claimants, Huck's situation becomes dangerous. Because of an implicit threat by the king, Huck has to defend the impostors:

> and so I knowed enough to talk on the right side. I sailed in, and begun to tell all about Sheffield, . . . (MS, 381)

The nautical metaphor, however, seems inappropriate, both for the earlier favorable associations with the raft and for the connotations of enthusiasm or energy. Twain accordingly simplified Huck's part so that the printed text reads only, "I begun to tell." But Twain saved the word, and the enthusiasm, because at the end of a five-page insertion (MS, 380A-1 to [misnumbered] 381-5), Twain assigns the metaphor to the proper subject: "Well, then they sailed in on the *general* investigation." As a result of the change, the reader perceives Huck as initially a less willing participant and the townspeople as enthusiastic questioners.

In several cases, Twain improved the novel immensely, changing acceptable phrases to adapt the descriptions to the particular locale and themes. At one point in the interrogation, the real brother tries to trap the king by asking what Peter Wilks had tattooed on his chest:

> I'm blamed if the king didn't have to brace up mighty quick, or he'd a kerflummuxed, it took him so sudden—and mind you it was a thing that was calculated to make most <u>anybody</u> kerflummux, to get fetched such a stunner as that without any notice . . . (MS, 391–92)

In print, however, the unusual word choice of "or he'd a kerflummuxed" becomes "or he'd a squshed down like a bluff bank that the river has cut under" (256). This brilliant but unusual simile refers to the locale and strikingly portrays a large, impressive facade slowly sinking. The final version assures the reader that "it was a thing that was calculated to make most *anybody* sqush to get fetched such a solid one as that without any notice." The reader certainly may regret the loss of such a 'stunner' of a word as "kerflummux," but must recognize the appropriateness of the new comparison. Twain masterfully seized an unusual word for a collapse into liquid and uses it twice.[1]

Larger thematic concerns also influence the descriptions. The king continues his attempt to brazen out the imposture:

> He whitened a little; he couldn't help it; and it was mighty still, in there, and everybody bending a little forward and gazing at him. Says I to myself, <u>Now</u> he'll throw up the sponge—there ain't no more use. Well, did he? I wish <u>I may</u> never stir if he did. (MS, 392–93)

But Huck's wish, unfortunately, parallels the stillness in the room and seems simply inappropriate for Huck as well. Twain canceled it and revised to, "I wish *I'm a nigger* if he did." The contrast to the king's whitening seems, at first, effective, but this phrasing would implicitly contribute to the disparagement of Black people. It would be contradictory to set up a Huck-Black contrast while Huck and Jim are becoming closer. The final version seems less personal, less as if Huck speaks, and more as if Twain uses ordinary prose to do its duty, more as if Twain reveals his own compositional difficulties:

> Well, did he? A body can't hardly believe it, but he didn't. (256)

Such a presentation does not offend; this vague, bland form fits into the book without disturbance.

Of course, there is a chance that Huck would be punished for the deception along with the swindlers, and this possibility causes real fear. After the rival claimants have each described the tattoo, the townspeople must disinter Peter Wilks's body to learn which "brother" had lied. The townspeople shout: "and if we don't find them marks, we'll <han> lynch the whole gang!" (MS, 398). Momentarily, Twain had planned to write "hang," then shifted to "lynch." Why? "Lynch" carries much stronger connotations of mob lawlessness and disregard for life; the change also emphasizes verbally the situational similarity to the other planned lynchings. The world of the completed novel contains, in fact, three planned lynchings: those of Sherburn, of Huck and the king and duke, and finally, of Jim after the escape from the Phelps farm. Clearly, Clemens/Twain's mind was concerned by this threat of illegal, violent mob action.[2] Moreover, the revision of this description to "lynch" fits the incident into a progression of increasingly outrageous plans: a contemplated lynching of a killer, Colonel Sherburn; a threatened lynching of an innocent victim, Huck; and an intended lynching of a heroic Black man, Jim. (In the period 1883–85, at least 347 lynchings of whites and 178 lynchings of Blacks occurred in the United States.) It is worth remembering that a comic variation of the lynch motif occurs when the duke chokes the king in their quarrel on the raft.

But at this one point, this possibility of death by lynching seems quite frightening to Huck, who says, "here was nothing in the world betwixt me and sudden death with a halter but just them little tattoo-marks" (MS, 400–401). This description on copy sheets is certainly concrete, and the critical reader may regret that Twain softened the impact of the passage by later dropping "with a halter" and "little." The final version still conveys Huck's worry, but in a slightly less memorable way.

With these general guidelines about revision of descriptive language in mind, we can proceed to two contrasting, ultimately complementary ways of reading. First we shall examine a storm and escape sequence to evaluate the descriptive and suspenseful story-telling powers appreciated by Twain's nineteenth-century readers. Later we shall consider Twain's command of patterns of animal and hand imagery to indicate what some schools of modern aesthetics value.

At the conclusion of the Wilks episode, Huck's anxiety contributed to the novel's extraordinary excitement. The descriptions of the walk to the graveyard in a storm and the escape reveal Twain's characteristic powers. The situation of a mob of people digging up a body in a storm provided a great opportunity for melodrama and exaggerated effects. On MS, 400 we find a very neat transcription, a copy sheet of what had presumably once been a page so heavily revised that it was almost illegible. The storm-escape sequence begins:

> Well, we swarmed along down the river road, just carrying on like wild-cats; and to make it more scary, the sky was darking up, and the lightning beginning to wink and flitter, and the wind to moan and shiver amongst the leaves.

The double infinitive style seems dramatic and effective, but in the printed version Twain dropped "moan," omitting the auditory and leaving only the visual and tactile descriptions.

But the auditory sense received other attention at the grave site in the early version:

> So they dug and dug, like mad; and it got awful dark, and the rain started, and the <li> wind swished and swushed along, and the lightning come faster and sharper, and the thunder boomed; . . . (MS, 402)

At first, Twain was going to mention the lightning immediately, "<li>," but instead he developed the wind sounds and concluded with the contrasting thunder booms. The printed version puts more emphasis on an increasing pace, for "the lightning come brisker and brisker." The partial repetition of "swished and swushed" resolves in the exact duplication of "brisker," and the final version gains tension by combining auditory contrast and increased speed. In all likelihood, Twain's original audience would be excited by these sensory descriptions.

After the diggers have uncovered the body and discovered the gold, Huck's captor releases his wrist. The boy says, "and the way I lit out and shinned for the road in the dark, was as near as I can state it, undescribable" (MS, 404). This first version has an odd mixture of the boy's tone with the novelist's problem and vocabulary. Twain, however, created a printed version to keep within Huck's colloquial expression: "There ain't nobody can tell" (258).

But of course Huck does tell—describing in a memorable way:

> I had it all to myself except <the company of the> the company of the solid dark, and the now-and-then glares, and the singing of the rain, and the thrashing of the wind, and the booming of the thunder; and you bet you I did clip it along! (MS, 405)

For a brief instant, Twain canceled "the company of the" but then restored it in running sequence. Possibly his mind was working with ways to describe the scene in terms of paradox: "all to myself" opposed to "the company of." He probably felt some inclusive term would subordinate the particular details, such as the "solid dark." But "the company of" could also be confusing because the king and duke could also be escaping. Thus a phrase—canceled and quickly, almost immediately, restored—could conceivably be the germ of a later plot complication. At any rate, Twain decided once more to excise the phrase in the printed version. In addition, the printed text has several clear improvements: the manuscript's "singing of the rain" becomes much less cordial when described as "buzzing." Furthermore, the original "booming of the thunder," hardly a fresh phrase, becomes "splitting of the thunder" (259), a change which conveys, perhaps synaesthetically, a fragmenting effect.[3]

The brief section describing Huck's arrival at the raft and the short flight downriver displays a sampling of Twain's creative skills. Here we find movement toward concrete language and suppression of confusion as well as change for thematic reasons. Huck relates that:

> As I hopped aboard I sung out:
>   "Out with you Jim, and cast her loose! Glory be to goodness, we're shut of them rapscallions!" (MS, 407)

Twain canceled "cast" in the manuscript and substituted "*set*," a change which lessens the energy associated with the raft's departure. Later, Twain changed "As I hopped aboard" to "As I sprung aboard," and the energy is properly placed with the boy, not the raft. The word "rapscallions" disappeared in print (259), part of a general pattern of diminishing the explicit criticisms of the frauds.

Huck informs us that:

> Jim lit out, and was a coming for me with both hands spread, but when I glimpsed him under the lightning, my heart flopped up in my mouth, and I went overboard backwards; for I had forgot he was old King Leer and a sick, solid-blue A-rab combined, and it most scared the livers and lights out of me. (MS, 407–08)

The original image of Jim with his "hands" spread could have been interpreted as threatening, and Twain substituted "*arms*" and wrote in, between the lines, "*he was so brim full of joy*." This change primarily creates the contrast between Jim's welcoming joy and Huck's fright. In the printed text we find evidence that Twain was still fiddling with the passage, dropping "brim" and having Jim appear not "under" lightning but "in" lightning. The printed text also shows significant changes: Huck's heart no longer "flopped-up," but instead "shot up," a change which describes the fright in more active terms. On the other hand, the concrete description of Jim as "a sick, solid-blue A-rab," Twain simplified to "a drownded A-rab," a description which implicitly refers to the river's constant threat (259). The change is, in context, effective, because Huck had fallen overboard.[4]

Actually, Twain imposed a major modification in the original favorable description of the river in order to prepare for a negative turn in the plot, the reappearance of the king and duke. The draft of the story continues:

> So, in two seconds, away we went, a sliding down the river, and <u>did</u> seem so good to be free again and all by our two selves once more, and the big friendly river stretching out so homelike before us! (MS, 409)

In all likelihood, Twain was composing rapidly at this point, because he later had to insert a word for clarity: "and *it* <u>did</u> seem so good." But the other changes had a thematic effect. For the book version, Twain changed "all by our two selves" by canceling "two," a revision which makes Huck and Jim more of a unit ("ourselves") by ignoring numbers.[5] "And the big friendly river stretching out so homelike before us!" goes through three significant changes: "friendly" is dropped; the image of the river "stretching out so homelike before us!" is omitted; what had momentarily been a sanctuary becomes a neutral area when Twain revised in a soon-to-be-contradicted plot preparation, "and nobody to bother us" (260). The dynamic shifts in description of the river from a friendly, inviting location to a setting which is only apparently without human antagonists seems apt at this point in the novel and, furthermore, at this point in the paragraph because the paragraph will end far differently. Perhaps Twain did not wish to present the river as deceptive and therefore had to modify away from the pleasant description.

Huck originally continued:

> Well, sir, I just <u>had</u> to skip around a bit, and jump up and crack my heels together a few times, I couldn't help it; but about the third crack, I noticed a sound that <u>I</u> knowed mighty well,—and cocked eye and ear, and listened and waited—and sure enough, when the next flash glared out over the water, here they come! (MS, 409)

The colloquial beginning, "Well, sir," is dropped, and the voice becomes a bit more purposive, less leisurely. Similarly, "together" vanished from the heel clicking, with a noticeable improvement in economy. The original "cocked eye and ear, and listened and waited" section sounds vaguely aggressive. But the passage in print has more emphasis on suspense: "and held my breath and listened and waited." At first, the lightning "glared," a verb which conveys an image of a stern, disapproving look. The final print description of the lightning, "busted out over the water," conveys only suddenness and violence. Accordingly, in these revisions the natural world changed from friendly and supportive to a non-deceptive, relatively neutral backdrop.

Huck's earlier happiness and sense of control over his own destiny collapse with the return of the king and duke:

> So I wilted right down onto the planks, then, and give up; and it was all I
> could do to keep from crying. (MS, 410)

The contrast between initial joy and concluding sorrow helps to hold this
effective, exciting section together. Moreover, once nature appears as a
neutral force, the full burden of rage for the intrusion falls upon the king
and the duke.

The presentation of these two swindlers can provide another micro-
cosmic case study, but this can be approached using not the supposed
values of Twain's original audience but the techniques of "new criticism."
In several instances Twain dropped explicitly derogatory words, such as
"rapscallions," or explicitly condemning diction, such as "derned," preferring to use descriptions which dramatize the evil qualities of the king and
duke. The most specific and limited pattern of revised iterative imagery
involves the careful use of animal comparisons to describe the pair. By
gathering several passages from different portions of the novel and contrasting the versions, we can observe the modulations in Twain's use of
animal imagery.

When the king is trying to impress Dr. Robinson, Twain, we recall,
writes:

> The king smiled, and ⟨put⟩ shoved out his paw and says: . . . (MS, 260)

Clearly the cancellation in the original composition sequence of "put"
indicates that Twain almost instantly had a better idea. Twain also dropped
the somewhat general animal image in "paw" and substituted "*flapper*," a
slang word that means *hand* as well as *flipper*. Twain also inserted "*eager*,"
which interrupts the rhythm of the sentence and heightens the comic
contrast with the Doctor: "The king smiled *eager*, and shoved out his
flapper, and says. . . ." The final description implies that the king resembles a
performing seal.

The hands of the thieves are also the subject of revision involving
animal imagery when Huck is explaining his and Jim's precarious situation
to Mary Jane Wilks:

> I got to travel with them a while longer, whether I want to or not—druther
> not tell you why—and although this town would get me out of their hands if
> you was to blow on them, I'd be all right, but there'd be another person that
> you don't know about who'd be in awful trouble. (MS, 335–36)

For the printed version, Twain changed "hands" to "claws," a word choice
which certainly makes the king and duke more bestial and threatening.

Moreover, in this section of the novel, Mary Jane Wilks had moved Huck by "laying her silky hand on ⟨mind⟩ mine in that kind of a way that I said I would die first" (MS, 334–35). In the context of these few pages "claws" creates an effective contrast.

All the revisions of animal imagery, however, do not achieve such vividness. After Huck persuades the other sisters to follow his plans, Twain writes:

> "All right," they said, and cleared out to lay for their cussed uncles, and ⟨tell⟩ give them the love and the kisses, and tell the old principal hog the message. (MS, 365)

In revision for print, "cussed" and "old principal hog" were omitted. Instead, the final copy has the flat functional phrase, "and tell them the message." Although some critics might say the shift is designed to include both "uncles," the substantial toning down of vivid, explicit contempt seems to be the primary effect.

But all animal imagery is not modified. Shortly before the genuine brothers arrive, Huck observes that:

> I never see such a girafft as that king for wanting to swallow <u>everything</u>. (MS, 368)

Twain let this precise, effective image remain.

Similar phrasing introduces Huck's opinion when the king tries to bluff about the tattoo:

> Well, I never see anything like that old rip, for clean out-and-out cheek. (MS, 394)

The word "rip" carries a variety of appropriate meanings, from slang for *reprobate*, to *worn out horse*, to a *treacherous water current*. But these meanings were lost when Twain simplified to "old blister."[6] The final description certainly seems acceptable—even inventive—for a swollen irritation, a prominent, hollow aggravation.

The harshest criticism of the king spews out of the duke's mouth. After the escape from the graveyard, the king and duke argue about how their scheme went wrong. As mentioned, the duke says:

> I never see such an old ⟨hog⟩ *ostrich* for wanting to gobble everything—and I a trusting you all the time, like you was my own father. You ought to ⟨be⟩ *been* ashamed of yourself to stand by and hear it saddled onto to a passel of poor

niggers and you never say a word for 'em. It makes me feel right down ridicklous to think I was soft enough to believe that rubbage . . . you unsatisfiable, tunnel-bellied old sewer! (MS, 420–21)

Regrettably, in my opinion, Twain decided once more to drop "hog," substituting "*ostrich*." This more polite description may be part of a general effort to change the king from fat to ordinary size. The vivid, splendidly disgusting sewer metaphor, unfortunately, does not appear in print.

A final example of revision involving animal imagery occurs in the transitional section. When Huck is trying to evade the duke in order to trace Jim, the boy says, "when I see the king in that gin-mill, yesterday" (MS, 449). Perhaps because it was to be a boys' book in need of a euphemism, or perhaps because "gin-mill" was not current in 1845, or perhaps to emphasize, by slang, the animalistic conditions, in print Twain twice renamed the "gin-mill" as a "doggery." Because the king and the duke are far from elevated characters, Twain uses animal imagery with great precision and humor to lower their standing. Unfortunately, the revised phrasing occasionally seems less compelling.

Two revisions in description may be chosen from the transitional section between the Wilks and Phelps farm episodes in order to illustrate two opposite types of revision, using different temporal reflexes, to achieve timeless artistry. As mentioned earlier, at the very instant of composition, Twain was alert enough to revise for consistent imagery:

> Well, early one morning we hid the raft in a good safe place about two mile below a little bit of a shabby village, *named Pikeville*, and the king he went ashore, and told us all to stay hid whilst he went up to town and smelt around to see if anybody had ⟨hear⟩ got any wind of the Burning Shame there yet. (MS, 428)

Shortly before concluding the word "heard" Twain self-critically changed his word choice to relate to the emphasis on sense of smell. Twain's artistic imagination, then, was able to censor mixed sense imagery in mid-word. However, such consistent olfactory imagery was concealed when, in print, the obscene romp was re-titled as "The Royal Nonesuch."

On the other hand, some revision comes later, perhaps in cool consideration of future necessity. For example, an important location on the Phelps farm—the area where Jim will be imprisoned—Twain first described as:

> three little log nigger-cabins in a row beyond the smoke-house; one little hut by itself, down against the back fence . . . (MS, 463)

Later, probably after he had determined more details of Jim's imprisonment, he added to the manuscript so that the single cabin is described as:

one little hut **all** by itself, **away** down against the back fence.

With admirable economy, with the magic of words, the cabin and the fence are moved and Jim's prison becomes more isolated; hence the tricks and deceptions become much more possible. One could even speculate that boys attempting to reach Jim would be able to conceal their approach behind the distant fence. Such care with description obviously makes certain plot possibilities more believable, as will be revealed by another twist of the kaleidoscope.

Notes

1. A similar sensitivity about word choice occurred in the Phelps farm section when Twain decided to revise Huck's "carpet bag" to his "*baggage*" (MS, 474). Similarly, Twain converted the word or dropped "carpet bag" on pages 475, 476, 487. Probably Twain considered that, in the post Civil War era, his first choice would carry distracting negative connotations, especially since Huck could be regarded as a semi-Northerner in southern Arkansas. In contrast, when the king had been planning to rob the Wilks family, he ordered Huck: "Now hustle back, right off, and fetch the duke up here *and the new carpet-bags*" (MS, 229). Thus Twain was careful to impose this provocative association only where it would do the most harm. The first description of the king and duke concluded a paragraph with "and both of them had big fat ratty-looking carpet bags" (161).

2. The topic of lynching had infuriated Twain for years. He wrote a vehement, sarcastic editorial protesting lynching for the *Buffalo Express* (Aug. 26, 1869). The headline read "ONLY A NIGGER." In fact, one later dialogue in the novel might have had a covert, almost private meaning for Twain, a meaning that mocks the culturally and regionally conditioned racism and careless disregard for the lives of Black people. When Aunt Sally Phelps cross-examines Huck about his trip down-river and the boy fabricates a steam boat explosion, he plays upon her attitudes:

Now I struck an idea, and fetched it out:
"It warn't the grounding—that didn't keep us back but a little. We blowed out a cylinder-head."
"Good gracious! anybody hurt?"
"No'm. Killed a nigger."
"Well, it's lucky; because sometimes people do get hurt." (280)

3. The manuscript's final assurance, "you bet you," becomes "sure as you are born." The notion of birth frequently occurs when Twain has reached a break-

through in the plot, either a resolution of a complication or a new possibility for involved fabling. The most well-known example is Huck's remark when he learns that he is thought to be Tom Sawyer, ". . . for it was like being born again, I was so glad to find out who I was."

4. The printed text has a balance of correction and modified, less formal tonality. The original reading, "I had forgot he was old King Leer and a sick, solid-blue A-rab combined," was changed. The "Leer" is not needed, because the sexual reference would be distracting, and "combined" is a bit too high-style for Huck. The printed text says simply, "I forgot he was King Lear and a drownded A-rab all in one." (The editors of the California text preserve the MS "Leer," an indication that they consider the first edition "Lear" a non-authorial correction.) Another effect of the allusion to "Lear" will become apparent in the chapter on Nobility and Individualism.

5. The idea of having the king and duke reappear probably first stirred in the depths of Twain's mind in the earlier ambivalence about "the company of the."

6. Other uses of "rip" occur with characters who merit some sympathy. Possibly Twain simply decided that the connotations of "rip" were too favorable to apply to the king.

6. Plot

> So far as I know, Mr. Clemens is the first writer to use in extended writing the fashion we all use in thinking, and to set down the thing that comes into his mind without fear or favor of the thing that went before or the thing that may be about to follow. I, for instance, in putting this paper together, am anxious to observe some sort of logical order, to discipline such impressions and notions as I have of the subject into a coherent body which shall march columnwise to a conclusion obvious if not inevitable from that start. But Mr. Clemens, if he were writing it, would not be anxious to do any such thing. He would take whatever offered itself to his hand out of that mystical chaos, that divine ragbag, which we call the mind, and leave the reader to look after relevancies and sequences for himself. These there might be, but not of that hard-and-fast sort which I am eager to lay hold of, and the result would at least be satisfactory to the author, who would have shifted the whole responsibility to the reader, with whom it belongs, at least as much as with the author.
>
> William Dean Howells, in *My Mark Twain* about Twain's
> travel books, 144–45

Although the quality of evidence permits us to make relatively precise conclusions about revisions of tone and imagery, the quantity of evidence allows only less definite conclusions about plot development. A revision of imagery almost always occurs on a single page, but an early discarded version of a plot line would typically take several pages. Because Twain did not save those extra pages, much of the evidence simply does not survive. Accordingly, some interpretations are likely to involve less evidence and more inference.

About plot revisions we usually have only hints: canceled lines or phrases, occasionally a canceled half page, and the complex polyvalent evidence of copy sheets, page renumberings, and insertions. But within these limitations, we nevertheless can perceive how Twain developed his plot.

He did not have a long-range plot conclusion in mind, but instead discovered his story, episode-by-episode, as he went along. For example,

Twain probably did not know, when he began the Wilks episode, precisely how it would end. Similarly, when he began the Phelps section, he probably realized that Huck could be mistaken for Tom Sawyer and that the two boys could provide many incidents. But he probably did not know early on that there would be a shooting or that Aunt Polly would reappear to straighten out the identities.

Howells's insight about Twain's mind seems accurate, while also suggesting that we should not apply traditional expectations to Twain's way of plotting. Apparently Twain preferred a plot with flexibility rather than a rigid, predetermined scheme or way to reach a resolution. Because he was quite adept at revising in props, characterizations, dialogue, and settings as anterior preparation for plot developments, Twain could write effectively, from episode to episode, trusting that as the exciting situations piled up a long-range plot would happen. This method fits well with the picaresque mode. Moreover, the largest plot insertion would be done for thematic reasons, as shall be explored in Chapter 9.

The notes and marginalia offer some corroboration. For example, Note A-10 states "Back a little CHANGE—raft only crippled by steamer." Clearly at that critical point Twain had first written the episode of the dramatic crash, then later decided to preserve the needed transportation for the voyage down river. Other notes indicate a number of plot alternatives that Twain may have explored but finally decided to omit. This matter has been carefully and perceptively analyzed by many, including Blair, DeVoto, and Franklin R. Rogers. Moreover, Blair and Fischer's new California edition presents the notes in facsimile and the marginalia in typescript. (Perhaps Twain's most explicit and amusing remarks about arbitrary and capricious plotting occur at the end of his "Notes on Those Extraordinary Twins", usually printed with *Pudd'nhead Wilson*.)

In the manuscript, the marginalia also preserve some evidence of plot confusion. During the Phelps farm section, where there are several references to letters from Sis, Twain scrawled in the top margin, "find out who Sis is" (MS, 745). We can safely infer that Twain either forgot or did not have in mind a definite plan for "Sis," Tom Sawyer's Aunt Polly, to enter at the end to resolve all the confusion. But the notes and marginalia also reveal the concrete practicality, the pragmatics of Twain's mind, with comments such as, "Provide him with a knife," and "They take along a lunch." These self-directions usually deal with plot-enabling details rather than with long-range goals of the plot.

The manuscript remains our best source of detailed evidence about changes in plotting. The original version of the Wilks will would have permitted the king and duke to rob $4,030 and get out of town quickly, but the revised will gave the thieves less cash and more items of property of lesser value to sell, hence providing them with a financial reason to remain in town longer. Quite probably the situation simply appealed to Twain's imagination, and he then decided to develop it in a leisurely fashion.

Similarly, plot considerations perhaps influenced the cancellation of the following passage in which Mary Jane Wilks explains about sleeping rooms:

> and she said ⟨they had two; so he said she <u>could</u> put his valley in the same bed with <u>him</u>—meaning me. He said in England it warn't usual for a valley to sleep with his master, but in Rome he always done the way the Romans done, and besides he warn't proud, and reckoned he could stand Adolphus very well. Maybe he could; but I couldn't a stood ⟨it⟩ ***him***, only I was long ago used to sleeping with the other kind of hogs. So Mary Jane showed us all up, and they was plain rooms but nice.⟩ (MS, 265–66)

Although one may again regret yet another loss of the hog comparison, this cancellation permits Huck to prowl around at night. In the revised section, the king and duke and Huck each have a separate room. Such a modification provides for much more flexibility in future actions.

Twain arranges to have the king use Mary Jane's room, increasing the sense of the king as an intruder. Revision supplied her room with props which could have an effect upon the plot:

> ***She said she would have her dresses and a lot of other traps took out of her room if they was in uncle Harvey's way, but he said they warn't. The dresses was hung along the wall, and before them was a curtain of calico that hung to the floor.*** (MS, 265 A–B)

This inserted description obviously creates the possibility for Huck to be accidentally caught in the king's room and then to eavesdrop on the scoundrels' plans from behind the curtain. It may well be that this room description was inserted as preparation after the eavesdropping incident was composed. Twain's practical, concrete mind made a number of such revisions which prepare for later plot developments.

Occasionally we may observe Twain casting around for the next plot development. Such a passage, with evidence of several false starts, occurs as Twain attempted to create a way to free Huck and Jim from the swindlers solely by using Huck's intelligence and integrity. Huck explains the situation to Mary Jane, but also tries to protect Jim:

I'd be all right, but there'd be another person that you don't know about who'd be in awful trouble. Well, we got to save him hain't we? Of course. Well then, we won't blow on them." ⟨Now another thing—the bag of money⟩
⟨I thought a while, and I had a mighty notion to tell her to⟩
Saying them words put a first-rate idea into my head. ⟨It was this⟩ I see in a minute how maybe I could get Jim and me rid of them frauds: get them jailed, here, and **then** give them the slip! (MS, 335–36)

Clearly Twain's mind, as well as Huck's, was exploring possibilities. At this point, the idea of the melodramatic appearance of the genuine brothers and the resultant doubling of "brothers" and the trial scene had probably not occurred to Twain.

Because Twain was uncertain about the plot's direction, he could not always initially judge the tonality of future events. At MS, 337 he originally wrote about Huck's involved scheme, "so I didn't want the circus to begin till pretty late to-night." But the connotation of play and the tone of sarcasm are modified in print because Twain revised "circus" to "plan," a change which attributes more control to Huck.

After the rival brothers do arrive and while the investigation is in progress, Twain made a most revealing change which is indicative of his freedom—or casualness—in plotting. The manuscript originally read:

We all got in a big room in the hotel, and fetched in the new couple, and there we had it, up and down, hour in and hour out, . . . (MS, 380)

This major change placed a five-page insertion *within the paragraph*, a decision which may weaken the novel in conventional aesthetic terms. But this addition indicates Twain's concern for dramatic excitement and his obliviousness to predetermined, goal-oriented plotting.[1] He canceled "and there we had it" and inserted a page direction, "Insert 381A +c" which opens:

First, the doctor says:
"I don't wish to be too hard on these two men, but I think they're frauds, and they may have complices that we don't know nothing about. If they have, won't the complices get away with that bag of gold Peter Wilks left? It ain't unlikely. If these men ain't frauds, they won't object to sending for that money and letting us keep it till they prove they're all right—ain't that so?" (MS, 380-A-1)

The doctor begins the battle of wits well. He summarizes the situation accurately, except that the accomplice, Huck, has actually *already* stolen the money *from* the frauds. The insertion continues.

Everybody agreed to that. So I judged they had our gang in a pretty tight place, right at the outstart. But the king he only looked sorrowful, and says:

"Gentlemen, I wish the money was there, for *I* ain't got no disposition to throw anything in the way of a fair, open, out-and-out investigation of this mournful business; but alas, the money ain't there; you can send and see, if you want to."

"Where is it, then?"

"*Well,* When my niece give it to me to ⟨keep⟩ keep for her, I took and hid it inside of the straw tick of my bed, ⟨calculating to wait⟩ not wishing to bank it for ⟨but⟩ the few days we'd be here, and considerin' ⟨that as⟩ *the bed a* safe place, we not bein' used to niggers, and supposin' 'em honest, *like servants in England*. The niggers stole it the very next morning, after I had went down stairs, and when I sold them, I hadn't missed the money yet, so they got clean away with it. My servant here can tell you about it, gentlemen."

The cancellation of "calculating to wait" slightly raised the king's deceitful self-characterization, since he presents Harvey Wilks publicly as less scheming, more socially elevated in his plans. The king's feigned naivete about theft is as ironic as the supposed innocence of "*like servants in England*" is amusing. All of this, of course, indicates that the king had believed Huck's story about the slaves coming out of the room. It is even more ironic that the king will direct the investigation toward Huck.

The king will have to depend for confirmation upon the person who has deceived him and who wishes ultimately to unmask him. This entire section prepares for Huck to take an active dramatic role in the trial. Although it is possible that Huck is fearful and genuinely attempts to fool the townspeople, it seems more likely that he wishes to betray the frauds while seeming loyal and helpful, as follows:

The doctor and several said "Shucks!" and I see nobody didn't altogether believe him. One man asked me if I see the niggers steal it. I said no, but I see them sneaking out of the room and hustling away, and I never thought nothing, only I reckoned they was afraid they had waked up my master and was trying to get away before he made trouble with them. That was all they asked me. Then the doctor whirls on me and says:

"Are you English, too?"

I said yes; and him and some others laughed, and said "Bosh!"

Well, then they sailed in on the *general* investigation, and there we had it,
up   (Manuscript directions are to "Run *back* to 380." Passage occurs from MS, 380-A-1 to [misnumbered] 381-5)

Huck's earlier deception of the king and duke had been achieved by being reticent, by slowly revealing, step by step, minor details and letting the king and duke think they were clever in forming their own conclusions. With that conversation demonstrating how adept at deception Huck can be, Twain in this insertion has Huck pretend to be an inept, talkative liar when he wishes to expose the frauds.

In this case, on the contrary, Huck becomes voluble and for a few moments seizes center stage. He talks quite freely for enough time to convince the king and duke, whom he must not antagonize, that he is trying to help, while he talks long enough to convince the doctor—and apparently more townspeople—that he is not English and that therefore fraud exists. Such ability to fool con men and to reveal the truth to truthseekers simultaneously is a rare talent, worth a slight digression in the trial scene.

This insertion seems to have grown, in part, from its immediate surroundings, MS, 381–82, in which the *same* situation occurs. Probably Twain wrote the following section first, then imaginatively elaborated upon it for the insertion:

> And by and by they had me up to tell what I knowed. The king he give me a left-handed look out of the corner of his eye, and so I knowed enough to talk on the right side. I sailed in, and begun to tell all about Sheffield, and how we lived there, and all about the English Wilkses, and so on; but I didn't get pretty far till *the Doctor begun to laugh; and* Levi Bell, the lawyer, says:
>
> "Set down, my boy, I wouldn't strain myself, if I was you. I reckon you ain't used to lying, it don't seem to come handy; what you want is practice. You do it pretty awkward."
>
> I didn't care nothing for the compliment, but I was glad to be let off, any way. (MS, 381–82)

Huck's practice and skill at lying are, as we know, vastly better than he reveals in the situation. Twain, characteristically, wishes to demonstrate Huck's ability to lie with deliberate clumsiness twice rather than once, by inserting five pages into the trial scene. The finished version shows how completely the king had believed and thereafter relied upon the boy who deliberately unmasked the fraud twice.

We may ask how these amusing episodes affect the plot. Basically, not at all! A conventional novelist—which Twain is not—who is careful about plotting would, after writing two similar passages, compare them to evaluate which is superior or which one is only "practice" for the other. Then the ordinary novelist would pick the better passage or combine and move quickly to a single scene with a resolution based on the information revealed. Twain did not. Instead, he kept both episodes; moreover, neither has any noticeable effect on the plot. This tendency to value episodes for their own sakes is both a cause of the curiously repetitive structure and an explanation of the unusually loose plotting of the novel.

After the critic has become immersed in the problems of the manuscript, it becomes apparent that Twain, in all likelihood, wrote from episode to episode. Most scholars would infer that he had not thought of the device of body marks and the exciting grave-opening episode which would conclude the Wilks section when he inserted Huck's inept lying.

This matter can also be explored in the important transition from the Wilks to the Phelps farm section. At this point in the story, at approximately what is now Chapter XXXI, Twain seems to have been casting about, seeking the best direction in which the story could proceed. Apparently Twain wished to separate Huck and Jim from the king and duke, perhaps because he knew that he had already amply satirized monarchy and religion in the Wilks section. His novelistic problems involved how to separate them, and what to use as a new plot complication.

It is necessary to attempt to speculate about what a novelist could do in this situation. The earlier parts of the book dealt with Huck's successful escapes from the widow, the Sunday school teacher, his father, the searchers from town, the Shepherdsons, Mr. Loftus, other slave hunters, and, most recently, Hines. But Huck had not been able to arrange to elude the king and duke during the Wilks part. Although Huck returns twice to the raft believing he has given them the slip, once after the grave-opening scene and once after Jim has been sold, Huck never really escapes from these rogues. His inability to escape from the king and duke casts a dark shadow over the rest of the novel. Although the rascals are ultimately caught, Huck could not save himself or Jim from them. Moreover, we realize that Huck's later escape from the Phelpses' neighbors is an imperfect escape, since one of his group suffers a wound which ends the flight. Perhaps Twain was facing disturbing realities in his fiction: it is impossible to escape from hypocritical exploitative greed, exemplified by the king and duke; perhaps it is impossible, outside of the romance escape fiction later parodied, for a young boy to bring a slave to freedom.[2]

We observe in this portion of the manuscript more marginalia, e.g., "This is lugged—shove it back yonder to where they escape lynching and regain raft" (MS, 429). A higher proportion of the pages are copy pages, comparatively clear transcriptions of what had probably become laboriously rewritten, almost illegible sheets. Moreover, we find a significant amount of renumbered sheets.

The manuscript pages which present Huck's moral debate about turning Jim in and his decision to tear up his note, concluding, "All right, then, I'll go to hell," are all copy pages (MS, 441–47). Thus this significant portion of the novel is the product of revision. Although we wish in vain for the earlier sheets, we can observe in the copy sheets Twain's attention to ethical problems, comparative disregard of plot machinations, and skill in joinery. Directly after the "I'll go to hell" passage, Twain continued on copy sheets 446 and half way down 447:

> It was awful thoughts, and awful words, but they was said. And I let them stay said; and never thought no more about reforming. I shoved the whole thing out of my head; and said I would take up wickedness again, which was in my line, being brung up to it, and the other warn't. And for a starter, I would go to work and steal Jim out of slavery again; and if I could think up anything worse, I would do that, too; because as long as I was in, and in for good, I might as well go the whole hog.
> Then I set to thinking over how to go at it, and turned over considerable many ways in my mind, and at last fixed up a plan that suited me. So then . . .

The text would flow smoothly to the plan we find on the bottom half of MS, 448. We can, however, develop a sense of what was in the earlier version by reading through the cancel marks to see the early version on the top half of MS, 448. The fragment covers some of the same ideas, but with noticeable differences. Huck must have stated that what he was hoping:

> ⟨for, and longing for, and pining for, always, day and night and Sundays, was a career of crime. And just that ⟨very⟩ thing was the thing I was a-starting in on, now, for good and all.
> When I got my plan fixed . . .⟩

Huck sounds, momentarily, like Tom Sawyer. The writing conveys a lifelike tone, and some of the rhetorical repetition sounds like Huck's way of creating extreme emphasis. But if the attitude of this canceled fragment had been allowed to stand without revision, the end of the novel in all likelihood would have been a series of high jinks, perhaps without thematic significance. Such events will be developed, but will be attributed to Tom, not Huck. Instead, the revised version has Huck sounding more deliberate about his vague plans; moreover, the revised version includes issues of thematic significance, such as the influence of heredity and environment upon Huck.[3]

Immediately after this section we find MS pages renumbered 448A and 448B along with a new page, 448C, insertions which present strong evidence of how efficiently Twain was exploring possibilities. He has Huck stroll past the Phelps' Sawmill.[4] It appears that Twain would frequently reconnoiter a new situation by means of descriptive passages, then happen upon a plot breakthrough, then within a few pages need to revise extensively to put in props or details that he had discovered would be needed. Evidence of this pattern may be found shortly after two important passages, the "All right, I'll go to hell" and the "It's Tom Sawyer. . . . It was like being born again" surprise.

Additional evidence about plot revision exists in the rewriting and renumbering of numerous pages of the MS between 493 and 517, the opening of the Phelps farm segment. As shall become clear, Twain probably realized fairly early that Huck could be mistaken for Tom. Twain originally planned to have two Phelps children, Phil and Mat, serve as Huck's helpers. But apparently Twain realized that Tom Sawyer could provide plenty of complications by himself. Instead Huck and Tom are the only people their age, and they have the run of the farm, the freedom to plot the "evasion" without interference by their peers.

Extensive study of this material leads one to conclude tentatively that Twain discovered his pliable plot as he went along, writing without a definite final resolution or plan in mind. His real interests were elsewhere—in writing memorable episodes and frequently in doubling the incidents or repeating the basic situation in varied forms. It is, accordingly, a supreme misreading of the novel to read for plot as plot. It is appropriate to the spirit and craftsmanship of the book to read for episodes, for doublings, for Twainings, finding relationships, repetitions, contrasts, and progressions between episodes. It is not that all significant events are repeated, but that the repetition of an event often signals its significance.[5] This plotting has one advantage; it permits Twain to revise in sections for thematic reasons. Indeed, his sixty-page insertion about the exploration of the *Walter Scott* and the debate about the French language will be considered as a thematic preparation rather than as a mere exciting incident.

Twain's *Huck* resembles a sequence of visions of brightly colored glass fragments—the traditional continuity resides in the boy's voice; the modernity involves the fragmentation and the shifting overlap. Our newly acquired knowledge of interacting stylistic matters, from voice to plot, prepares for an understanding of relatively unnoticed but significant themes. The integrity of Twain's artistic imagination, combined with his enormous stylistic control, compels him to struggle with the more difficult issues of his interrelated themes. Both the stylistic and the thematic revisions dynamically create meaning.

Notes

1. In this portion, time and atmosphere were modified slightly by inserting *"and lit up some candles."* Twain also put in an earlier reference to *"sundown."* He frequently and freely shifts time of day in his revisions, adding or subtracting a half an hour or an afternoon or a few days, exercising a fairly arbitrary control.

2. One of the Clemens family house guests, G. W. Cable, was quite concerned about the very high proportion of escapes from the Southern convict-lease system.

3. Twain's typical concern about the mechanical details is preserved by two marginal notes at the top of MS, 448 about the skiff. For other comments on the passage, see Walter Blair, *Mark Twain and Huck Finn*, and Henry Nash Smith, *Democracy and the Novel*, 113.

4. It is noteworthy that Huck puts on store-bought clothes and originally wishes to approach the Phelps' farm from the south, perhaps planning to duplicate, in miniature, the king's arrival at the beginning of the Wilks section.

5. A cogent statement on the role of intentionality in the creative process can be found in Hershel Parker's *Flawed Texts and Verbal Icons*:

> For now, the most compelling recent descriptions of the creative process in literature (aside from some descriptions by writers themselves) is in the writings of a few aestheticians (notably Murray Krieger), and in the writings of a few clinical psychologists and psychiatrists (notably Albert Rothenberg); as it happens, both Krieger and Rothenberg are indebted to the philosopher John Dewey's *Art as Experience*. The evidence presented by these three (like Searle's evidence) suggests that authorial intentionality is built into the words of a literary work during the process of composition, not before and not afterwards. Dewey's account laid great stress on the artist's moment-to-moment control over the relationships between what he has already done, what he is about to do, what he actually is doing, and what he knows, at least vaguely, that he must do later on. If what the writer puts down at a given moment does not "retain and sum up what has gone before as a whole and with reference to a whole to come," Dewey said, there will be "no consistency and no security" in what the writer later puts down. While genuine art is coherent, it can never be fully plotted out in advance; all finer artists "learn by their work, as they proceed, to see and feel what had not been part of their original plan and purpose." (23)

Thematics

Mark Twain on Writing a Novel:

A man who is not born with the novel-writing gift has a troublesome time of it when he tries to build a novel. I know this from experience. He has no clear idea of his story; in fact he has no story. He merely has some people in his mind, and an incident or two, also a locality. He knows these people, he knows the selected locality, and he trusts that he can plunge those people into those incidents with interesting results. So he goes to work. To write a novel? No—that is a thought that comes later; in the beginning he is only proposing to tell a little tale, a very little tale, a six-page tale. But as it is a tale which he is not acquainted with, and can only find out what it is by listening as it goes along telling itself, it is more than apt to go on and on and on till it spreads itself into a book. I know about this, because it has happened to me so many times.

And I have noticed another thing: that as the short tale grows into the long tale, the original intention (or motif) is apt to get abolished and find itself superseded by a quite different one. It was so in the case of a magazine sketch which I once started to write—a funny and fantastic sketch about a prince and a pauper; it presently assumed a grave cast of its own accord, and in that new shape spread itself out into a book. Much the same thing happened with *Pudd'nhead Wilson*. I had a sufficiently hard time with that tale, because it changed itself from a farce to a tragedy while I was going along with it—a most embarrassing circumstance. But what was a great deal worse, was, that it was not one story, but two stories tangled together; and they obstructed and interrupted each other at every turn and created no end of confusion and annoyance.

Lincoln in the Lincoln-Douglas debate:

That is the issue that will continue in this country when these poor tongues of Judge Douglas and myself shall be silent. It is the eternal struggle between these two principles—right and wrong—throughout the world. They are the two principles that have stood face to face from the beginning of time; and will ever continue to struggle. The one is the common right of humanity and the other the divine right of kings. It is the same principle in whatever shape it develops itself. It is the same spirit that says, "You work and toil and earn bread, and I'll eat it."

No matter in what shape it comes, whether from the mouth of a king who seeks to bestride the people of his own nation and live by the fruit of their labor, or from one race of men as an apology for enslaving another race, it is the same tyrannical principle. . . .

breff mos' hop outer me; en
I feel so — so — I doan know
how I feel. I crope out,
all a-tremblin', en crope
aroun' en open de do' easy
en slow, en poke my head in
behine de chile, sof' en still,
en all of a sudden I says
pow! jis' as loud as I could
yell. ^She never move'! O, Huck, I bust out
a-cryin', en grab her up in
my arms en say, 'O de po'
little thing! de Lord God Almighty
fogive po' ole Jim, kaze
he never gwyne to fogive his-
seff as long as he live!" O, she
was plumb deef en dumb, Huck, plum
deef en dumb — en I'd ben a treat'n her so!"

9. Manuscript p. 210.

spoke

on that boat? — & suppose
he ~~pops~~ [steps] in here, any minute, & ~~Yells~~ [Sings] out my name
before I can ~~toss~~ [throw] him a
wink to keep quiet? & let
~~on that he's somebody~~
~~else?~~ Well, I ~~ask~~ couldn't
have it that way — it
wouldn't do, at all. I must
go up the road & waylay him.
So I told the folks I reckoned
I would ~~could~~ [go] up to the village & fetch down my ~~carpet~~
~~well~~ bag [gage]. The old gentleman
"Walk?" says cousin
Phil. "'deed you won't, Tom!

10. Manuscript p. 487.

11. Thomas Nast's cartoon about Twain's efforts to secure a Canadian copyright for *The Prince and the Pauper*.

12. Twain posing at the window of the Quarry Farm study during a 1904 revisit.

7. The Conflict Between Nobility and Individualism

> I will say this much for the nobility: that, tyrannical, murderous, rapacious, and morally rotten as they were, they were deeply and enthusiastically religious. Nothing could divert them from the regular and faithful performance of the pieties enjoined by the Church.
>
> *Connecticut Yankee*, Chapter XVII

It should by now be expected that just as Twain improved his novel in stylistic ways through revision, he also created greater depth and resonance by the changes that incrementally affected themes and built meanings. In fact, some of these topics are relatively unnoticed or completely misunderstood. Attention to thematic revision increases the fun of reading *Huck*, because one can observe precisely how Twain attempts to whack more accurately at his targets.

In these next four chapters some well-recognized themes, such as the conflict between slavery and freedom or between conformity and individualism, will be seen as existing in a much more complex context. Twain was, in his own relatively unschooled but incisive, fiercely intelligent way, attempting to think through a cluster of interrelated problems, including the role of birth-determined hierarchy in a supposedly democratic culture and the conflict between heredity and environmental training. A philosophical deepening seems to occur, as if Twain wishes to know, "What explains human nature?" Similarly, the roles of shame, guilt, and positive reinforcement for right action also occupied his mind.[1] In addition to what may properly be considered individual issues, Twain was also concerned with larger, more systemic topics, such as national literacy and reading habits, copyright problems, and perhaps most important, independence from European literary models. We can, in fact, untangle some of these interrelated, serious threads, while still taking pleasures from the texts, enjoying both the old and new meanings in this surprisingly rich, continuously rewarding novel.

In order to explore this richness, it is necessary to draw upon some external information and to isolate factors, beginning with what is probably the simplest. Most treatments of the king and duke deal with the two frauds as stock figures of Southwestern humor, tramps, jour-printers, drunkards, pretenders, regional representatives of the world of local-color humor that Twain knew and loved. But why did Twain decide to call them the king and the duke? In this chapter we shall observe a collection of material that has more to do with Europe, a group of changes, usually additions, Twain made that seem to transcend the local American stock figures.[2]

Let the primary opposition be stated baldly: a hierarchical stratification of names and titles would place Jim and the orphaned boys, Huck and Tom, toward the bottom of a pyramid, under the Judge, the Grangerfords, and the Doctor. At the top of the nominal stratification, one finds, of course, the titles of the king and the duke. These titles and these characters act to oppose or suppress the inherent worth of every person. A simple bi-polar opposition exists between comically fraudulent representatives of "nobility," whose claimed status is determined by birth and religious sanctions, and two orphaned white boys and a decent, ethical, unsophisticated Black adult. Instantly this paradigm becomes complicated because the two orphaned lads contrast greatly with each other in their education, literacy, practicality, and reverence for "nobility." Moreover, Jim, who is separated by slavery from his own children, extends his parental concern to the two lads.

Some repetitions shape these thematics. The king and duke as well as Tom Sawyer act selfishly to harm Jim. The king and duke imprison Jim on the raft heading downstream, shamming that he is an escaped slave who must be tied. Similarly, Tom knowingly engages in selfish, immoral deceit to extend Jim's imprisonment on the Phelps farm. Moreover, although Twain's mind usually works through oppositional values, the mobs which function at the ends of both the Wilks and Phelps episodes are equally dangerous, lethal, mistaken. The resulting oppositions, then, are not simply hierarchy against mobs but hierarchy and mobs against the individual as well as slavery and imprisonment against freedom.

The individualism in question may be influenced by heredity or environment, by shame, by positive reinforcement for right action, by chance, and by reading. In the cases of successful individualism, a genuine self-transformation occurs, permitting Jim and Huck, but not Tom, to view the world from another's point of view. Although Twain was trying to figure out such issues without the benefits of reading abstract theories of genetics, psychological reinforcement, or behaviorism, he was able to observe how these issues developed in his real and fictional world. What was right action when he was a child? How does a person decide? What shapes a person?

Is one person innately better than another? The Clemens family background included, according to family legend, the Lambtons, Earls of Durham, and, at the other end of a political spectrum, the man who signed the order of execution for King Charles I of England. Such a contradictory ancestry, whether true or not, suggests a complex attitude about inherited nobility and traits. In all probability, most of the Clemens family looked upon their "heritage" with pride. But if the adult Sam Clemens considered the legends with his usual probity, he may have experienced such a heritage as a burden; one side of the ancestry would encourage unrealistic great expectations in the J. Leathers or Colonel Sellers fashion, while the other side would deride those delusions. In August 1879, Twain wrote a note, "'Our Old Nobility' from Echo," reminding himself about an article that had criticized the "palpable absurdity" of the "hereditary principle" (*Notebooks and Journals* 2, 339).

If an adult Sam Clemens realistically assessed his own development, the helpful formative influences would seem to have been not ancestral status or "blood," but intelligence, wit, compassion, and a judgmental temperament. Many today would consider his intelligence to be determined or partially influenced by heredity and the remaining factors to be primarily developed by his environment, as shaped by his mother's witty personality and his father's judgmental, evaluative style. Yet there was always the issue of his siblings. How could Jane and John Marshall Clemens have created someone with Orion's infuriating stupidity, with Pamela's dull literalness, or with Sam's active mind?

Moreover, a glance at his country would reveal that Clemens/Twain lived in a putative democratic system which was verbally opposed to ideas of inherited nobility but nevertheless had been willing to grant privileges of high birth status to Southern aristocracy or First Family of Virginia personalities. Does higher birth lead to or justify lower morality?

As a sophisticated traveler, Twain would know that kings, emperors, and sovereigns reigned; over thirty-six countries were then governed by people with inheritable noble titles. Twain had visited several and, at different times, closely observed royalty. Remarks in *The Innocents Abroad* about Napoleon III, Abdul-Aziz, and the Czar of Russia indicate ambivalence—a Tom Sawyerish fascination with show or privilege balanced by suspicions about cruelty or a compassionate realization of shared humanity.

In general, Twain was by the 1880s in theory categorically and vehemently opposed to the system of nobility but able to recognize and respond favorably to titled individuals.

In *Life on the Mississippi* Twain wrote about the harmful effects upon American Southern culture of aristocracy and hierarchy as embodied in the "Sir Walter [Scott] disease." But, in connection with his efforts to secure Canadian copyright protection for this work by visiting Canada, he came into contact with the British royal family. A rather imperious invitation announced that:

> The Aide-de Camp in waiting is commanded by His Excellency the Governor General and Her Royal Highness The Princess Louisa to invite Mr. S. L. Clemens to dinner on May 24th, 1883.*3

Although Twain apparently enjoyed the occasion, his artistic imagination would repeatedly mock the systems of nobility, rank, and privilege.

The nobility-commoner conflict appears consistently in his fiction, especially in *The Prince and the Pauper* and "1002 Night," as well as in *A Connecticut Yankee* and *The American Claimant*. While working on *Huck*, Twain was also writing a play with Howells, "Colonel Sellers as a Scientist," which involves Sellers's idiotic pretensions to an English title.

Twain was, apparently, indeed trying to think through several complex, interrelated questions. What is the relative importance of heredity and environment? How do nature and nurture interact? What are the effects of determinism and free will? What shapes ethical behavior? It should be emphasized that when wrestling with such issues Twain did not have, in 1883 and 1884, the advantages of reading Mendel or Pavlov. But he was, in a primitive way, aware of what we would call psychological reinforcement as an influence on behavior. He was, to some extent, discovering the problems within his own family and exploring the issues as he created his fiction.4

In attempting to deal with these serious topics, Twain explored the conflict between birth-determined status and individualism by contrasting characters of supposed nobility and low morality with people of low status and better morals, such as Jim and Huck. Indeed, the novel includes many characters who have a birth-determined status: the Shepherdsons and Grangerfords, the genuine Wilks brothers, and, supposedly, the king and duke. In contrast, Jim, his family, and all the slaves have a birth-determined low status, while Huck, orphaned son of poor whites, and Tom, a motherless orphan, have somewhat uncertain low social placement.

Many revisions emphasize the criticism of inherited "nobility." This theme also carries, by extension, nationalistic, anti-European meanings of increasing importance. In this book "nobles," who have in combination foreign birth, religious sanction, pretension, and stylistic luxuriance become targets for authorial scorn. Many revisions are inexplicable except as evidence that Twain's satiric wit desired to lash nobility and notions of inherited status. As will become clear, Twain was especially scornful of those Americans like the king, duke, and Tom who sham, ape, or admire "nobility."

For most modern American readers, this nationalistic theme in the novel now seems curiously reduced or flattened. The satire on nobility frequently seems merely quaint, and most readers regard the king and duke as only pompously deceptive, missing the absolute domination they exert over Huck and Jim on the southward trip.[5] Certainly, the king and duke are greedy con-men, tramps, stock rascal characters from the Southwestern fiction Twain enjoyed, but an additional important theme involves the emphatic criticism of all forms of inherited nobility. The king and duke control the morally superior Huck and Jim, taking them further downriver, away from possible freedom into more dangerous or hostile areas. For example, if a slave raised his hand against a white man, the penalty in Missouri was thirty-nine lashes, but in Louisiana the penalty was one hundred lashes, a frequently fatal punishment. A sensitive reader may react to the king and duke with a democratic revulsion similar to that felt when an American citizen—instead of shaking hands—kneels before a foreign sovereign. Or with an anger similar to that felt when Tom's imagination keeps Jim, a freedman, a prisoner on the Phelps farm. By using in *Huck* these extremes of social stratification, from self-ascribed inherited nobility to orphanhood and slavery, Twain could indeed explore human nature.

One indication of how completely the nobility theme has been misunderstood and how strong the subservient attitude remains can be found in the frequency with which American publishers, scholars, and journal editors insist on capitalizing "the King and the Duke" or "the Duke and the Dauphin." But Huck's voice does not grant this status in either the manuscript or first edition. Twain probably would have preferred to set these non-honorific titles only in lower case!

The sense of ridicule aimed toward hierarchy and birth privilege encourages a contrasting acceptance of democratic values, mutual understanding, and reciprocal decency. This theme contributes significantly to the novel's national and international appeal. Moreover, if Twain was suspicious about inherited hierarchical systems, he was equally critical of mobs, especially lynch mobs, as similarly opposed to genuine justice and individualism.

To work out versions of individualism, Twain uses three life conditions that are ostensibly ignoble: slavery, poverty, and orphanhood. A great many memorable characters in world fiction spring from these conditions; many are children without parents, orphans raised by relatives, abandoned children who live by their wits, or children who have mistaken identities and thus the wrong parent. To be "orphaned," in this general sense, is to be without origins. For Twain this condition opened the possibility for the character to be a self-creating person. Huck can adopt the guise and guile of an auto-autho-biographer, making up stories of his past, duplicating, at the same time, some activities of a novelist. Instead of being determined or defined by the past, as nobility is, the orphaned or abandoned child must, like the novelist, continually create a past and a self.

The theme of self-transformation provides several contrasts. The king and duke falsely claim the undeserved, meretricious high status of noble birth. They wish the unearned deferences and predetermined roles accorded to nobility. And they also claim the higher status given to travelling Englishmen or ministers; whenever possible, these amoral men use their status to control others. Huck, on the other hand, usually makes up for himself only low status fictions: "Sarah Williams," "Mary Williams," "George Peters," or "Gorge Jaxon." Relatively high status roles, such as "Adolphus" or "Tom Sawyer," are put upon him by others. Similarly, Jim's transformations as a sick Arab in King Lear's outfit and as the "natural son of Louis XIV" are also imposed upon him by others.

But both Huck and Jim do engage in genuine individualistic ethical self-transformation, genuine acts of imaginative sympathy, when each person, in a time of crisis, thinks of the situation from another's point of view, leading to individually correct moral action. Jim's self-transformation will be explored in this chapter and Huck's, which will demand some emphasis on religion and more psychological theory, will be examined in the next. As shall gradually become apparent, the last portion of the novel deals with three overlapping narratives: the liberation of Jim, of Huck, and of American values.

With this preliminary knowledge in mind, it is appropriate to consult the manuscript. Let a hitherto neglected fact of the novel's composition signal the importance of inherited "nobility" as a motif. Twain wrote a coherent segment on royalty, upbringing, and cultural differences, originally numbering the pages 1–15 and then adding two pages. This segment was later revised and fitted into another, longer insertion and renumbered.[6] Moreover, since this segment was written on Old Berkshire Mills paper, we can determine that it was written or copied late in the creative process, but placed relatively early in the novel, obviously to prepare for the following material, creating a foundation for several important themes. Note C-4 states: "Back yonder, Huck reads and tells about monarchies and kings etc. So Jim stares when he learns the rank of these 2" (*Huck*, 1988, 740). Basically, prior to this insertion, the text which corresponds to the first thirteen chapters had not had much development along anti-nobility or anti-European lines, except for a brief comment in the raftsmen's conversation "about what a king had to do, and how much he got."

The significant sequence begins with what is now the second paragraph of Chapter XIV and continues through to the end of the chapter, forming an unusually coherent thematic statement:

> *I read considerable to Jim about kings, and dukes, and earls and such, and how gaudy they dressed and how much style they put on, and ⟨how⟩ called each other your majesty, and your grace, and your lordship, and so on, 'stead of Mister; and Jim's eyes bugged out, and he was interested.* (MS, 81-44)

The opening emphasis on reading as a way of knowing carries, as shall become clear in Chapter 9, great thematic importance. Later in this segment, Jim questions the American situation: *"dey ain't no kings here, is dey, Huck?"* (MS, 81-54). Jim argues for the power of environment or situation over heredity when he says about "King Sollermun:"

> *"Blame de pint! I reckon I knows what I knows. En mine you, de real pint is down furder—it's down deeper. It lays in de way Sollermun was raised. You take a man dats got on'y one er two chillen: is dat man gwyne to be waseful o' chillen? No, he ain't; he cain't 'ford it. He know how to value 'em. But you take a man dat's got 'bout five million chillen runnin' roun' de house, en it's diffunt. He as soon chop a chile in two as a cat. Dey's plenty mo'. A chile or two, mo' er less, warn't no consekens⟨e⟩ to Sollermun, dad fetch him!"* (MS, 81-52–53)

The thematic concerns focus upon the evils of monarchy and upon the influence of training. Jim's characteristic concern about the welfare of someone else's children affects our emotional response when we later learn that his own child had been afflicted by disease. And the splitting of a child, as proposed by Solomon, may be considered a metonymy for what actually happens to Huck in his later ethical conflicts.[7]

Of more immediate importance, however, is the portion of the insertion in which Huck declares:

> *I told about Louis Sixteenth that got his head cut off in France long time ago;
> and about his little boy the dolphin, that would a been king, but they took and
> shut him up in jail, and some said he died there.* (MS, 81-54)

Twain inserted this section in the manuscript and used it to introduce the
royal family that re-appears—substantially modified for satiric purposes—
several times in the finished novel.

Twain ended this section with the now famous debate between Jim
and Huck about the French language, with Jim's eloquent—although
culturally limited—view that all men are or ought to be the same.[8] Jim can
differentiate between species, but he insists on shared humanity and communication:

> . . . *"Is a Frenchman a man?"*
> *"Yes."*
> *"Well, den! Dad blame it, why doan he talk like a man?—You answer me
> dat!"* (MS, 81-60)

Twain placed this long insertion in a significant place in the novel, right
before the fog separates Jim and Huck, with Jim's despair about losing the
boy, Huck's subsequent trickery, Huck's humbling himself to Jim, and
Huck's battle with his conscience about betraying Jim. The portion we now
read as Chapters XV and XVI thus contains or evokes much more resonance and reverberation because we know more of Jim's humanity and
because we know that this Black man's feelings reflect a common humanity,
transcending national or cultural definitions or status stratification.[9]

Furthermore, the placement of the insertion offers opinions of European nobility before Twain tests out, through Huck, the ethics of the
American quasi-aristocracy, the Grangerfords, in an episode replete with
courtesy, breeding, manners, sentimentality, and senseless killing in a blood
feud of unknown origin. The feud presents a concrete, vicious example of
the destructive influences of heredity and environment, in combination.

Shortly after Huck escapes from the Grangerford-Shepherdson shoot-
ings, he rescues the two fleeing sharpers. The younger fraud manipulates
the group, first managing to gain status by fabricating an impressive mystery. As Blair has noted, Twain may have been influenced by reading
Horace W. Fuller's *Noted French Trials: Imposters and Adventurers*, a book he
purchased and signed in June 1882 (*Mark Twain and Huck Finn*, 327). In a

chapter devoted to "The False Dauphins," Twain could have read about several pretenders to noble status, including an American, Eleazor the Iroquois, who is told of his "royal" heritage in Green Bay, Wisconsin. The language used in Fuller's scornful account includes a phrase, "the secret of my birth" (141), which is identical to the one used by Twain in the fraud's self-proclamation. But a certain verbal source cannot be claimed because both of Twain's speakers sound like walking compilations of cliches from romantic fiction:

> "Ah, you would not believe me; the world never believes—let it pass—'tis no matter. The secret of my birth—"
> "The secret of your birth? Do you mean to say—" (163)

The grotesquely improbable situation continues:

> "Gentlemen," says the young man, very solemn, "I will reveal it to you, for I feel I may have confidence in you. By rights I am a duke!"
> Jim's eyes bugged out when he heard that; and I reckon mine did, too. Then the baldhead says, "No! you can't mean it?"
> "Yes, my great-grandfather, eldest son of the Duke of Bridgewater, fled to this country about the end of the last century, to breathe the pure air of freedom; married here, and died, leaving a son, his own father dying about the same time. The second son of the late duke seized the title and estates—the infant real duke was ignored. I am the lineal descendant of that infant—I am the rightful Duke of Bridgewater; and here am I, forlorn, torn from my high estate, hunted of men, despised by the cold world, ragged, worn, heart-broken, and degraded to the companionship of felons on a raft." (163)

The stylistic elevation of the con man's claim, his use of literary cliches, and his self-dramatizing attitudes each imply his moral failings. The duke uses his claim of nobility—even within a democracy—to suppress Huck and Jim.

At first, Jim and Huck pity the duke and make a fuss over him. But the older scoundrel soon resents the attention and responds by competitively claiming not only nobility of his own, but higher rank:

> "Yes, my friend, it is too true—your eyes is lookin' at this very moment on the pore disappeared Dauphin, Looy the Seventeenth, son of Looy the Sixteen and Marry Antonette." (164)

The combination of an executed king, an orphaned child, and claimants to hereditary privilege must have fascinated Twain; the chances to parody romantic literature's grand style and sentimental tones also must have been appealing. Moreover, the dual claims provide another example of Twain's characteristic doubling because the satire even includes a pair of aquatic puns: "Bilgewater" and "dolphin."

Huck, as usual, quickly perceives: "It didn't take me long to make up my mind that these liars warn't no kings nor dukes, at all, but just low-down humbugs and frauds. But I never said nothing." On the other hand, Jim, at first, believes. His trusting attitude is partially justified by the manuscript insertion in which Huck, whom he believes, had introduced the concept of nobility and the story of the dolphin. But Jim gradually, individualistically, makes up his own opinion:

> "Huck, does you reck'n we gwyne to run acrost any mo' kings on dis trip?"
> "No," I says, "I reckon not."
> "Well," says he, "dat's all right, den. I doan' mine one er two kings, but dat's enough. Dis one's powerful drunk, en de duke ain' much better."
>
> I found Jim had been trying to get him to talk French, so he could hear what it was like; but he said he had been in this country so long, and had so much trouble, he'd forgot it. (176)

The earlier insertion, with its section on the French language, prepares for Jim's credulousness and for his open-minded curiosity in exploring the topic with the king.

The rascals attempt to stage plays about nobility, such as *Richard III* (which can be thought of as a comic variation of the killing of Buck by the Shepherdsons), *Romeo and Juliet* (an obvious duplication of the love affair within a feud as experienced by Sophia Grangerford and Harney Shepherdson) and Hamlet's spectacularly garbled soliloquy. But, of course, all the theatrical efforts by the king and duke fail to turn a profit, and they finally sink to performing a nude cavort, a crude exhibitionistic show and swindle, originally called "The Burning Shame" but retitled in revision "The King's Camelopard" or "The Royal Nonesuch." Both modified titles, significantly, include references to nobility; in addition, the bestial form uses a combination word to refer to a giraffe, an animal which is also used to characterize the king; in the second title, "nonesuch," can mean either *without equal* or *no such thing*. Both titles for the nude display severely limit the concept of royalty. But the idea of an undressed king on stage may have resonated in Twain's head.

Jim gradually begins to suspect the villains and confides his doubts to Huck who responds in part by advising the illiterate Jim to read:

"Don't it sprise you, de way dem kings carries on, Huck?"

"No," I says, "it don't."

"Why don't it, Huck?"

"Well, I [sic] don't because it's in the breed. I reckon they're all alike."

"But Huck, dese kings o' ourn is reglar rapscallions; dat's jist what dey is; deys reglar rapscallions."

"Well, that's what I'm a-saying; all kings is mostly rapscallions, as fur as I can make out."

"Is dat so?"

"You read about them once—you'll see. Look at ⟨Charles Second; this'n⟩ Henry the Eight; this'n 's a Sunday school superintendent to <u>him</u>. And look at Charles Second, *and Louis Fourteen and Louis Fifteen*, and James Second, and Edward Second, and Richard Third, and forty more; besides all them Saxon heptarchies that used to rip around so in old times and raise Cain. (MS, 197–98)

Twain apparently first canceled, then later included in the running sequence, the line one of his own ancestors supposedly judged. At some later time, Twain also included the line of French kings claimed as ancestors by the elderly fraud and mentioned as a model by young Tom Sawyer.

This conversation leads naturally into a fairly lengthy catalogue of Huck's thoughts about the misdeeds of kings, especially Henry the Eighth, who Huck somehow thinks was a son of the Duke of Wellington. The potpourri of misinformation ends with Huck's conclusion: "All I say, is, kings is kings, and you got to make allowances. Take them all around, they're a mighty ornery lot. It's the way they're raised" (MS, 204). Huck traces the evils of royalty to the "breed" and to "the way they're raised," colloquial, concrete ways of expressing what a modern reader would call heredity and environment.

The ensuing dialogue between Huck and Jim deals with the way the king smells and the way the duke drinks. Huck offers an opinion about the duke that neatly conflates the two: "When he's drunk, there ain't no near-sighted man ⟨can tell⟩ could tell him from a king" (MS, 204). Jim's opinion grows more negative about the scoundrels:

"Well, anyways, I doan hanker for no mo' un um, Huck. Dese is all I kin stan'."

"It's the way I feel, too, Jim. But we've got them on our hands, and we got to remember what they are, and make allowances. Sometimes I wish we could hear of a country that's out of kings."

I went to sleep, and Jim didn't call me when it was my turn. (MS, 205)

Into this section Twain inserted, for the printed version, an entire paragraph which emphasized his already obvious theme of disgust for nobility, compelling evidence of his intended meanings. After the wish about a country that is "out of kings" (clearly America is not), Twain added this unmistakable linking statement:

> What was the use to tell Jim these warn't real kings and dukes? It wouldn't a done no good; and besides, it was just as I said; you couldn't tell them from the real kind. (201)

Thus the increased emphasis on criticism of nobility also occurred as late as the preparation for print stage.

Although Twain's treatment of phony nobility, birth privilege, and European pretension within a democracy has been, to this point, relatively straightforward and negative, the next permutation of the theme is quite subtle and indeed has not, to my knowledge, previously been detected. Huck's opinions about kings lead into the emotionally powerful presentation of Jim's feelings about his family and Jim's discovery of his daughter's affliction, after scarlet fever, with deafness and muteness.[10] Strange as it may seem, a reflective reader may well re-read Jim's description in the light of the famous tragic scene of King Lear holding Cordelia's body. Jim relates that he had punished the child for disobedience and that she did not hear the door slam:

> "—en my lan', de chile ⟨nuvver⟩ *never* move'! My breff mos' hop outer me; en I feel so—so—I doan know how I feel. ⟨So⟩ I crope out, all a-tremblin', en crope aroun' en open de do' easy en slow, en poke my head in behine de chile, sof' en still, en all of a sudden I says pow! jus' as loud as I could yell. *She never move'!* O, Huck, I bust out a-cryin', en grab her up in my arms en say, "O de po' little thing! de ⟨l⟩Lord God Amighty fogive po' ole Jim, kaze he never gwyne to fogive his-seff as long as he live!' O, she was plumb deef en dumb, Huck, plumb deef and dumb—en I'd ben a treat'n her so!" (MS, 209–10)

On note B-2, Twain had told himself: "Let Jim say putty for 'pretty' and nuvver for 'never,'" but while revising this emotionally powerful scene, Twain twice wrote "*never*," and one of the changes is the highly unusual modification of dialect form to standard language. Moreover, in another unusual action, Twain wrote in the left margin, in pencil, "This expression shall not be changed." At this point the possible allusion to King Lear's tragic situation with Cordelia and his famous line, "Never, never, never, never, never," could be interpreted to mean that tragic emotions can occur in the life of a low-status, traditionally voiceless person such as Jim just as they can in those of higher birth. For a moment Twain has created, in this richly allusive context, a dramatization of immense, irreparable human sadness, the inconsolable grief about a sick child that can torment any parent. This suffering, limitless in depth, transcends cultural status and racial boundaries to serve as the best argument in favor of Jim's shared humanity.

Moreover, Twain's surprising mind moves to a similar complex literary revision, probably affecting plot, only two paragraphs later. In a heavily revised, re-ordered paragraph, the duke first dresses Jim up as Richard III. But then, inarguably, Twain decided to change the costume to the previously unmentioned "*King Leer's outfit*," (MS, 212[1/2 A]), thereby summoning a completely different constellation of allusive meanings. Thus we, as readers, first experience the genuine emotion in an individual situation, then see an explicit identification in a comic version.

But the full use of the Shakespearean story occurs in the subsequent plot situation, because Twain creates in the entire Wilks episode an inverse repetition of *King Lear*. In Twain's version a false king attempts to steal the inheritance of three orphaned daughters; there is a false duke; there is a true and false brother, in fact a pair of them; there is a trial scene and a stormy heath scene in which a body is uncovered. And, at the end of the story, as if to punctuate the extended parallel, when Huck returns to the raft, King Lear is mentioned yet again in the reference to Jim's outfit. The inclusion of enough elements to create an observable resemblance also creates a progression from the burlesque of relevant Shakespeare plays in the earlier sections to a subtle, perhaps accidental, parody of the Wilks episode. Huck, of course, never realizes that he may be wandering around in a parodic situation.

How does Twain use literature? At this point let us say only that he uses allusions to literary titles effectively, and that in the case of *King Lear* Twain recognizes the genuine emotion of a grieving father but recreates this feeling in Jim, a politically and racially contrasting human. The overwhelmingly negative attitude toward nobility may contribute to the notion of a rascal king on stage in the nude or to the outlandish distortion of Jim in King Lear's outfit. The honored piece of literature is absorbed, transformed, made into a quite new and quite different thing as the king and duke attempt to swindle three orphaned girls. This significant use of literature prepares for the blatant—and all encompassing—parody of literature in the Phelps farm sequence.[11]

After the king and duke have been caught, tarred, and feathered, the satire on "nobility" seemingly becomes more diffuse, if only because the king and duke disappear.[12] Thereafter, the basic point is that Tom Sawyer, an American orphaned child with European hierarchical values, uses notions of captivity and escape—from books about nobility and courtiers—to suppress a legally free person. Just as the king and duke have controlled and tied Jim, Tom Sawyer, fully aware that Jim is legally free, takes Jim—as well as Huck—hostage to his veneration for European values and literature. Moreover, we know that Jim has emotions of great—even Shakespearean—intensity. That makes the extended imprisonment, the continuation in slave status, even more appalling.

The criticism of "nobility" in the Phelps farm episode relies primarily upon parodic treatment of literature about titled European aristocracy, e.g., *The Count of Monte Cristo* and Baron von Trenck. Yet Twain also continued the theme by sarcastic uses of the word "noble." In Tom Sawyer's ethic or language system, "noble" carries favorable connotations, and accordingly Twain frequently revises it into highly inappropriate contexts:

> Then we went to the nigger cabins, and while I got Nat's attention off, Tom shoved a piece of candlestick into the middle of a corn-pone that was in Jim's pan, and we went along with Nat to see how it would work, and it just worked first-rate: when Jim bit into it it most mashed all his teeth out. (MS, 601)

When the section appeared in print, "first-rate" had been taken out and "noble" appeared in its place (313).

Similarly, the manuscript presents a description of the materials the boys steal for the prank:

> Silas had a *noble* brass warming pan which he thought considerable of, because it belonged to his ancestors with a long wooden handle that come over from England with William the Conqueror in the Mayflower, *or one of them early ships* ⟨,⟩ and was hid away up garret with a lot of other old pots and things that was valuable, not on account of being any account, because they warnt but on account of them being relicts, you know. (MS, 633)

In this section, Twain played with tradition, at one moment spelling the word "ancestors" as "anzesters." Moreover, Huck uses the word "noble" to describe the pack of rats in the cellar (MS, 622 same as 319).

Within the Phelps episode, Jim's situation is peculiar; he is a man of genuinely noble spirit harassed by Tom's childish, destructive, ignoble, European, immoral bookish notions about nobility and imprisonment. A grotesquely comic contrast occurs when Tom insists that Jim, who cannot read or write, must have a coat of arms, and Jim replies:

"W'y, mars Tom, I ain'⟨t⟩ got no coat ⟨er⟩ ⟨*no*⟩ *o'* arms; I ain' got ⟨noth'n⟩ *nuffn* but dish-yer *ole* shirt, en you know*s* I got to ⟨do⟩ *keep* de journal on dat." (MS, 637)

The coat of arms is savagely appropriate because Tom says it must include:

crest, a runaway nigger, <u>sable</u>, with his bundle over his shoulder on a bar sinister, ⟨*with*⟩ *and* a couple of gules for supporters, which is you and me. (MS, 639–640)

The boys are both not gules (heraldic for red), but gulls, for Huck is deceived about Jim's imprisonment, and Tom is deceived about the value of the literature he has read.[13] Huck asks Tom:

"What's a bar sinister?"
"Oh, <u>I</u> don't know. But he's got to have it. All the nobility does."
That <u>was</u> just his way. If it didn't suit him to explain a thing to you, he wouldn't do it. You might pump at him a week, it wouldn't make no difference. (MS, 641)

The humor involves attributing the bar sinister of illegitimacy to all the nobles, with a final duplicitous comment: Tom has this ignorant, damaging way of dealing with all texts; and Twain seems to be content to allude to bastardy in a way which may or may not be understood.

The French royal family reappears when Tom gets emotionally involved by petting his own sentimentality and creating a series of stylistic gradations, which climaxes in calling Jim "<u>a noble stranger, natural son of Louis XIV</u>" (MS, 644). Jim is, in fact, noble and decent, a natural embodiment of humane consideration for another. Most readers, however, skip over the moments of Jim's ethical transcendence.

Later in the novel, after Tom has been shot and the escapees are on the raft, Tom rants on fantastically:

I wish <u>we</u>'d a had the handling of Louis XVI, there wouldn't a been no 'Son of St. Louis, ascend to heaven!' wrote down in <u>his</u> biography: no, sir, we'd a whooped him over the <u>border</u>-that's what we'd a done with <u>him</u>—and done it just as slick as nothing at all, too ⟨, dont chu know⟩. Man the sweeps—man the sweeps!"
But me and Jim was consulting—and thinking. And after we'd thought a ⟨while⟩ *minute*, I says:
"Say it, Jim.
So he says:
"Well, den, dis is de way it look to ⟨Jim⟩ *me*, Huck. ⟨If⟩ Ef it wuz <u>him</u> dat ⟨w⟩

'uz bein' sot free, en one er de boys wuz to git shot, would he say, 'Go on en save me, nemmine 'bout a doctor for to save dis one?' ⟨Would⟩ Is dat like mars Tom Sawyer? Would he say dat? You <u>bet</u> he wouldn't! <u>Well</u> den is ⟨Jim gwyne⟩ <u>Jim</u> gwyne to say it? No, sah—I ⟨don't⟩ **doan'** budge a step out'n dis place, 'dout a <u>doctor</u>; not ef it's forty year!" (MS, 709–10)

This segment is actually fairly complex; Tom makes a wish contrary to fact about literature; Huck and Jim function in the real world, "consult" wordlessly, understand one another perfectly, and are in agreement. Significantly, Huck trusts Jim to "say it"; surprisingly, Jim—with a dignity almost palpable—phrases his concern for the wounded Tom in Tom's own language. But Jim's self-transformation is done to explain his decision and to persuade in a non-oppressive fashion. Actually, Tom has been sacrificing not himself, but Jim during the entire escapade. Jim and Huck and generations of readers have indeed been imprisoned or held hostage by Tom's veneration for nobility.

Jim does not need noble status or European bookish authorities to determine the best course of action from a moral point of view. Jim—of his own free will but phrased in Tom's style—is heroically but foolishly endangering his only chance for freedom and, as far as he knows, re-entering the world of slavery and punishment in order to protect the dependent, foolish boy who says that he wishes to free the slave but actually torments him. Jim's ethical but self-sacrificial decision is an apt demonstration of the morality of the golden rule, a flexible, considerate morality of mutual respect, an absolute contrast to the destructive ethics of social stratification, hereditary rank, heroic adventures, noble sentiments, and bookish precedents. Jim shares such freedom from selfishness and from convention with Huck. Huck, as a white semi-literate child, can add greater freedom to plan, to arrange, and to criticize, as he also works out his own individual morality.

Notes

1. Twain's short story, "Edward Mills and George Benton: A Tale," presents issues of positive and negative reinforcement in skeletal form. Blair has written brilliantly about the influence upon Twain of reading W. E. H. Lecky's *History of European Morals from Augustus to Charlemagne*, in *Mark Twain and Huck Finn*, especially 131–45. Lecky favored the view that people have an innate intuitional preference for moral behavior; Twain's marginal annotations demonstrate that he disagreed and instead believed that environmental forces determine morality.

2. Three studies may be recommended as particularly useful background: Blair's "The Duke and the Dauphin," Chapter XIX in *Mark Twain and Huck Finn*, 270–84; Howard Baetzhold's "The Bright and the Dark (1882–1885)" in *Mark Twain and John Bull: The British Connection* 68–101. In addition Sherwood Cummings in *Mark Twain and Science*, which appeared after these chapters were completed, offers an interpretation consistent with mine in these next four explorations.

3. Invitation in *The Mark Twain Papers*. A later letter dated June 8, 1883, from Major Arthur Collins, provides information about the mutual cordiality of the visit and the human ordinariness of life near nobility. Collins informs Twain that the Princess was delighted by Twain's "salute," probably a brief greeting speech or toast. The letter also conveys Major Collins's favorable opinions about Twain's writings, especially about Saal and the Prophets, Issac, and the story of the boy who pretended to be a spy because of his reading spy literature, "A Curious Experience."

Collins also offers a literary opinion: "Youth will be served ⟨if only⟩ in more ways than one, and for freshness of humor and for that charm of all charms—unconsciousness of it—I note how all of you have to draw on the font of youth." He continues by confiding that the Governor General's son, when asked about plans for a seaside vacation, replied: "I really think we must escape the mosquitoes; mother's legs are in a terrible state, she has 28 bites on them." Collins enjoyed the "directness of the information, the numerical minuteness of it—what is more entrancing, and though I had to wait for half an hour for my laugh, not a smile played on my lips till we parted."*

4. Several entries from "A Record of Small Foolishnesses" may be cited as indicative of his observations. The family tried to train the girls to avoid fighting by using candy as positive reinforcement for domestic tranquility. But once Clara misinterpreted the providing of a cracker during punishment as a positive reinforcement for negative behavior. Then, when she wanted another cracker, she invented a bad behavior to entitle her to the food.

For another exploration of the conflicting roles of heredity and reinforcement, see Lee Clark Mitchell's "'De Nigger in You': Race or Training in *Pudd'nhead Wilson*."

5. In my teaching experience, foreign students often appreciate immediately Twain's satire against royalty as an attack on the corruption of absolute power. Several foreign students (from countries at opposite ends of the political spectrum) who have relatives feared by the absolute powers have read *Huck* with rare insight and resonance.

6. The bibliographical facts follow: MS, 81–43 concludes half way down the page with the statement, now in Chapter XIV, that Jim *"had an uncommon level head for a nigger."* There is a crossed out direction to:

Read [XXX] from book to Jim

MS, 81-44 begins, *"I read considerable to Jim about kings, and dukes, and earls. . . ."* This page was originally numbered 1. The next page, 81-45, has a canceled 2 under the 8. The following pages are all renumbered: original 3 appears as 81-46, original 4 as 81-47, etc., through 81-53, which has a canceled 10, up through the original 15, which was renumbered 81-58 (emphasis added). Original 15 ended midway on the page in the dialogue about how French people talk. There was trimming and revision at this point because page 81-60 was originally renumbered 16 and then 17. The page ends with "*You can't learn a nigger to argue*," with "*So I quit*," the end of Chapter XIV, squeezed in at the right bottom margin. Thus, all of what is now Chapter XIV, except the first paragraph, was composed as a unit, with some revision at the end.

A possible thematic connection with the conclusion of *Tom Sawyer* exists because Huck may have once needed to learn about dukes and nobility in order to be included in Tom's gang. Huck pleads and Tom then responds:

> "Can't let me in, Tom? Didn't you let me go for a pirate?"
> "Yes, but that's different. A robber is more high-toned than what a pirate is—as a general thing. In most countries they're awful high up in the nobility—dukes and such." (*The Adventures of Tom Sawyer*, Chapter XXXV)

If Twain did cut a chapter from the end of *Tom Sawyer*, it may conceivably have dealt with Tom's and/or Huck's notions about robber gangs and nobility.

7. At the time of composition, after the death of his only son, and later in his life after the death of Susy, it might have been extremely painful for Sam Clemens to write or to read Jim's comment about King Solomon.

8. "A Record" has "parlez vous Francais Polly wants a cracker"* written and erased on the inside cover. This resembles Huck's hypothetical question to Jim: "*Spose a man was to come to you and say Pollyvoo-franzy—what would you think?*" (MS, 81-56)

9. Among the many rich treatments of Jim's personality, special mention must be made of Neil Schmitz's *Of Huck and Alice*, and his "Twain, *Huckleberry Finn* and the Reconstruction," as well as Forrest Robinson's "The Characterization of Jim in *Huckleberry Finn*."

10. Twain may have been influenced by the reality of this disease. His coachman's child was made deaf, and Twain's own family was quarantined by the feared disease. See *Mark Twain-Howells Letters*, Vol. 1, 465–66. "A Record of Small Foolishnesses" reveals that Jean had scarlet fever in December 1882. For Twain's fictional rendition of the frightening illness, see "Tom Sawyer's Conspiracy" in Blair, ed., *Mark Twain's Hannibal, Huck and Tom*, 185–88. Note A-11 preserves his original source for the touching moment:

> Put in
> L. A. punished her child several days for ⟨disobedience⟩ *refusing to answer* and inattention (5 yr old) then while punishing discovered it was deaf <and dumb> and dumb! (from scarlet fever. ⟨T⟩ It showed no reproachfulness for the whippings—kissed the punisher and showed non-comprehension of what it was all about.

11. In one of those sheer coincidences which occasionally haunt our language, Albany says at the conclusion of *King Lear* to Kent and Edgar:

"Friends of my soul, you twain
Rule in this realm, and the gored state sustain."

It is also worth noting that Clemens himself had three daughters and was called "King" by a servant. I speculate that late in his life, after the death of Susy, portions of *King Lear* must have been, to Sam Clemens, unendurable. The centrality of the family to Sam Clemens should affect the way we read his fiction about a child seeking a father or about a father seeking a child. It is regrettable aesthetically, but understandable psychologically, that the father of Langdon Clemens agreed to drop the raftsmen section with the story of the dead child pursuing the father.

12. At one point Twain must have considered extending this material into the Phelps section. Note C-6 describes the gossiping Arkansas women and plans: "Let em drop in ignorant remarks about monarchs in Europe, and mix them up with Biblical monarchs." But Twain decided in the Phelps section to limit this topic to Tom.

13. This heraldic device may allude to the one at the end of *The Scarlet Letter*, forming a contrasting pair: just as *The Scarlet Letter* is a book about a letter, *Huck* can be considered as a letter about books. Moreover, Jim's sale by the king and imprisonment on the Phelps farm can be considered as a reverse captivity narrative, in which a free Black adult is captured and tormented by whites before being restored to his family.

8. Christianity in Conflict with Morality

> The church has never started a good work, and has always been the last
> to relinquish an evil one. American slavery's last and stubbornest friend
> and champion in the North was the church.
>
> Twain's marginal comment in Quarry Farm copy of
> Lecky's *History of the Rise and Influence of the Spirit
> of Rationalism in Europe* I, 141

> The most permanent lessons in morals are those which come, not
> of booky teaching, but of experience.
>
> *A Tramp Abroad*, XX

I

In this chapter we shall trace Huck's development as Twain makes him
grow increasingly independent from conventional Christianity and as the
boy experiences his own self-transformations that lead, ultimately, to
an admirable but not controlling moral position. Crucial issues include
Twain's attitudes toward conventional religion, as well as his exploration of
the formative influences of heredity and environment, psychological reinforcement, avoidance of shame, truth-telling, and self-transformation.

A relatively unknown nineteenth-century religion of Sam Clemens's
Uncle John Quarles and a controversial modern theory about stages of
moral development in male children will be introduced as two useful
paradigms. In addition, a unity can be traced: repeatedly Huck sees a
situation from one or more other points of view, and this imaginative
sympathy helps his moral growth. Although the novel is limited to the
boy's narrative point of view, Huck's mind readily and sympathetically
includes many other characters' perceptions. Because this chapter presents
a thesis about development, it will be necessary to present evidence in
narrative order.[1] By now some of the pieces of glass in the kaleidoscope, the
manuscript evidence, will be familiar, although the pieces may appear
differently when viewed not in a stylistic but in a thematic light.

Most Americans in Clemens's parental generation and many in his own generation would regard "religion" and "morality" as almost identical in meaning, but Clemens/Twain's attitude was far more complex. A typical modern reader must study extensively in diaries, journals, and autograph books of the period to realize how extensive and pervasive an influence conventional Christianity had—and how individualistically independent this author's attitudes were.

Early in his career, the trip to the Holy Land sharpened Twain's eye and ear for hypocrisy among the pilgrims, and the travel letters which became *Innocents Abroad* are frequently irreverent. Twain found the travel letter form particularly suitable for scathing attacks on religion, traditions, and society. This novel—which concludes, "The End. Yours Truly, Huck Finn."—can be seen, finally, as an extended example of the travel letter.

Twain received several letters from strangers in 1883 and 1884 urging Christianity upon him. Because the tones vary from delusional to assaultive, I consider these documents to be "crank" letters. One informed him that Jesus would come knocking at the door of his heart that week, and another asked him to open his life to Jesus. One letter from Hartford was filled with misspellings and religious cliches; Twain scrawled on the envelope, "self-righteous ROT."* In several incoherent, delusional letters, Mary Reily told Twain about her visions, assuring him that John Wilkes Booth was really John the Baptist's successor. On one of her envelopes, Twain wrote, "That lunatic."*2 Many famous people receive such correspondence, but these letters must have been particularly irritating to Twain because he did not share his generation's veneration for and acceptance of religion. In his fiction, Twain dramatizes the notion that cloaks of sanctity frequently can conceal delusion, stupidity, foolishness, greed, selfishness, and deceit.

He had also observed and recorded some of his own children's struggles with Christianity. Susie once asked, honestly and innocently, how Langdon, the first child who died at about eighteen months, would recognize his family in heaven. In what must have been an equally poignant moment, Susie once had Clara play a game in which Susie was the angel taking a little dead baby up to heaven. The complicated words of religion were, upon occasion, misunderstood, as happened when Susie assured her parents that, "I never was at church except that one day that Bay was crucified." (i.e., christened).* Susie also was able to shift to another's point of view; when she heard the biblical story of Joseph and the killing of the baby goat to stain the garment with blood, Susie reacted, "Poor little kid!"* Susie at one point had an attitude of trust, feeling no need to be specific or mechanistic, "I hardly ever pray now; when I want anything I just leave it to Him—He understands."* But later, after making the relativistic perception that Indians had prayed to their own gods, she said, "So now I only pray that there may be a God and a heaven—or something better."* Once Clara, a quite practical child, listened while Livy sat to hear Susie's bedtime prayers. When Livy said it was Clara's turn, the younger child just rolled over, saying, "Oh, one's enough."*[3] In the summer of 1883, Clemens lived with and loved precocious children, who had grown to ages nine and eleven, who were exploring their own involvement with religion.

As we observe Huck's growth from religion to morality, we must be aware of several contributory issues. As indicated earlier, Huck, an historian of the self, attempts to figure out the influences on his personality of his heredity and his environment without the guidance of sophisticated theories such as we would now associate with Mendel or Pavlov. Instead, this abandoned child, perceptive but relatively unschooled, tries to figure out the interactions, the sources of his own behavior, under the shadow of an unrealistic, irrelevant, or deceitful religion. Huck behaves as a recently illiterate, now minimally literate, boy struggling in conflict with a society that uses books to pass on values. Moreover, Huck respects Tom Sawyer partially because Tom has read so much and holds "the rules" in memory. The telling of the truth or of a lie recurs as an issue; another complex topic involves the formative effect on personality of shame, guilt, and positive reinforcement after moral action.[4] In this context, Huck's explicit debates about his values and his reasons for his values compel the readers' sympathetic attention, generation after generation.

II

We shall at first concentrate not upon the comparatively well-understood conventional Christianity which young Sam Clemens experienced at the Old Ship of Zion Methodist Church in Hannibal but upon the less well-known but relevant beliefs of Universalism, the religion of Sam's uncle, John Quarles. His farm, in Missouri, where young Sam spent summers, was the model for the fictional Phelps plantation. Similarly, Uncle John and Aunt Patsy served Twain's imagination as models for Silas and Sally Phelps, just as one of their slaves, Uncle Daniel, was a partial model for Jim.

Young Sam Clemens's religious and ethical development probably was affected, on a primary level, simply by the existence of an alternative system;

regular religion could be set against summer religion; the relatively urbanized Hannibal morality could be set against the more rural and perhaps nature-centered morality. The fact that John Quarles's Universalism happened to be a comparatively tolerant, rational, humane alternative probably had an immense influence upon the boy and upon the adult author.

Universalism drew upon the intellectual background of Deism and Jeffersonian thought, urging that Biblical scriptures be interpreted in the light of rationalism (Cassara, *Universalism in America*, I). Works by Ethan Allen and Tom Paine contributed to this religion. Universalism tended to deemphasize the trinitarian notions of conventional Christianity; the leader, Hosea Ballou (1771–1852) thought that the trinitarians believed in "infinity multiplied by three."

Universalism's most important aspect involves the controversial belief that salvation can be granted to all souls. Of course, this doctrine of Universal Salvation offended many other religions which insisted upon special or exclusive salvation for their own believers, their own "elect." But Universalists disagreed, contending that the "limitarians" or "partialists" mistakenly underestimated God's power and desire to save souls.

Universalists disagreed among themselves about man's free will and determinism. Similarly, some Universalists believed that evil-doers and sinners are punished only when alive, while others believed that after death sinners would be "purified" in Hell for up to 50,000 years before being "restored" to God's salvation. Thus, whether a person would go to Hell for some period or whether no one would might be a topic of debate among Universalists. Although most Universalists shared an emphasis on tolerance and reason with the Unitarians, the Universalists tended to be less wealthy, less educated, and more exclusively Biblical in focus, lacking the cultural relativism of the more sophisticated Unitarians.

Some Universalists, such as Dr. Benjamin Rush (1745–1813), had advanced anti-war, anti-slavery, and pro-education beliefs, but this faith did not try to enforce uniformity of belief. By the 1840s there were approximately three hundred Universalist "preachers," but many Universalists did not attend churches, perhaps partially to avoid debating one another about their differing individual principles of conscience and belief.

Yet the Universalists differed enough from conventional Christians to suffer discrimination and, in some cases, attacks. Perhaps because members of his religion upon occasion endured persecution, Hosea Ballou picked as his favorite Biblical verse, Acts 17:11, a verse which praises the open-mindedness of some ancient unbelievers who listened long enough to be converted. (We may recall, with surprise, that Uncle Silas Phelps has been "a-studying my text in Acts seventeen, before breakfast" (MS, 619).) Ballou recommended verse eleven as helping him when he has been "troubled by unbelief." In this section the apostles Paul and Silas went into a synagogue in Berea to face a potentially hostile audience:

> These were more noble than those in Thessalonica, in that they received the word with all readiness of mind, and searched the scripture daily, whether these things were so.

Although it is hard to know exactly what beliefs shaped the daily thoughts and Biblical searchings of John Quarles and his family on the Missouri frontier, when his nephew Sam would visit, we may presume that the scriptures and some form of Universal Salvation would be emphasized.

Universalism's 1803 Winchester Profession appears relatively simple, with only three Articles. Article II stated:

> We believe that there is one God, whose nature is love, revealed in one Lord Jesus Christ, by one Holy Spirit of Grace, who will finally restore the whole family of mankind to holiness and happiness.

For many Universalists, the "whole family of mankind" included both other religions and other races. Many Universalists opposed slavery, and in 1841 and 1843 anti-slavery petitions and resolutions were passed.

The Universalists' Article III stated:

> We believe that holiness and true happiness are inseparably connected, and that believers ought to be careful to maintain order and practice good works; for those things are good and profitable unto man.

In frontier Missouri, in 1845, such thoughts might be considered progressive to shocking, and the Universalists had already allowed for flexibility in adapting the Articles to local circumstances. Huck, who repeatedly feels threatened with Hell, often feels drawn to doing "good works," and his thinking about Jim's family may represent, in this context, relatively greater open-mindedness and consideration than the presumed cultural norms.

It should be stressed that Clemens/Twain would have also been familiar with the Romantic notions which see the earliest stages of childhood as the most innocent and most "moral." Moreover, his sensitivity and attention to his own children's intellectual and ethical development command admiration and remain relevant to his treatment of Huck.

In addition to the religious approach, we may utilize a ground-breaking, comprehensive evolving theory drawn from developmental psychology. Because refinements and qualifications of this illuminating theory appear frequently, the validity of this chapter need not be linked to the theory; but the illuminating strength, almost like a high-powered searchlight operating from an angle, whites out some details and creates large shadows while casting other feature into bold relief. As a secondary aid, a subsidiary oblique approach, the theory merits attention.

While we follow the counterpoint between wide-ranging satire on conventional Christianity and the construction of an individual morality, it may also be helpful to put Huck's progress alongside an admittedly modern, admittedly controversial paradigm, Lawrence Kohlberg's theory about six stages of ethical and moral development in adolescent males. Such comparison does not imply that Twain cleverly, presciently, has Huck scamper up a ladder of definitions, but a careful analysis reveals that Huck does grow in congruence with this modern, easily understood theory. As is true for most adolescents, Huck is not perfectly consistent. Moreover, each stage in his behavior includes elements of the earlier stages. Significantly, this theory helps explain clearly the final ethical contrast between Huck and Tom.[5]

In Kohlberg's framework, the first two stages can be called "premoral." In stage one the child has a simple orientation to punishment and obedience, obeying simply to avoid punishment. Stage two involves naive instrumental hedonism; the child conforms to obtain rewards or to have favors returned. Stages three and four involve conventional role conformity: a stage three child conforms to avoid disapproval or dislike by others, while a stage four boy acts to uphold authority, conforming to avoid censure by recognized authorities. Tom Sawyer might be labeled as usually performing at this level in his slavish obedience to literary authorities. Only at levels five and six are self-accepted moral principles involved. Only at the fifth stage does the child consider the morality of the contract, the individual rights, and the accepted laws. At this stage the individual seeks to conform to maintain the respect of a presumed impartial spectator judging in terms of community welfare. This stage creates a tortuous situation for Huck when he debates writing to Miss Watson about Jim's location. Only at the sixth, highest level of moral development, does the child's thinking include the morality of individual principles of conscience, as the individual acts to avoid self-condemnation. A possible reason for widespread discomfort on readers' parts with the novel's ending is that Huck, who has reached stage six values, frequently submits to Tom's stage four behavior. Although Huck becomes much more openly, explicitly critical of Tom in the Phelps episode, he does follow Tom's leadership. Twain's genius about childhood encompassed the range and progression posited by Kohlberg, along with the complexity of the real situations in which his created characters functioned. Because Huck seems so open, so unrestrained as he confides his story, his history, we follow his development through difficulty with admiration.

III

How quickly does the concern for morality and religion surface in the novel? We recall the initial references to an earlier novel and to the moral issues of lying and truth-telling:

> You don't know about me, without you have read a book by the name of "The Adventures of Tom Sawyer," but that ain't no matter. That book was made by Mr. Mark Twain, and he told the truth, mainly. There was things which he stretched, but mainly he told the truth. That is nothing. I never seen anybody but lied, one time or another, without it was Aunt Polly, or the widow, or maybe Mary. . . . (17)

The central concerns of Christianity and morality dominate the first chapter, with truth-telling, religious cliches such as "a poor lost lamb," and a grumbling grace over food. The widow attempts to indoctrinate Huck in the Judeo-Christian tradition by reading from the Bible the story of "Moses and the Bulrushers." Huck listens attentively perhaps because he at first thought the story involved people who charged at bulls, probably an eventful kind of story. Of course, the story actually deals, appropriately enough, with hereditary status, religion, an abandoned child on a water journey, and liberation from slavery. But Huck experiences two disillusionments: he learns that the story is not what he expected but concerns "dead people," and he quickly realizes that the widow's restrictions about tobacco are hypocritical and not based on experience.

Huck's direct conflict with books and with conventional religion occurs as Miss Watson criticizes Huck's behavior and warms to her subject. We can observe a contrast between her volubility and Huck's increasing reticence:

> Her sister, Miss Watson, a tolerable slim old maid, with goggles on, had just come to live with her, and took a set at me now, with a spelling-book. She

worked me middling hard for about an hour, and then the widow made her ease up. I couldn't stood it much longer. Then for an hour it was deadly dull, and I was fidgety. Miss Watson would say, "Dont put your feet up there, Huckleberry;" and "dont scrunch up like that, Huckleberry—set up straight;" and pretty soon she would say, "Don't gap and stretch like that, Huckleberry—why don't you try to behave?" Then she told me all about the bad place, and I said I wished I was there. She got mad, then, but I didn't mean no harm. All I wanted was to go somewheres; all I wanted was a change, I warn't particular. She said it was wicked to say what I said; said she wouldn't say it for the whole world; *she* was going to live so as to go to the good place. Well, I couldn't see no advantage in going where she was going, so I made up my mind I wouldn't try for it. But I never said so, because it would only make trouble, and wouldn't do no good. (19)

Huck's behavior and attitude in the opening chapter correspond to Kohlberg's definition of the first stage of moral development, simple deference to a superior force or authority. Despite coercive predictive threats and, later, internalized fears about damnation in hell, Huck will create his own integrity; he will even become willing to go to hell. His autonomy develops as he learns to withhold his opinion, as he experiments with the adolescent habit of controlling the interaction or situation by his silence.

Repeatedly Huck's common sense and naive literalism combine with his perceptiveness to lead him to observe silliness in society. When he questions the tradition or rules of religion (or of Tom Sawyer's romantic fiction), Huck is branded as a fool. A countermotif develops, however, because frequently Huck is silent: "But I never said so." Accordingly, this fiction uses a contrast between Huck's reticence or inarticulate withdrawal from many other characters and his fluent revelations to the reader.

Huck submits himself to the civilizing influence at the widow's house only intermittently. Prior to the novel's opening he had "lit out," and he takes another chance to leave, temporarily, that first evening for some adventures with Tom. But when he returns he reveals a more complex response to each adult's reactions. To Miss Watson, who treats him harshly, he reacts in a way which shows an instrumentalist-functionalist view of the world (Kohlberg's second stage); but to the disappointed widow, who treats him kindly, he reacts by attempting to be good:

Well, I got a good going-over in the morning, from Old Miss Watson, on account of my clothes; but the widow she didn't scold, but only cleaned off the grease and clay and looked so sorry that I thought I would behave a while if I could. Then Miss Watson she took me in the closet and prayed, but nothing came of it. She told me to pray every day, and whatever I asked for I would get

> it. But it warn't so. I tried it. Once I got a fish-line, but no hooks. It warn't any good to me without hooks. I tried for the hooks three or four times, but somehow I couldn't make it work. By-and-by, one day, I asked Miss Watson to try for me, but she said I was a fool. She never told me why, and I couldn't make it out no way.
>
> I set down, one time, back in the woods, and had a long think about it. I says to myself, if a body can get anything they pray for, why don't Deacon Winn get back the money he lost on pork? Why can't the widow get back her silver snuff-box that was stole? Why can't Miss Watson fat up? No, says I to myself, there ain't nothing in it. (29)

Huck tries these prayers because of a practical need, attempting as a naive literalist to make a new trick work and expressing his needs in short simple sentences. His rational thoughts about other persons' prayers reveal a prescient skepticism. Huck may subconsciously calculate that a Deacon Winn's prayers just lose, although they ought to be more effective than the average person's.[6] The final devastating proof of the inefficacy of prayer occurs in the combination of personal and material concern in the animal terminology of Miss Watson's inability to "fat up."

The next step in Huck's progress appears as he turns to the kindly parental figure, the widow:

> I went and told the widow about it, and she said the thing a body could get by praying for it was "spiritual gifts." This was too many for me, but she told me what she meant—I must help other people, and do everything I could for other people, and look out for them all the time, and never think about myself. This was including Miss Watson, as I took it. I went out in the woods and turned it over in my mind a long time, but I couldn't see no advantage about it—except for the other people—so at last I reckoned I wouldn't worry about it any more, but just let it go. (29–30)

As we shall see repeatedly, Huck's ability to see things from another person's point of view is crucial to his developing character, to his sympathy, to his morality. Ultimately, Huck does come to have "spiritual gifts," because he unselfishly attempts "good works," trying to help the robbers on the *Walter Scott*, the Wilks girls, the king and duke, and, most important, Jim. Huck's intuitive kindness and decency grow to become dominant parts of his personality—parts which are in clear conflict with the actual observed practices of the conventional Christians.

The conflict between two attitudes toward religion appears to Huck:

> Sometimes the widow would take me one side and talk about Providence in a way to make a body's mouth water; but maybe next day Miss Watson would

take hold and knock it all down again. I judged I could see that there was two Providences, and a poor chap would stand considerable show with the widow's Providence, but if Miss Watson's got him there warn't no help for him any more. I thought it all out, and reckoned I would belong to the widow's, if he wanted me, though I couldn't make out how he was agoing to be any better off then than what he was before, seeing I was so ignorant and so kind of low-down and ornery. (30)

Amusingly, Huck thinks about the two Providences rather as he would about two rival gangs.[7] Characteristically, Huck does not abase himself before a god-figure, but attempts to think *from* each Providence's point of view, calculating what he would add to the side. Such an implied equality of Huck's personality and Providence helps the novel appeal to a nation with democratic, practical, individualistic values. In the early chapters, prayer, Sunday school, and religion appear as children's games; Huck's effort to summon a genie works no more successfully than the prayer for fish hooks. The attempt to rob a caravan of rich Arabs smacks of bookish romance, but the robbery actually attacks a Sunday school picnic. Praying and playing actually involve similar fantasizing, both based upon unrealistic bookish authorities. Even Pap Finn's brief reformation includes attention to both bookishness ("turn over a new leaf" and signing his pledge) and history ("the holiest time on record"). Of course, his religious reformation fails.

Twain's satire on Christianity takes many forms, creating a pervasive criticism. Huck's father yells about "the Angel of Death" while trying, in his alcoholic delusion, to kill Huck. Although the Christian story gives honor to an almighty father who permits his son's death as a requirement for others' salvation, the reality of a murderous father frightens Huck. Although the Christian society had consented to his virtual imprisonment in his father's cabin, Huck, using his practical intelligence, escapes from this captivity to a limited form of freedom. Further, the religious phrase "bread upon the waters" refers to the baker's bread with plugs of quicksilver cast upon the water to locate Huck's drowned body. This loaf finds Huck not because of divine or supernatural guidance, but because the hungry lad pragmatically studied the current and knew where the bread would pass close enough to grab.

Later, after the interpolated episode aboard the *Walter Scott*, Huck tricks a steam-ferry owner into attempting to rescue the criminals. Twain wrote in the manuscript:

But take it all around, I was feeling ruther comfortable, on accounts of the trouble I had took for that gang. I wished the widow knowed about it. I

> judged she would be proud of me for helping these rapscallions, because rapscallions and dead beats is the kind the widow and good people takes the most interest in. (MS, 81–38)

Apparently Twain wished to emphasize Huck's humanity and to satirize Christianity because the author revised the first sentence to read, ". . . comfortable, on accounts of *taking all this* trouble for that gang, *for not many would a done it*." Huck—ever the realist—knows that most people would pass up the chance to practice good works. Without vanity, he does try "to be good" for her, action typical of a child at what Kohlberg would identify as the third stage.

Although Huck's values include empathy and helpfulness, he becomes more deviant from the stated and practiced values of his society. Whenever he tries a Tom Sawyerish prank, such as putting a dead snake in Jim's blanket, boarding the *Walter Scott*, or fooling Jim about being lost in the fog, the prank turns out to be not funny or fun but, contrary to Huck's expectation, destructive. The most forceful early example of Huck's disillusionment with Tom's style of prank occurs in Chapter XV, after he has fooled Jim about being lost in the fog. Jim uses the mode of a sermon to rebuke Huck, interpreting the situation in terms of a personal narrative and his keenly felt emotions rather than by citation of conventional authorities:

> Jim looked at the trash, then looked at me, and back at the trash again. He had got the dream fixed so strong in his head that he couldn't seem to shake it loose and get the facts back into its place again, right away. But when he did get the thing straightened around, he looked at me steady, without ever smiling, and says:
>
> "What do dey stan' for? I's gwyne to tell you. When I got all wore out wid work, en wid de callin' for you, en went to sleep, my heart wuz mos' broke bekase you wuz los', en I didn' k'yer no mo' what become er me en de raf'. En when I wake up en fine you back agin', all safe en soun', de tears come en I could a got down on my knees en kiss' yo' foot I's so thankful. En all you wuz thinkin 'bout wuz how you could make a fool uv ole Jim wid a lie. Dat truck dah is *trash*; en trash is what people is dat puts dirt on de head er dey fren's en makes 'em ashamed."
>
> Then he got up slow, and walked to the wigwam, and went in there, without saying anything but that. But that was enough. It made me feel so mean I could almost kissed *his* foot to get him to take it back.
>
> It was fifteen minutes before I could work myself up to go and humble myself to a nigger—but I done it, and I warn't ever sorry for it afterwards, neither. I didn't do him no more mean tricks, and I wouldn't done that one if I'd a knowed it would make him feel that way. (121)

Shame and mistreatment of a friend function as the cardinal evils of Huck's world. The mistreatment of Jim in the final portion of the novel will be perceived as such an outrage precisely because of passages like this. The repetition of the religious allusion, "to kiss the foot," creates an equivalence between the two, a relation of humility, mutual consideration, and reciprocal compassion. Huck's ability to transcend conventional behavior grows after such an incident.

In the next chapter, Huck faces more severe moral tests when he realizes his own complicity in helping Jim escape:

> Jim said it made him all over trembly and feverish to be so close to freedom. Well, I can tell you it made me all over trembly and feverish, too, to hear him, because I begun to get it through my head that he *was* most free—and who was to blame for it? Why, *me*. I couldn't get that out of my conscience, no how nor no way. It got to troubling me so I couldn't rest; I couldn't stay still in one place. It hadn't ever come home to me before, what this thing was that I was doing. But now it did; and it staid with me, and scorched me more and more. (123)

The initial identity of symptoms reveals how similarly Huck and Jim react. As the passage continues, the language changes to resemble that of a conventional sermon, and the heat imagery for discomfort ("trembly and feverish") recurs in "scorched." The conflict between his intuitive sympathy and the expectations of society tortures Huck. When Jim discusses buying or stealing his own wife and children, an extension of the same situation, Huck says, "It most froze me to hear such talk." Twain embodies the feelings in contradictory, and therefore confusing, temperature imagery.

Huck decides to turn Jim in and feels momentarily relieved, but Jim's farewell comment to him revives the conflict:

> "Pooty soon I'll be a-shout'n for joy, en I'll say, it's all on accounts o' Huck; I's a free man, en I couldn't ever ben free ef it hadn' ben for Huck; Huck done it. Jim won't ever forget you, Huck; you's de bes' fren' Jim's ever had; en you's de *only* fren' ole Jim's got now."
>
> I was paddling off, all in a sweat to tell on him; but when he says this, it seemed to kind of take the tuck all out of me. I went along slow then, and I warn't right down certain whether I was glad I started or whether I warn't. When I was fifty yards off, Jim says:
>
> "Dah you goes, de ole true Huck; de on'y white genlman dat ever kep' his promise to ole Jim."
>
> Well, I just felt sick. . . . (124–25)

Jim praises concisely; by saying "ole," Jim implicitly summons up the experiences they share; Jim's word "true" carries favorable but dangerous connotations for Huck; momentarily Jim raises Huck to the status of a "genlman," and, most important, Jim recognizes Huck's uniqueness, his individuality. Huck's feelings of heat, sickness, and chills reappear transformed in the immediately following exchange with the slave-hunters as he fools them into believing that his raft carries smallpox. The men are frightened off and, in a morally problematic situation, give forty dollars and advice about how to conceal the terrifying disease down river as "fever and chills." Thus the imagery used to describe genuine conflicting emotions changes, under the pressure of society's unethical norms, to embody a sham disease.

Huck learns immediately from this experience and thinks about the roles of environmental training, positive reinforcement, and of his own values:

> They went off, and I got aboard the raft, feeling bad and low, because I knowed very well I had done wrong, and I see it warn't no use for me to try to learn to do right; a body that don't get *started* right when he's little, ain't got no show—when the pinch comes there ain't nothing to back him up and keep him to his work, and so he gets beat. Then I thought a minute, and says to myself, hold on,—spose you'd a done right and give Jim up; would you felt better than what you do now? No, says I, I'd feel bad—I'd feel just the same way I do now. Well, then, says I, what's the use you learning to do right, when it's troublesome to do right and ain't no trouble to do wrong, and the wages is just the same? I was stuck. I couldn't answer that. So I reckoned I wouldn't bother no more about it, but after this always do whichever came handiest at the time. (127–28)

Although in his confused state the emotional wages may appear the same, Huck has just received a tremendous financial reward, forty dollars, for intuitive action. The modern equivalent is between $572 and $693 in the purchasing power of 1990 dollars.[8] One assumes that amount would make a noticeable impression on a poor, homeless lad. Current research indicates that for normal children, moral conduct may be regulated less by fixed guilt feelings and more by ego strength, moral judgment, situational expectations, and reinforcement. Although Huck tells his entire story retrospectively, the backward temporal direction of guilt seems not as influential as the forward-directed impetus Huck has to avoid shame. From this point onward, until Tom Sawyer reappears, Huck will use his own intuitive judgment in responding to each situation. When he does experience more evil in the world, his evolving values seem to require kindness and concern for the individual, as well as avoidance of personal shame, rather than any veneration for the culture's abstract rules.

Such moral growth does not appear during Huck's sojourn with the Grangerfords, but there is a chance for both subtle and obvious satire on conventional religion. Huck characterizes the home:

> There was some books too, piled up perfectly exact, on each corner of the table. One was a big family Bible, full of pictures. One was "Pilgrim's Progress," about a man that left his family it didn't say why. I read considerable in it now and then. The statements was interesting, but tough. (137)

The perfect placement of the books suggests that, prior to Huck's arrival, they were not often read, that the books were on display rather than frequently consulted. But Huck does consult both; in fact, the two books reflect his predicament. The Bible clearly represents conventional Christianity, but Huck apparently spent more time with *Pilgrim's Progress*, attempting to find out about the application of Christian methods in a fictional world. Huck's tersely eloquent evaluation is, of course, reflexive. His own narrative is also about a youth "that left his family," and we are told why.

Huck reveals, in his own literalist, naive way, the hypocrisy of the Grangerford's Christianity:

> Next Sunday we all went to church, about three mile, everybody a-horse-back. The men took their guns along, so did Buck, and kept them between their knees or stood them handy against the wall. The Shepherdsons done the same. It was pretty ornery preaching—all about brotherly love, and such like tiresomeness; but everybody said it was a good sermon, and they all talked it over going home, and had such a powerful lot to say about faith, and good works, and free grace, and preforeordestination, and I don't know what all, that it did seem to me to be one of the roughest Sundays I had run across yet. (148)[9]

The surface irony about gun-toting, feuding people listening to a sermon on brotherly love is apparent; the service involves love, but Eros not Caritas. The two lovers use the service to make their elopement arrangements which, in this feuding situation, will result in the deaths of many relatives. And it does turn out to be the roughest Sunday for Huck, because it leads to the death of Buck, his friend.

Twain manages, as usual, to throw in a bit more sarcasm about orga-

nized religion when Huck unknowingly runs the errand for Sophia Grangerford which will lead to the slaughter:

> . . . and there warn't anybody at the church, except maybe a hog or two, for
> there warn't any lock on the door, and hogs likes a puncheon floor in summer-
> time because it's cool. If you notice, most folks don't go to church only when
> they've got to; but a hog is different. (149)

Although the criticism of Christianity to this point seems random, the
possibilities changed when the king entered the novel.

IV

The king's deceptive, exploitative personality provided a perfect vehicle for
satire. He claims many religious skills, saying, "Preachin's my line, too; and
workin' camp-meetin's; and missionaryin around" (162). The deception of
the camp meeting occurs first, followed by the extended, focused satire
when the king poses as a preacher. In Chapter XX, Twain describes the
behavior of the Pokesville natives at camp-meeting, criticizing their enthusiasm and gullibility.[10] The king exploits the religious fervor, posing as a
reformed pirate and using many cliches of religion to bilk the crowd of
$87.75 (modern equivalent well over $1,200). This situation duplicates Pap
Finn's reform. Neither Pap nor the deliberately deceptive king makes any
moral development; those who believe in the reformations simply appear
foolish and exploited.

The king's masquerade as a preacher, the Reverend Elexander Blodgett, leads smoothly into his role as the Reverend Harvey Wilks, bereaved
English "dissentering minister." As indicated earlier, Twain probably relished the chance to present the fraudulent royalty, the king and duke, as
involved with exploitation under a religious guise. But the king's blatant
immorality seemed to cause extremely harsh satire on religion, and Twain
rather consistently tried to moderate his attack.

A familiar piece now reappears in the kaleidoscope. In the scene of the
false brothers viewing the coffin, Twain made several changes which are
relevant to the conflict between religion and morality. The first manuscript
version states:

> Then one of them got on one side of the coffin, and 'tother on 'tother side, and
> they knelt down and rested their foreheads on the coffin, and let on to pray, all
> to their selves. Well, when it come to that, it was so moving that everybody

went to sobbing right out loud—the poor girls, too; and every woman, nearly, went up to the girls, without saying a word, and kissed them, solemn, on the forehead, and then put their hand on their head, and looked up towards the throne, with the tears running down, and ⟨then let go⟩ then busted out and went off sobbing and swabbing, and give the next ⟨heifer⟩ **woman** a show. I never see anything so disgusting. (MS, 240–41)

The king and duke observe the forms of devotion, but they are patently hypocritical. The phrase "was so moving" acknowledges the genuine emotion appropriate to the situation. But Twain revised the passage for print by substituting, "worked the crowd like you never see anything like it" (212), a phrasing used twice about the camp meetings, emphasizing the moral degeneracy of the impostors in exploiting gullible townspeople. Although the townspeople seem more manipulated, the guilt remains squarely on the king and duke. Twain manipulates the reader's emotions, using the techniques of Huck's point of view, his word choice, exaggeration, and comic repetition so that the targets of the writing, the king and later Tom Sawyer, become objects of the reader's contempt and disgust.

Similarly, Twain shifted the king's long cliche-filled speech as Rev. Wilks from the manuscript's direct quotation to the printed version which presents Huck's framing opinions and his moisture-filled paraphrase. The shift to Huck's third-person retelling in the finished version makes the criticism of religious conventions weaker, more indirect, but the king becomes ludicrously evil.

Twain balances his criticism of the king by also criticizing the local town leaders, the Reverend and the Doctor, who must deal with a similar situation:

> **Rev.** Hobson and Dr. Robinson was down to the end of the town, hunting together; ⟨where⟩ that is, I mean the doctor was shipping a sick man out of the world, and the preacher was pinting him right. (MS, 244–45)

Significantly, Twain did not give the genuine minister an active role in detecting the frauds. The wildly incongruous phrase, "hunting together," presents Huck's sarcastic evaluation. These local men give an alternative version of the facing of death; they are doing their unpleasant duty, but only the Doctor will participate in unmasking the frauds.

Apparently Twain's mind linked preachers and kings as emblems of laziness. We recall that Huck had told Jim that kings mostly just "sit around" and "lazy around." Joanna Wilks elicits Huck's opinion about the way preachers spend their time:

Well, then, what does the rest of 'em do?"

"Oh, nothing much. Loll around, pass the plate—and one thing or another. But mainly they don't do nothing."

"Well, then, what are they <u>for</u>?"

"Why, they're for <u>style</u>. Don't you know nothing?" (MS, 274–75)

Twain's mind, one suspects, perceived a connection between monarchy, religion, and stylistic luxuriance. As the novel progresses, Tom Sawyerish stylistic luxuriance also becomes more obviously evil.

On the other hand, the positive moral values of Huck's universe seem slightly more difficult to pin down. Mary Jane Wilks, who represents one type of virtuous action, criticizes her sister Joanna and expresses the values of kindness, consideration, sympathy, and avoidance of shame:

"It ain't right nor kind for you to talk so to him, and him a stranger and far from his people. How would you like to be treated so?"

"That's always your way, Maim—always a-sailin⟨g⟩' in to help somebody before they're hurt. <u>I</u> hain't done nothing to him. He's told some stretchers, I reckon; and I said I wouldn't swallow it all; and that's every bit and grain ⟨that⟩ I <u>did</u> say. I reckon he can stand a little thing like that, can't he?"

"I don't care whether 'twas little or whether 'twas big, he's here in our house and a stranger, and it wasn't good of you to say it. If you was in his place, it would make you feel ashamed; and so you oughtn't ⟨to ever to⟩ to say a thing to another person that will make <u>them</u> feel ashamed."

Why, Maim, he said—"

It don't make no difference what he <u>said</u>—that ain't the thing. The thing is for you to treat him <u>kind</u>, and not be saying things to make him remember he ain't in his own country and amongst his own folks." (MS, 279–81)

Mary Jane also possesses an unusual self-transformative ability to sympathize, to put herself in another person's place. Moreover, the orphaned, abandoned, abused Huck must hear her statements with emotional force. Making people feel ashamed is a cruelty; Jim's magnificent statement after the separation in the fog echoes in our mind: "Dat truck dah is *trash*; en trash is what people is dat puts dirt on de head er dey fren's en makes 'em ashamed." The girls' kindness and decency impress Huck, leading him to comment upon the "beauty" of how the sister with the hare-lip asked his pardon. His values thus permit him to get beyond the normal cruel categories frequently used by youths about people with deformities. In addition, Huck—a self-blaming child of an alcoholic—accuses himself of complicity in the king's deception and vows to steal the money from the frauds. Huck's mind moves quickly from decision to actions.

In contrast, when the frauds attempt to make plans, there are only a few moral considerations. Part of the duke's reluctance is a tactical desire to clear out quickly, but part sounds minimally compassionate:

> The duke he grumbled; said the ⟨money⟩ *bag of gold* was enough, and he didn't want to go no deeper-didn't want to rob a lot of orphans of <u>everything</u> they had.
> "Why, how you talk!" says the king. "We shan't rob 'em of anything at all but jest ⟨this⟩ their money. The people that <u>buys</u> the property is the sufferers; becuz as soon as it's found out that we didn't own it—which won't be long after we disappear—the sale won't be valid, and it'll all go back to the estate. These-yer orphans 'll get their house back again *and that's enough for <u>them</u>*: ⟨and⟩ they're young, and spry, and can easy earn a livin'. <u>They</u> ain't agoing to suffer. Why just think ⟨of the⟩—there's thousands and thousands that ain't *nigh* so well off." (MS, 290–91)

Momentarily, the king has become a reverse preacher and, in contrast to Huck and to Mary Jane's compassion, offers lamely justified greed. Because the king is characterized as an "ostrich," an "old hog," and a "tunnel bellied old sewer," Twain's insertion of "*and that's enough for <u>them</u>*" creates an obvious comedy.

The king-minister performs another highly immoral action when he separates the slave family:

> So the next day after the funeral, along about noontime, the girls' joy got its first jolt; a *couple of* traders come along, and the king sold ⟨him the three⟩ *them the* niggers reasonable, for ⟨cash⟩ *three-day drafts*, and away they went—the two sons up the river to Memphis, and their mother down the river to Orleans. I thought them poor girls and them niggers would break their hearts for grief; they cried around each other, and took ⟨on, so, it⟩ on so it most made me down sick to see it. The girls said they hadn't ever dreamed of seeing the family separated or sold away from the village. I can't ever get it out of my memory, the sight of them poor girls and niggers hanging around each other's necks and crying; and I reckon ⟨I'd been been bound⟩ *I couldn't a stood it at all but would a had* to bust out and tell on our gang if I hadn't knowed the sale warn't no account and the niggers would be back home in a week or two. (MS, 313–15)

Here we are at some depth in the mind of Clemens/Twain; the separation of a slave family occurs in "A True Story," Jim's situation, and, in a way, in *Pudd'nhead Wilson*. A king posing as a minister can impose such cruelty. Yet, interestingly, Twain frequently chooses for his moral actor an orphaned or abandoned self-creating character, precisely the kind of character least likely to have the behavioral or cultural restraints expected of a member of the nobility or clergy. At this point Huck does not feel compelled to interfere directly, trusting to the legal system. But his discomfort does lead to progress in the plot.

Mary Jane Wilks's grief about the separation of the family leads to another of Huck's explicit self-debates about truth-telling. He comforts her by saying that the slaves will soon be reunited. Mary Jane's sympathetic grief and Huck's compassionate reaction lead quickly to the next plot breakthrough, his "good work" of revealing the fraud to Mary Jane:

> Laws, it was out before I could think!—and before I could budge, <u>slam</u> comes her arms around my neck, and she kissed me right on the mouth, and told me to say it <u>again</u>, say it <u>again</u>, say it <u>again</u>.!
> I see I had shot my mouth off once too often, and was in a mighty close place. I asked her to let me think, a minute; and she set there, mighty impatient and excited and beautiful, but looking kinder happy ⟨.⟩ *and eased-up like a person that's had a tooth pulled out*. So I went to studying it out. I says to myself, ⟨a⟩ I reckon ⟨that⟩ a body that *ups and* tells the truth ⟨,⟩ when he is in a tight place, is taking considerable many risks; though I ain't had no experience, and can't say for certain; but it looks so to me, anyway; and yet <u>here's</u> a case where I'm blamed if it don't look to me like the truth is ⟨better than a lie⟩ better, and actually <u>safer</u>, than a lie. I must lay it by in my mind, and think it over some time or other, it's so ⟨curious⟩ ⟨*queer*⟩ *curious* and unregular. I never see anything like it. Well, says I to myself, at last, dog my cats if I don't chance it; I'll up and tell the truth this time, or bust—though it does seem most like setting down on a kag of powder and touching it off, just out of curiosity to see where you <u>will</u> go to. (MS, 328–30)

For telling the truth, Huck receives the reward of kisses on the mouth. To an adult, this response would be a reward, but many young boys would consider it an embarrassment, cause of confusion, or punishment. The hugs and kisses were, however, removed by the time the passage appeared in print. With the suppression of the kisses, the proper emphasis remains on the theme of the risk involved in telling the truth. Twain had originally written that, in this situation, it seemed to Huck "like the truth is better than a lie." Then, immediately, Twain canceled the last four words and wrote instead "better, and actually <u>safer</u>, than a lie." Huck seems startled by the possibility that truth could be not dangerous, but safe. His previous condition in society had, of course, made most truth dangerous. The final evaluation about the risk of telling the truth creates a comparison with an explosion. The keg of powder exactly duplicates the method Twain had used in the satiric story, "The Good Little Boy," to destroy the truth-teller.

Telling the truth surrenders Huck's ability to control the world by controlling the fictions. He has recently lied most adroitly to the king and duke; he has lied with dexterity to Joanna. He cannot, it seems, lie to Mary Jane. Why? Is it because affection is involved? It seems that the truth can be explosive, that revealing the truth has unforeseen consequences, probably bad, and that the truth can only be revealed to good people. Such a world view places Huck or a novelist in a difficult or untenable position. To the extent that Twain could sympathize with Huck in the fictional situation, Twain could also put himself in a difficult position as a novelist. The very act of creating a truth-telling fiction could become morally questionable.

Characteristically, this view does not stand unmodified. After the full explanation, Huck tells Mary Jane a quite insignificant lie. She agrees to go along with the plot, but refuses to have her love given to the frauds:

> ⟨"The rest⟩ *"Gone to see a friend* is all right, but I won't <u>have</u> my love given to them!"
> "Well, then, it shan't be." It was well enough to tell <u>her</u> so—no harm in that. Then I says: "There's one more thing—that bag of money." (MS, 346)

But on the back of MS, 346, Twain inserted a brief disquisition on morality to go after "no harm in that":

> *It was only a little thing to do, and no trouble; and it's the little things ⟨that help⟩ that smoothes people's roads the most, down here below; it would make Mary Jane comfortable, and wouldn't cost nothing*

The addition offers a good example of a balancing, a contrary repetition, a Twaining. Huck has previously told the truth at great discomfort and at great cost to his companions because of his loyalty and his own kind of integrity. Yet Twain has him wriggle around to tell a small white lie—to make her comfortable, at no cost. The morality of the undertaker, with his "soothering" ways, seems relevant here. Huck's tone in this passage sounds unusual, as if he were repeating or testing out other peoples' ideas, moral codes, and community standards. We expect the compassion from Huck, but the semi-theoretical justification does not seem characteristic.

Huck's desire to be considerate of Mary Jane complicates his arrangements because he does not want to tell her that the bag of money lies on her uncle's corpse. He finally decides to write her a note, which she can read later. The parting is an emotional moment, in a way analogous to the burial of Buck Grangerford:

It kinder made my eyes water a little, to remember her crying there all by herself in the night, and them devils laying there right under her own roof, shaming her and robbing her; and when I folded it up and give it to her, I see the water come into her eyes, too; and she took me by the hand, hard, and says: . . . (MS, 349–50)

The two honest adolescents almost seem to merge, as if they realize they are each isolated in an evil world. Shame functions as a very negative force, even parallel to the actual robbery. The vocabulary of religion, "devils," carries great power. It is possible that, for Twain, a split occurs; the description of evil in religious terms seems accurate and even convincing, while the description of good action and characters in religious terms seems incomplete or inaccurate.

Mary Jane's final words to Huck and his reflections on the parting support this interpretation. She says:

"Good-bye—I'm going to do everything just as you've told me; and if I don't ever see you again, I shan't ever forget you, and I'll think of you a many and a many a time, and I'll pray for you, ⟨too⟩ too!"—and she was gone.

Pray for me—good land! I reckoned if she ⟨'d a⟩ knowed me she'd tackle a job that was *more* nearer her size. But I bet you she done it, just the same—she was just that kind. She had the grit to pray for Judas Iscarott if she took the notion—there warn't no back-down to her, if I know a girl by the rake of her stern; and I think I do. You may say what you please, but in my opinion that girl had more sand in her than any girl I ever see; in my opinion she was just full of sand. *It sounds like flattery, but it ain't no flattery*. And when it comes to beauty—and goodness-she lays over them all. I hain't ever seen her since that time that I see her go out at that door, ⟨and turn at the stairs and kinder throw a kiss back at me;⟩ *like light and comfort agoing out of a body's life;* no, I hain't ever seen her since; but I reckon I've thought of her a many and a many a million times, and of her saying she would pray for me; and if ever I'd a thought it would do any good for me to pray for her, I'm dum'd if I wouldn't a done it or bust. (MS, 350–52)

Her offer to pray for Huck presents a statement of devotion, an almost love-like commitment, but his reaction simply doubts the efficacy of prayers for him. He does, however, paradoxically confirm her determination, independence, and individualism by saying that she would pray for the least valued person in the Christian tradition. Although the male-female relationship is recognized and suppressed, the youths do share a vocabulary of "a many and a many a time" and reciprocal notions of prayers. The difference, of course, is that Mary Jane thinks her prayers will help while Huck doubts the power of his. But he has grown from praying for fishhooks to feeling the desire to pray for unselfish purposes. In the manuscript Twain has Huck say, "I'm dum'd if I wouldn't a done it or bust," but the slang reference to damnation is weakened in print to "blamed." Clemens/Twain as an ironic artist can think of having a character say in slang, "damned if I wouldn't pray for her," yet decide to say "blamed" in print. The negative reaction to religion remains, but the irony is less sharp. The human paradox appears in that Huck thinks his own case too vast for her prayers while his prayers for her are probably not needed because of her goodness; moreover, his prayers may be useless because they would come from such an imperfect person. Significantly, Huck grows to feel some equality of personality with this older, respected young woman.

Huck manages to arrange the plot quite cleverly, saying, in the manuscript:

> I felt good; I judged I had done that thing pretty neat—I reckoned Tom Sawyer couldn't a done it no neater, *himself*. Of course he would a slung more style into it, but I can't sling style very handy, not being brung up to it. (MS, 366)

Huck's self-assessment undergoes some changes. Huck says, "I felt very good," in the printed version, and the improvement increases his self-esteem. And in this explicit self-comparison with Tom, Twain drops the repeated phrase "sling style." Instead, in print Huck says that Tom "would a throwed more style into it, but I can't do that very handy, not being brung up to it" (249).[11] The importance of training remains undeniable. Huck believes Tom carries authority and thinks he has done the task well enough to earn Tom's approval. Twain has explicitly compared Huck's problem-solving ability with Tom's, but Huck still feels, incorrectly, inferior because of Tom's superior reading and socialization. We admire the dexterity and compassion of Huck's plans before the sudden arrival of the genuine Wilks brothers renders all his plans useless.

The final critical reduction of conventional Christianity in the Wilks episode occurs when the king participates in an auction in such a way that religion is totally discredited:

> Well, they held the auction, in the public square, *along towards the end of the afternoon*, and it strung along, and strung along, and the old man he was on hand a looking his level piousest, up there longside the auctioneer, and chipping in a little ⟨dab⟩ ⟨Scrip⟩ dab of Scripture, now and then, or a little goody-goody remark, of some kind, . . . (MS, 367)

First Twain wished to refer to a small amount, then to the Scriptures in general, but then he hit upon the memorable phrase, "a little dab of Scripture," a phrase which likens the words of conventional religion to paint, a material which can be applied to a surface in small amounts, easily separated. Scripture thus becomes only a decorative, deceptive commentary. Unfortunately, by the time the book was set in print, Twain softened the phrase back to "a little Scripture." Such modification toward decreasing the explicit criticism of religion occurs within the context of the use of the king a sham preacher. The overall effect is that the satire in the Wilks episode becomes more unified, but less extreme in tone.

Conclusions about Huck's moral development in this section appear less clear-cut. His stealing is not morally reprehensible since he regains money stolen by the impostors; moreover, he has no personal greed, and he manages to protect Jim throughout the Wilks episode. Huck's action parallels his behavior in the inserted *Walter Scott* episode, but his behavior is motivated not for the sake of the adventure but by the desire to help. Huck tries to arrange the trickery as Tom Sawyer would have and feels, momentarily, that he had done well.

For Huck, the elements of good seem to be compassion, sympathy, identification, reciprocal trust and action, and avoidance of shame; the elements of evil include deception for gain, hypocrisy, greed, and exploitation. For Twain, religion can be easily appropriated for deceptive purposes, but apparently conventional religion is unnecessary or powerless for beneficial purposes. Moreover, telling the truth may be dangerous. These ideas contribute to the novel's strong fascination for generations of Americans. But just as Huck was soon to face a moral crisis, Twain was soon to face a similar difficulty in his attitude toward the values derived from books.

V

After the king and duke sell Jim into captivity for $40, Huck has to reassess the entire situation; his thinking leads him to the novel's major crisis involving Christianity and individual morality. Twain recopied much of this section from earlier sheets. We may reasonably infer that the section had been revised extensively, making the original sheets too difficult to read and therefore making recopying necessary. And his revising process continued, to some extent, on these copy sheets. By following Huck's thought in this rather lengthy and complicated moral crisis, we obtain insight about the interaction of religion and morality.

Huck begins by thinking about Jim's situation from each *other* person's point of view. Such thinking may be considered sequential sympathy, a combination of thought, imagination, and emotion:

> Once I said *to myself* it would be a thousand times better for Jim to be a slave at home where his family was, as long as he'd got to be a slave, and so I'd better write a letter to Tom Sawyer and tell him to tell Miss Watson where he was. But I soon give up that notion, for two things: she'd be mad and disgusted at his rascality and ungratefulness for leaving her, and so she'd sell him straight down the river again; and if she didn't, everybody naturally despises an ungrateful nigger, and they'd make Jim feel it all the time, and so he'd feel ornery and disgraced. (MS, 436–37)

In this extraordinary passage, Huck thinks sequentially from each point of view: Jim's, Miss Watson's, the townspeoples', and Jim's again. This mature, empathic thought progression convinces him that the situation would not be improved for Jim. Then Huck applies the same process to his own situation:

> And then think of me! It would get all around, that Huck Finn ⟨had⟩ helped a nigger get his freedom; and if I was to ever see anybody from that town again, I'd be ready to get down and lick his boots for shame. (MS, 437–38)

At this point, Huck has apparently internalized what he perceives to be the dominant social ethic—that such a person is utterly shamed. We notice, with dismay, that the possible gesture of shame ("lick his boots") presents a degrading variation of the "kiss the foot" emotion of humility Huck felt toward Jim after the "trash" speech. At this, Kohlberg's fifth stage, Huck attempts to think through the situation to earn the approval of a disinterested person who shares the community's values.

Huck has only a partial, confused sense of the motives or reasons for his moral choices, and what knowledge he does have is cloaked in the confusing rhetoric of religion. When he starts to generalize about his situation, his thinking process gradually shifts from societal norms toward personal norms, the sixth stage:

> That's just the way: a person does a low-down thing, and then he don't want to take no consequences of it. Thinks as long as he can hide it, it ain't no disgrace. That was my fix exackly. The more I thought about this, the more my conscience got to grinding me, and the more ⟨bad,⟩ **wicked**, and low-down and ornery I got to feeling. (MS, 438–39)

The canceled "bad" presented too simple a view and "**wicked**" becomes another motif-word. Moreover, the words "disgrace" and "ornery" actually verbally equate Huck's feelings with his projection of Jim's feelings if he were to be turned in to Miss Watson. This process of generalization leading precisely to shared individual emotions is, however, momentarily thwarted by Huck's recognition of the role of conventional religion. The long peri-odic sentence captures Huck's emotions:

> And at last, when it hit me all of a sudden that here was the plain hand of Providence slapping me in the face and letting me know that my wickedness was being watched all the time from up there in heaven, whilst I was stealing a poor old woman's nigger that hadn't ever done me ⟨any⟩ **no** harm, and now was showing me that ⟨'s always⟩ ⟨**th**⟩ there's One that's always on the lookout, and ain't agoing to allow no such miserable doings to go only⟨s⟩ just so far and no further, I most dropped in my tracks I was so scared. (MS, 439–40)

Clearly Twain had some hesitation, did some casting about, before he could say "there's One that's always on the lookout." Later in the chapter Twain will use "Him" to refer to a deity.

Immediately, Huck shifts the ground of discussion to the familiar nature-nurture conflict, examining the influence of his environment upon his ideas:

> Well, I tried the best I could to kinder soften it up somehow for myself, by saying I was brought up wicked, and so I warn't so much to blame; but something inside of me kept saying, "There was the Sunday School, you could a gone to it; and if you'd a done it they'd a learned you, there, that people that acts as I'd been acting about that nigger goes to everlasting fire." (MS, 440)

The chance for improvement existed, but Huck passed it up. This concern about hell occurs, peculiarly enough, in close connection with "acts" and "acting," right before a paragraph in which the situation resembles the prayer scene in *Hamlet*, when Claudius tries unsuccessfully to pray:

> It made me shiver. And I about made up my mind to pray; and see if I couldn't try to quit being the kind of boy I was, and be better. So I kneeled down. But the words wouldn't come. Why wouldn't they? It warn't no use to try to hid it from Him. Nor from me, neither. I knowed very well why they wouldn't come. It was because my heart warn't right; it was because I warn't square; it was because I was playing double. I was letting on to give up sin, but away inside of me I was holding on to the biggest one of all. I was trying to make my mouth say I would do the right thing and the clean thing, and go and write to that nigger's owner and tell where he was; but deep down in me I knowed it was a lie—and He knowed it. You can't pray a lie—I found that out. (MS, 441–42)

The important psychological discovery in the passage involves the equivalence of God's knowledge and Huck's knowledge. Huck certainly contains severe conflict, but there is no conventional self-abasement, no commitment of self to God no matter what, no attitude of *in manuas tuas*. Instead, we see Huck's realization that it does no good to hide the truth *from himself either*. That basic perception, that self is equal to God in insight and importance, forms the core of Huck's morality. This respect for individual conscience contributes to the novel's appeal to our culture. And we shall soon see how destructive "letting on" can be.

Immediately after he discovers that "you can't pray a lie—I found that out," he turns to writing:

> Miss Watson, your runaway nigger *Jim* is down here two mile below Pikesville, and Mr Phelps has got him, and he will give him up for the reward if you send.   <u>Huck Finn</u>. (MS, 443)

The letter reveals a rudimentary, additive, unsubordinated style. The elements occur as equivalent, and the simple style does not equal the complexity of his thought as later conveyed in the novel. Huck's letter simply offers information, with little subordination, coherence, or self-involvement except his signature. But the letter prompts in him a feeling of reform, like his father's false conversion; in this case, however, a fascinating shift gradually occurs as the language of religious cliches gives way to more concrete, detailed, personal involvement:

> I felt good and all washed clean of sin for the first time I had ever felt so in my life, and I knowed I could pray, now. But I didn't do it straight off, but laid the paper down and set there thinking; thinking how good it was all this happened so, and how near I come to being lost and going to hell. And went on thinking. And got to thinking over our trip down the river; ⟨but⟩ and I see Jim before me, all the time, in the day, and in the night-time, sometimes moonlight, sometimes storms, and we a floating along, talking, ⟨and glad⟩ *and singing, and laughing*. But somehow I couldn't seem to strike no places to harden me against him, but only the other kind. I'd see him standing my watch on top of his'n, stead of calling me—so I could go on sleeping; and see him how glad he was when I come back out of the fog; and when I come to him again in the swamp, up there where the feud was; and such-like times; and would always call me honey, and pet me, and do everything he could think of for me, and how good he always was; and at last I struck the time I saved him by telling the men we had small-pox aboard, and he was so grateful, and said I was the best friend old Jim ever had in the world, and the only one he's got now; and then I happened to look around, and see that paper. (MS, 443–45)

Twain creates a fine blend of additive sequentiality, with the "but" phrases carefully placed to change the flow of the thought. Apparently the part, "but somehow I couldn't seem to strike no places to harden me against him" was originally to have come earlier, where "but" is canceled. Twain was probably merely transcribing the paragraph, to make a clear copy, when he decided to add the part of "and I see Jim before me, . . ." In that sequence, Twain even modified the original, non-parallel "talking and glad" to the parallel action of "talking, *and singing, and laughing*." Huck's thinking and remembering ability provides us with a brief recapitulation of the book and finally argues around to emphasize Jim's *gratefulness*, the exact opposite of the earlier perception from Miss Watson's point of view. Thinking from Miss Watson's point of view, Huck considers Jim to be ungrateful; but thinking from his own individual experience, Huck remembers Jim to be grateful. Should thinking or experience be distrusted? Is the truth nothing?

Huck feels trapped, confined by the emotions associated with words such as "ornery," "disgraced," "ungrateful," and "wicked." Moreover, some of the words could be used by two opposed people about the same situation. When Huck trembles, the shaking letter is a tactile, visual image of moral ambiguity:

> It was a close place ⟨, it was.⟩. I took it up, and held it in my hand. I was a trembling, because I'd got to decide, once and forever, betwixt two things, and I knowed it. I studied a minute, sort of ⟨held⟩ holding my breath, and then says to myself:
> "All right, then, I'll go to hell—" and tore it up. (MS, 445–46)

The phrase "close place" had been used earlier to describe Huck's difficulty in talking to Mary Jane Wilks. Twain's original repetition of "it was" did literally box in this "close place" by surrounding it. Huck's paradoxical phrase "once and forever" captures the seriousness of the moment, but Twain simplified it, in print, to "forever." The change from "held" to "holding" emphasizes the tension and urgency of the continuous present tense. Huck decides, quite literally, between the letter and the spirit of the Christian law.[12] This momentous decision obviously repeats in a more serious fashion the damnation motif from the first chapter. For the conventional nineteenth-century American Christian, the pains and torments of hell seemed quite real; certainly an ordinary person would not immerse his or her body voluntarily. Too often modern readers seem to minimize the anticipated physical torments of Huck's choice:

It was awful thoughts, and awful words, but they was said. And I let them stay said; and never thought no more about reforming. I shoved the whole thing out of my head; and said I would take up wickedness again, which was in my line, being brought up to it, and the other warn't. And for a starter, I would go to work and steal Jim out of slavery again; and if I could think up anything worse, I would do that, too; because as long as I was in, and in for good, I might as well go the whole hog. (MS, 446–47)

In the printed version, Twain pays attention to pronunciation and, indirectly, the issue of training, by shifting "brought up" to "brung up" (272). The sentence structure moves back to the additive but now possesses subordination and a lifelike modulation of emphasis. Huck's statement acknowledges his past experiences and asserts a healthy coherence of individual commitment in non-religious but causal, concrete terms.[13] Probably Twain, Huck, and the reader each breathe a sigh of relief, knowing that the story can continue, with the same goal and with the integrity of Huck's personality reaffirmed in contrast to conventional Christianity. As his individualism develops, Huck has moved beyond wanting to be "good" boy to please someone else. Huck no longer wishes—even minimally—to be the good boy.

VI

What awaits Huck will test his newly won autonomy because a new, highly defined identity will be thrust upon him as he struggles with an enemy-brother, Tom Sawyer. The Phelps family believe Huck to be Tom Sawyer, and when Tom appears they believe him to be Tom's half-brother, Sid. Furthermore, Huck's difficulties increase because he has tremendous admiration for Tom's great knowledge of literature. Huck will attempt to maintain his own high stage of moral development in conflict with Tom, who functions almost constantly at a less mature level. Tom seems intensely involved with only the fourth stage, with attempting to deal with the world by using literary authorities, precedents, and rituals. Of course, in the Phelps section, most of Tom's authorities come from European adventure and escape books. Huck's conflict with Tom's self-abasement to books presents a thematic climax rather than a tedious, flawed ending. Both orphan boys were once equally lovable and equally malleable: Huck has been "brung up" to value common sense; in contrast, Tom has been trained to value European literature. Most readers would prefer that Huck's moral development would lead to his recognition, acceptance, and, finally, domination of Tom. That would, in the minds of many readers, make a better book.

After the breakthrough of Huck's decision to "go to hell," the explicit importance of religion diminishes somewhat, but the focus shifts to the influence of reading directly upon Tom's morality and secondarily upon Huck and Jim.

When Huck arrives on the Phelps farm, a revision occurs which relates to earlier religious references. We remember Huck's thought that there must be two Providences and the king's advice, in the Wilks episode, to trust in Providence. The first manuscript version reads:

> I went right along, not fixing up any particular plan, but just trusting in Providence to put the right words in my mouth when the time come; for I had noticed that Providence always did put the right words in my mouth, if I left it to him and just let him fix it his own way. (MS, 465)

In the manuscript Twain canceled both uses of "Providence" and substituted "*luck*," then in the printed version restored "Providence." Did Twain find the "him" phrase awkward and not think of "it"? Unlikely. Did Twain briefly wish to keep Providence out of this section? Did "*luck*" seem too flippant after the seriousness of the moral decision about Jim? Perhaps Twain wished to demonstrate repeatedly that two diametrically opposed characters (the king and Huck) can call upon two Providences, as Huck had determined in the early chapter. Twain also made a similar revision thirteen pages later in which Huck, puzzled by Mrs. Phelps's actions, prepared to give up and admit that she has mistaken him for someone else:

> Well, I see I was up a stump—and up it good. ⟨Providence⟩ **Luck** had stood by me this far, all right, but I was hard and tight aground, now. I see it warn't a bit of use to try to go ahead—I'd <u>got</u> to throw up my hand. So I says to myself, here's <u>another</u> place where I got to resk the truth. I opened my mouth to begin; but she grabbed me and hustled me in behind the bed, and says: . . . (MS, 478)

Clearly Twain considered having all these uses of "Providence" be "luck," but finally returned to the more religious word. Perhaps a convoluted irony exists in the inappropriateness of Providence as an accomplice to attempted theft.

After Mrs. Phelps has played a trick on Silas, she gives Huck his new name:

"It's Tom Sawyer!"

By jingo, I most slumped through the floor. But there warn't no time to swap knives: ⟨the whole biling went for me⟩ ⟨and such another hugging I never got before. And how⟩ *the old man grabbed me by the hand and shook, and kept on shaking; and* all the time, how the woman did dance around and laugh and cry; and *then* how they *both* did ⟨all⟩ *fire off questions about Sid, and Mary, and the rest of the tribe.*

But if they was joyful, it warn't nothing to what I was; for it was like being born again, I was so glad to find out who I was. (MS, 484–85)

The word "Providence" and the phrase, in context, "like being born again," both carry clearly religious connotations. Huck had decided to go to hell, to obey his intuition, to follow his conscience and disobey the letter of the law. This decision is admirable, and he is once more rewarded, this time with a religious renewal and with the identity of a person he admires tremendously—but wrongly. Now Huck experiences externally bestowed transformation, in name only, to the lad who is widely respected. Huck will be able to try out Tom Sawyer's identity, a weird amalgam of notions about aristocracy, morality, and literary romance, under Tom's tutelage.

Twain has once more duplicated a situation. In the Wilks episode, two false brothers try to steal under the guise of religion, and in the Phelps episode, two false brothers also try to steal under the influence of bookish romance. But the conflict becomes complicated because the second pair, Huck and Tom, are increasingly opposed in attitude and value structure. They are enemy-brothers, fighting over the proper methods for escape because Tom's superior literacy divides the boys.

The events on the Phelps farm are also complicated because Clemens/Twain had an ambivalent attitude. Clemens remembered his uncle, John Quarles, a Universalist and the partial model for Silas Phelps, as one of the best men he had ever met. Apparently he regarded his days with Uncle John and Aunt Patsy Quarles with a great fondness that permits the familial pranks to be amusing and accommodates the aggravating literary pranks demanded by Tom. Twain apparently wished to use the episode for some mild satire on southern living, some random satire on religion, and some extreme satire on Tom Sawyer's unrealistic notions about European adventure books. The satire on literature will be more fully explored in the following chapter.

Twain's description of Uncle Silas blends fondness and satire about religion:

He was the innocentest best old soul I ever see. But it warn't surprising; because he warn't only just a farmer, he was a preacher, too, and had a little

> one-horse log church down back of the plantation, which he built it himself at his own expense, for a church and school house, and never charged nothing for his preaching, **and it was worth it, too.** There was plenty other farmer-preachers like that, and done the same way, down South. (MS, 497–98)

Clemens/Twain values the unselfishness and charity of the dedication, yet he adds a stinger, Huck's priceless, naive, devastating evaluation of the sermon's value.

Twain also uses Uncles Silas to satirize Biblical religion in a quite subtle way, demonstrating that someone can read the Bible devotedly yet certainly not apply the information to his own situation. When the boys are in the midst of stealing objects for Jim's planned escape, Uncle Silas mentions that he "was a-studying my text in Acts seventeen, before breakfast," (MS, 619; First Edition prints "Acts Seventeen," 319). Although Twain probably realized the striking suitability of Acts, neither Huck nor Uncle Silas ever seems aware of such appropriateness. Presumably Uncle Silas has been reading, in the last few days, Acts 1–16, and would therefore have been studying the writing addressed to Theophilus (lover of God) about the actions and difficulties of the apostles between A.D. 33 and 53.

Among many relevant parallels between Acts and *Huck* are several references to imprisonment and escapes; in Acts 12, after two angels get Peter out of prison, Herod threatens to kill the ineffective jailors. Later in Acts 16, after a memorable—or perhaps grotesque—debate about adult circumcision, the apostles Paul and Silas pray for release and God shakes the prison so that all may go free, but the worried jailor considers suicide. Paul and Silas, however, are considerate and do not flee and accordingly the grateful jailor is converted. In Acts 16:36–39, the unjustly imprisoned will not agree to go quietly free out of jail but instead—in Tom Sawyer fashion—insist upon a prison release ceremony.

"Acts Seventeen" has sections about Paul and Silas being accused of creating chaos: "Those that have turned the world upside down are come hither also." Although Uncle Silas Phelps has just read that God "hath made of one blood all the nations of men for to dwell on all the face of the earth," and other Universalist-type verses such as 27 and 28, he does not seem to apply the Biblical values to his own role in imprisoning Jim. Uncle Silas does not even have enough sympathetic imagination to think about what imprisonment was like for his own Biblical name-parallel and transfer or apply that feeling to Jim. On Note C-10, Twain had considered but apparently decided against adding a dimension to Silas's character:

> Uncle S wishes he would escape—if it warn't wrong, he'd set him free—but its a too ⟨r⟩ gushy generosity with another man's property. (*Huck*, 1988, 746)

Perhaps Clemens/Twain was sympathizing with the moral dilemma and contradictions of a man, John Quarles, whom he loved and respected, but who had kept slaves. Although Uncle Silas read the Bible for religious guidance, he could not notice or interpret the scriptural resemblances.

Moreover, soon Uncle Silas will read, in the remainder of Acts, about the capture and imprisonment of Paul in Jerusalem that also resembles, as it turns out, the captivity of Jim. Paul, like Jim, narrowly escapes torture and death because of his free status. Uncle Silas, as another amusingly inefficient jailor, soon will experience a confusing escape of his prisoner, after reading about at least three relevant Biblical parallels. Twain could not have chosen any other selection of the Bible with more application.

Are these parallels mere chance? Very doubtful. Conventional reliance on the Bible may expose readers to relevant meanings, but the parallels are not noticed or not understood. The Bible's meaning has been ignored. It is, therefore, hardly remarkable that later, after the entire confusing escapade, when Tom and Huck's identities are declared by Aunt Polly, Twain writes:

> Aunt Sally she was one of the mixed-upest looking persons I ever see; except one, and that was uncle Silas, when he come in, and they told ⟨him⟩ it all to him. It kind of made him drunk, as you may say, and he didn't know nothing at all the rest of the day, and preached a prayer meeting sermon that night that give him a rattling reputation, because the oldest man in the world couldn't a understood it. (MS, 775–76)

The old man's confusion links directly to the boy's notion of the most impressive sermon, apparently an incomprehensible presentation. Uncle Silas possesses a basic decency and kindness, but combined with an ability, like the king's, to not comprehend and to give worthless sermons.

On Uncle Silas Phelps's farm, the real conflict occurs between Huck's morality of decency, kindness, and common sense and Tom's insistence that the "evasion," the stealing of Jim, be done "regular," according to the literary authorities. Explicit comments on religion become comparatively rare, almost as if conventional Christianity had lost its power after Huck's decision to go to hell—but the moral concerns become omnipresent because Huck becomes an unwitting, increasingly critical accomplice in the re-enslavement of Jim. It seems that Twain did link, as in a constellation, the following of hollow, meaningless, or destructive forms in monarchy, religion, and literary adventures. We might recall Huck's comment in Chapter III inspired by Tom's earlier reading: "It had all the marks of a Sunday school" (33).

When Huck learns, toward the beginning of the Phelps farm episode,

that the king and duke have been found out, he initially wishes to warn the
frauds. On the back of MS, 520 Twain added that Huck wants to help:

> *for I didn't believe anybody was going to give the king and the duke a hint, and
> so if I didn't hurry up and give them one, they'd get into trouble, sure.*

Huck's "good works" extend even to these criminals; his decision to attempt to alert the scoundrels seems wrong. The basis of Huck's decision is,
of course, sympathy; earlier Huck was willing enough to have the rascals
caught by the townspeople in the Wilks episode. But now Huck wishes to
extend kindness to the crooks even though they had sold Jim into captivity.
This unwillingness to hold people responsible for their evil actions occurs
because his sympathy is all-encompassing, undiscriminating.

The boys are too late to help the frauds. But the scene they witness
provides a good combination of description and Huck's emotional reaction:

> . . . I see they had the king and the duke astraddle of a rail—that is, I knowed it
> was the king and the duke, though they was all over tar and feathers, and didn't
> look like nothing in the world that was human—just looked like a couple of
> monstrous soldier-plumes. Well, it made me sick to see it; and I was so sorry
> for them poor pitiful rascals, that it seemed like I couldn't ever feel any
> hardness against them ⟨again⟩ *any more* in the world. It was a dreadful thing to
> see. Human beings <u>can</u> be awful cruel to one another. (MS, 521–22)

The scene pictures the ultimate doubling of the king's disguise in the Royal
Nonesuch. This dehumanization extends to the limit. The change in manuscript, from "again" to "*any more*" serves to make Huck's compassion less
time-bound, more general. In the printed version, Twain described them as
resembling "a couple of monstrous big soldier-plumes" (291), a change
which lessens the emphasis on deformity and makes Huck's tone more
child-like. Huck's conclusion has the emphasis on "can," the human capac-
ity for cruelty.

Huck is confused and upset by this event, and his thoughts reflect his
moral confusion between sympathy and conscience. Twain initially wrote
this section as part of a longer paragraph, then revised to make it a separate
unit:

> So we poked along back home, and I wasn't feeling so brash as I was before,
> but kind of ornery, and humble, and to blame, somehow—though <u>I</u> hadn't
> done nothing. But that's always the way: it don't make a blame bit of differ-

ence whether you do right or wrong, a person's conscience ain't got no sense, and just goes for him <u>anyway</u>. If I had a yaller dog that didn't know no more than a person's conscience, I would pison him. It takes up more room than a person's bowels, and ain't no good, no how. Tom Sawyer he says the same. (MS, 523–24)

"Bowels" is perhaps too concrete, and the printed version has "more room than all the rest of a person's insides" (292). The revised form makes conscience all-pervasive, and the resulting phrasing seems more general, more inclusive. This confusion of sympathy and conscience encourages Huck to hand over the control of the situation to Tom Sawyer whom, regrettably and indicatively, he quotes particularly as a confirming authority.

VII

In the remainder of the novel, however, Huck does not simply accept Tom's notions as he had in Chapters II and III. Instead, Huck constantly presents common sense alternatives and continuously, independently, debates the use of Tom's plans. Part of Huck's appeal lies in his creating his own unique morality in conflict with the cruelty of other people. It is a sign of some moral development in the final portion of the novel that Huck disagrees with Tom's methods, despite great feelings of inferiority based on his unfamiliarity with heroic nobles and escape literature.

Twice in the manuscript Tom ridicules Huck's practicality in terms of religion. But Twain changed both of them. Tom had originally said that Huck's plan to free Jim is "as mild as Sunday School" (MS, 529–30), but Twain changed the comparison to read in print, "as mild as goose-milk" (294). Tom also once criticized Huck by saying:

"Well, if that ain't just <u>like</u> you, Huck Finn. ⟨!⟩ You <u>can</u> get up the ⟨Sunday⟩ *infant*-schooliest ways of going at a thing. Why, hain't you ever read any books at all?—Baron Trenck, nor Casanova, nor Benvenuto Chelleeny, *nor Henri IV*, nor none of them heroes?" (MS, 556)

Tom originally used these religious comparisons to ridicule Huck, but Twain consistently canceled them. Perhaps such ridicule was thought to be unacceptable to Twain's audience, but I doubt it. The attitude toward religion was Twain's and Huck's, and the novelist decided not to have Huck be criticized in such terms by, of all people, Tom. But Twain definitely does permit Tom to ridicule Huck for his ignorance of certain books.

Conversely, the ridicule using religion flowed the other way. Once Huck brands as religious Tom's attitude toward doing things in accord with the authorities when he says: "Tom, if it ain't ⟨o⟩*un*regular and irreligious to sejest it," I says, "there's an old rusty saw-blade around yonder . . ." (MS, 584). Twain and Huck label Tom's following of empty forms and unrealistic traditions, by implication, as religious.

The Phelps episode does not have many explicit references to religion, as such, but it does explore the age-old moral problem of the difficulty of doing ethically correct action which deviates from social norms. Huck has a quite difficult time believing that Tom will actually help to steal Jim out of slavery. To some extent, the reader can observe that Twain also explores the possibility of right moral action of a socially condemned kind not only by the orphan outcast, Huck, but also by a "good" boy with social connections. Again training and shame are important considerations:

> Well, one thing was perfectly dead sure; and that was, that Tom Sawyer was *in* earnest, and was actually going to help steal that nigger out of slavery. That⟨s⟩ *was* the thing that was too many for me. Here was a boy that was respectable, and well brung up; and had a character to lose; and folks at home that had characters; and he was bright and not leather-headed; and knowing, and not ignorant; *and not mean, but kind hearted;* and yet here he was, without any more pride, or rightness, or feeling, than to stoop to this ⟨low-down⟩ business, and make himself a shame, and his family a shame, before everybody. I couldn't understand it, no way at all. It was outrageous, and I knowed I ought to just up and tell him so; and so be his true friend, and let him quit the thing right where he was, and save himself. And I did start to tell him; but he shut me up, ⟨square,⟩ and says: . . . (MS, 531–33)

Twain's identification process increases as he inserts: "*and not mean, but kind hearted*." The passage seems quite touching, for Clemens/Twain has created Huck's integrity, partially aided by the outcast status. Now Twain wishes to explore the possibilities for a person who had respectability and desired success. The sadness involves Twain's realization that the Tom Sawyer personality can only do the right action when it is safe. The social context of "shame" limits Tom's actions, and Huck remains completely puzzled. In a way, the re-introduction of Tom Sawyer and his behavior in the last section of the novel compellingly demonstrate Twain's artistic intuition that Tom was the wrong sort of boy to trace to maturity. Instead Tom dramatizes a particular kind of moral corruption, a combination of subservience to his authorities and absolute, arrogant, disregard for his companions.

There are other, lesser moral complications in the episode, particularly

involving the morality of stealing material to help in the escape. We recall
that earlier Huck and Jim had solved their problems about the morality of
stealing by making a category of things which they absolutely would not
steal; of course, as it happened the chosen objects were conveniently quite
undesirable—crabapples and unripe persimmons. This moral code about
stealing served Huck and Jim well because, despite its apparent rigidity, it
permitted them to do as they wished while "protected" by a seemingly
definite code. But in the Phelps farm episode, Tom thinks the boys can steal
only on behalf of the prisoner. Huck says: "I called it borrowing, because
that was what pap always called it; but Tom said it warn't borrowing, it was
stealing" (MS, 571). Tom clearly prefers the more dramatic name. At one
point, Tom makes Huck give the slaves ten cents for a watermelon Huck
had stolen for his own purposes. Tom's standard of judgment seems much
more complicated than Huck's because he judges each case by its literary
antecedents and intended usages. All of this creates what Huck calls "a lot
of gold-leaf distinctions." The manuscript pages which cover this section of
Chapter XXXV (MS, 571–74) appear to be fair copies, with no changes.
This circumstantial evidence thus hints that this amusing contrast in morality may be the product of extensive revision.

Such a contrast in morality occurs as conditions gradually force Tom
to be slightly realistic in his choice of tools for the escape. Tom squirms
with the morality of his decision, deciding "to <u>let on</u>"; the retentive reader
may recall the passage in which Huck considers the difficulty of "letting on
to give up sin" and exposing Jim in a letter to Miss Watson. The contrast is
striking; Tom begins:

> "I'll tell you. It ain't right, ⟨but⟩ and it ain't moral, and I wouldn't like it to
> get out—⟨I⟩ but there ain't only just the one way: we got to dig him out with
> the picks, and <u>let on</u> it's case-knives."
> *"Now you're ⟨shouting, I says.⟩ **talking**!" I says*; Your head gets leveler and
> leveler all the time, Tom Sawyer," I says. "Picks is the ticket, moral or no
> moral; and as for me, I don't care shucks for the morality of it, no how. When I
> start in to steal a nigger, or a water melon, or a Sunday school book, I ain't no
> ways particular how it's done, ⟨as lon⟩ so it's done. What I want is my nigger;
> or what I want is my watermelon; or what I want is my Sunday school-book:
> and if a pick's the handiest thing, that's the thing I'm agoing to dig that nigger
> or that watermelon or that Sunday school book out with; and I don't give a
> cuss what the authorities thinks about it, neither. (MS, 588–90)

Tom's solution, "letting on," or pretending, relates, of course, to lying,
except that "letting on" involves fictionalizing, not to others, but to oneself.
It seems that Twain was writing this segment partially to criticize the

fictional mode, and Tom's self-deception stands in contrast to Huck's deception of others and his pragmatism. Tom has confused "morality" with "authority," and Huck senses the opposition and opts for results. In a way, the catalogue of things to be stolen summarizes the book, especially the fairly involuted irony of how to steal a Sunday school book. The concluding effective phrase, "I don't give a cuss," directly conflicts with the Sunday-school authorities. But Twain changed the final version to read: "I don't give a dead rat what the authorities thinks about it nuther" (310). The "dead rat" is more concrete, and "nuther" is Huck's own individual way of talking, but "cuss" might have been preferable for the contextual irony.

Tom attempts to maintain control of the situation. As he continues his confusion of morality with authority, his voice begins to sound like the sanctimonious, condescending king:

> "Well," he says, "there's excuse for picks and letting-on, in a case like this; if it warn't so, I wouldn't approve of it, nor I wouldn't stand by and see the rules broke—because right is right, and wrong is wrong, and a body ain't got no business doing **wrong** when he ain't ignorant and knows better. It might answer for <u>you</u> to dig Jim out with a pick, <u>without</u> any letting on, because you don't know no better; but it wouldn't for me, because I do know better. . . . (MS, 590–91)

In this case, Tom equates moral action with action in accord with previous authorities, clearly an attitude shared by most conventional religions. Rigid and inflexible in his view, he adapts his "rules" to reality by self-deception.

Twain's most devastating criticism of Tom's morality involves false naming, when Tom refuses to call a pick a pick. Words have lost their meaning—a situation perhaps quite handy for maintaining a rigid authoritarian morality but threatening and debilitating for a novelist. Tom says:

> ". . . Gimme a caseknife."
> He had his own by him, but I handed him mine.(") He flung it down, and says:
> "Gimme a <u>caseknife</u>."
> I didn't know just what to do—but then I thought. I scratched around amongst the old tools, and got a pick-***axe*** and give it to him, and he took it and went to work, and never said a word.
> He was always just that particular. ***Full of principle.*** (MS, 591–92)

The first insertion insists on the contrast, and the sarcastic final stinger evaluates Tom's immorality.[14]

Both boys are confused in their statements. Huck confuses his sympathy for the king and duke by calling it "conscience"; Tom confuses his authority about literary models and tactics by using the word "moral." For Twain, it would be close to the truth to say that sympathy is a form of morality but that conscience is a form of authority. (In 1895, Twain would jot down a comment about the novel: "a book of mine where a sound heart and a deformed conscience come into collision and conscience suffers defeat" (M.T.P., Notebook 28A, 35). The dilemma, formed and reinforced by conventional Christianity, is that moral sympathy seldom conforms to authoritative conscience. Huck endures, with difficulty, Tom's extreme, stage-four-style devotion to authorities. But most readers would wish Huck to have a final clear-cut victory at this stage, leading to a conventional, unqualified moral triumph.

VIII

The conflict between sympathy and authority does resolve, but most readers have not recognized Huck's role in this resolution. Actually, a genuine personal equivalence exists when, for a moment, a morality of sympathy functions. Philosophers have speculated that the test of a moral society is whether the designers of the society could with equanimity take any position in the society. As indicated earlier, such a society exists, briefly, after Tom has been wounded when Huck *and* Jim perceive, almost as if they were one person, what to do to help Tom. The sympathy begins in a thought of both Huck and Jim, and Huck trusts both Jim and the situation enough to ask Jim to express it:

> But me and Jim was consulting—and thinking. And after we'd thought a ⟨while,⟩ *minute*, I says:
> "Say it, Jim."
> So he says:
> "Well, den, dis is de way it look to ⟨Jim⟩ *me*, Huck. ⟨If⟩ Ef it wuz <u>him</u> dat ⟨w⟩'uz bein' sot free, en one er de boys wuz to git shot, would he say, 'Go on en save me, nemmine 'bout a doctor for to save dis one?' ⟨Would⟩ Is dat like mars Tom Sawyer? Would he say dat? You <u>bet</u> he wouldn't! <u>Well</u> den—is ⟨Jim gwyne⟩ <u>Jim</u> gwyne to say it? No, sah—I ⟨don't⟩ *doan'* <u>budge</u> a step out'n dis place, 'dout a <u>doctor</u>; not ef it's forty year!" (MS, 709–10)

Huck is not authoritarian, as Tom had been, but is authoritative. Huck's tone is not commanding but implies his consent. Huck does not know exactly what Jim will say but trusts his companion and urges him to "say it," transcending racial categories to give authority to the most experienced but least literate person. Jim's eloquent self-transformation, placing himself in Tom's situation and Tom in his own, involves a genuinely moral insight, giving an individual basis for sympathy and right action. The ethic of self-sacrifice and total commitment, rising above Tom's torment of Jim and foolish risk taking, is achieved by this process of sympathetic identification. Momentarily the two healthy fugitives create a small society, an inclusive triad, of non-exploitative trust in which one could with equanimity take any role, confident about being treated morally. Moreover, Jim's gentle, considerate phrasing even attributes some dignity to Tom.

The story of Huck and Tom contains many deeds of death, ranging from the grave robbery, stabbing, and starvation in *The Adventures of Tom Sawyer*, through the real and imagined deaths of Huck's many parents, to Pap Finn's delusions about "the Angel of Death," the shooting of Boggs, and the murder of the Grangerford boys. Now that Tom has been shot in the escape attempt and has a fever and delirium, his prognosis without medical intervention would be unmistakable in the days of pre-sulfa medicine: blood poisoning, gangrene, and death. Moreover, delay in calling a doctor will increase the likelihood of suppuration, amputation, and death.

Once the Doctor arrives, Jim could easily wait quietly or drift away—deciding that the Doctor is now fully in charge. But he stays. Although we could follow the process of Huck's thinking as he debated and finally decided to "go to hell," we observe no debate as Jim makes an equally momentous decision to reveal himself, to risk the real torment of recapture, to suffer the hell of recapture in the South. Huck's hell was a future dystopia; Jim, experienced in the ways of slavery, would know what he faced.

The way that Jim helped was heavily revised on manuscript pages 751, 752 (recto and verso), and 753. The Doctor explains to Jim's captors how the slave came to his aid:

> "Don't be no rougher on him than you're obleeged to, because he ain't a bad nigger. When I got to where I found the boy, I see I couldn't cut the bullet out without some help, and he warn't in no condition to leave, to go and get help; and when I says this, out crawls this nigger from behind the wigwam or somewheres, and says he'll help, and the boy was mad, and told him to clear out, and said he wouldn't have no strange niggers meddling around him, but the nigger. . .

However, Twain changed the section substantially by the cancellation of everything after "to go and get help." The original version simply related the scene; the revised section presents more detail about Tom while he is delirious. One effect of the change is to offer three versions of how people act when delirious: Jim after the rattlesnake bite, Pap Finn when drunk, and Tom after the gunshot. More importantly, the changed version juxtaposes for dramatic contrast Tom's silly fantasizing verbosity with Jim's simple eloquent speech and action. In the last manuscript version, the Doctor reports that:

> . . . he got a little worse and a little worse, and after a long time he went out of his head *and wouldn't let me come anigh him ⟨ever⟩ any more, and said if I chalked his raft he'd kill me, and no end of wild foolishness like that, and I see I couldn't do anything at all with him; so* ⟨and⟩ I says, I got to have <u>help</u>, somehow; and the minute I says it, out crawls this nigger from somewheres, and says he'll help; and he done it, too, and done it very well. (MS, 752 recto and verso)

Twain has inserted more of Tom's romantically inspired foolishness and significantly made Jim's lifesaving help immediately forthcoming, "the minute I says it." Clearly, Jim's action is genuinely heroic, unselfish, in utter contrast to Tom's bookish "style." The doctor's evaluation of Jim's help includes a religious word: "I never see a nigger that was a better nuss *or faithfuller*, and yet he was resking his freedom to do it" (MS, 754). Significantly, here Twain applied the religious word to a human relationship. At this point, Jim demonstrates self-sacrifice, the opposite of Tom's selfish concerns, and Jim's action ends the danger-of-death motif.

Huck still has the nagging question in his mind about why Tom participated. We realize that the "good boy" can do a socially deviant act only when it is safe and that Tom's confusion of morality with past authority severely limits his integrity. Tom is a creature of literate, conventional society, quite unable to handle Huck's or Jim's individual morality. When Tom learns that Jim has been captured, that his game has ended, he reacts indignantly and amazingly selfishly:

> "They hain't no <u>right</u> to shut him up! <u>Shove!</u>—and don't you lose a minute. Turn him loose! he ain't no slave, he's as free as any cretur that walks this earth!"
> "What <u>does</u> the child mean!"
> "I mean every word I say, aunt Sally, and if somebody don't go, I'll go. I've knowed him all his life, and so has Tom, there." (MS, 770–71)

Utterly mistaken in his solipsistic way, Tom regards the older Jim as only an object in Tom's universe, not as a person with an existence apart from, or prior to, his own. Tom lacks the imagination to have sympathy; his complicity without sympathy seems destructive. (We recall with some bitter humor how Tom had earlier wished to prolong Jim's captivity so his children could set Jim free.) Now Tom's urgency is not genuinely on Jim's behalf, but only because a rule is being broken, a rule which Tom had himself knowingly broken for the sake of "adventure."

The actual freeing of Jim had happened because of shame. Shame functions as the opposite of self-transformation. When "shamed," a person is trapped, caught, characterized by previous action; but when self-transformed, a person's past and social identity can be re-created, self-created. Accordingly, we can realize that Clemens/Twain's and Huck's self-transformations are ways of avoiding shame and maintaining creativity of personality. Tom explains:

> "Old Miss Watson died two months ago, and she was ashamed ⟨that⟩ she ever was going to sell him down the river, and said *so*; and she set him free in her will."
>
> "Then what on earth did you want to set him free for, seein' he was already free?"
>
> "Well that is a question *I must say*; and just like women! Why, I wanted the adventure of it; and I'd a waded neck-deep in blood to—goodness alive, aunt Polly!" (MS, 771–72)

The insertion of "*I must say*" gives Tom a superior, condescending tone of voice, in a way the root of the problem. Tom's exaggerated offer to wade neck deep in blood dramatizes his blatantly immoral imagination as this would primarily have to be other peoples' blood. The word "adventure" carries a bitter sound as the novel demonstrates how enslaving "adventures" can be.

Once Huck has his social identity pinned upon him by the insertion of "*Tom's aunt Polly she told all about who I was, and what . . .*" (MS, 776) it is no longer possible for the now-defined Huck to exist in that society for long. His chance for self-transformation there has ended. Jim's revelation of Huck's father's death takes one step toward removing some social definitions of Huck; at least he is no longer Pap Finn's boy in the eyes of society. Setting out for the Territory offers the chance for continuing self-transformation and for the avoidance of shame. Although Huck has reached an independent, considerate, mature morality, and although he recapitulates that experience in writing the book, he also knows the difficulty of moral action in that society. A shadow falls, darkening the kaleidoscope.

A few concluding ironies may be catalogued. Jim's original flight to avoid being sold downriver leads to his eventual imprisonment downriver, a final irony comparable to the conclusion of *Pudd'nhead Wilson*.[15] Huck had originally said that he did not take stock in dead people, yet the wills of Peter Wilks and of Miss Watson both work as important plot devices, ways that dead people shape the action. As mentioned, in the Wilks and Phelps episodes two false brothers try to rob; the king uses noble status and religion to steal; Tom uses "noble" adventure books. Each technique is revealed to be utterly immoral. Consequently, although the word "Adventures" carried favorable connotations in the title of Tom Sawyer's novel and at the inception of Huck's story, "adventures" developed unfavorable meaning as the novel progressed. Several other ironies are unexpected. Who would have thought that an author would title a book *Adventures of Huckleberry Finn*, then emphasize the harmful effect of adventures in the last section? And, furthermore, who would have thought that the last section, a satire on bookish inspiration, would be widely regarded by readers as a following of empty forms, a blemish on an otherwise fine adventure? Twain's discoveries in the last two-thirds of *Huckleberry Finn* resemble the darkness of vision evident in *Connecticut Yankee*, *Pudd'nhead Wilson*, and other late works.

Notes

1. The reference in Twain's letter to Howells of October 5, 1875 about the bottles of "graded foetuses" may indicate his interest in human development (*Twain-Howells Letters*, Vol. 1, 105).

2. Samples of religious crank letters can be found in the Mark Twain Papers for the following dates, e.g., February 13, 1883 (Bessie Stone); December 15, 1883 (M.V., a Hartford resident); January 23, 1884 (Mary Reily).

3. These incidents may be found in "A Record of Small Foolishnesses," 14–15, 75–77, 27, 25, 39, 89, 39.

4. An example of accidental positive reinforcement for negative behavior actually occurred as follows:

> May '77 A month or more ago the Bay was naughty in the nursery and did not finish her dinner. In the evening she was hungry and her mamma gave her a cracker. I quote now from a letter written to me by mamma when I was in Baltimore 2 or 3 days ago:
> "Last night, after George had wiped off her sticky fingers in the china closet, Bay came out with her little, sad, downcast look, and said, 'I been littl' naughty up 'tairs, can I have a cacker?' [I found that the naughtiness had been invented for the occasion]." ("A Record," 16–17)*

5. Lawrence Kohlberg's theory has appeared in several different publications. Most accessible is his essay in *Phi Delta Kappan* (June 1975). See also Lawrence Kohlberg and Donald Elfenbein "Development of Moral Reasoning and Attitudes toward Capital Punishment," *American Journal of Orthopsychiatry* (Summer 1975) and Kohlberg's "Moral Stages and Moralization: The Cognitive-Developmental Approach" in *Man, Morality, and Society*, ed. Thomas Lickona (New York, 1976). Twain's views on the role of training and reinforcement in influencing behavior occur in skeletal, unillusioned form in his short story "Edward Mills and George Benton: A Tale."

6. Some adults retain this instrumentalist view; Twain mentioned a "Church of the Holy Speculators."

7. Also see Edgar Branch's treatment in *The Literary Apprenticeship of Mark Twain* 199, et seq.

8. Prices in 1835–1845 and in 1884 were relatively similar; calculations are based on *Historical Statistical Abstracts*, I, E135–166 and *Statistical Abstracts*, 1988, 451.

9. A crank letter with phonetic spelling was sent to Twain by a "W. Wilkins Micawber," dated September 24, 1883. In one portion the letter contains the spelling "4 ordenashun."* Perhaps this phrasing influenced the novel's "preforeordestination." Twain wrote "Dam fool"* on the envelope.

10. Victor Fischer has created a brilliant hypothesis, forthcoming, that the camp meeting may have been inserted into the king and duke's dramatic practice. The insertion would follow "then he give the book to the king and told him to get his part by heart," (Chapter XX, 171) and fit in before "When he had got it pretty good, him and the duke begun to practice it together" (Chapter XXI, 177). I consider this suggestion to be utterly convincing.

11. Once, when Clara was about three or four, she said, "Mamma, I brang you these flowers"—paused, then corrected herself—"No, I brung them." ("A Record," 62).* Twain, inconsistently, first has Huck say, in another passage about training, "I was brought up wicked" (MS, 440), but changed the printed version to, "I was brung up wicked" (270).

12. An incident from the children's lives reveals Clemens's understanding of "the letter and the spirit" of an agreement:

> (Dec. 1880) Bay and Susie were given candy this morning for not having quarreled yesterday—a contract of long standing. Bay began to devour hers, but Susie hesitated a moment, then handed hers back, with a suggestion that she was not fairly entitled to it.—Momma said, "Then what about Bay? She must have quarreled too, of course." Susie said, "I don't know whether Bay felt wrong in her heart, but I didn't feel right in my heart."
>
> ⟨Susie made a pretty nice distinction here—she had kept the letter of the contract ⟨not⟩ to not quarrel, but had violated the spirit of it; she had felt the angry words she had not spoken.⟩
>
> No, I got it wrong. Susie meant that Bay's talk might have been only chaff and not ill-natured; ⟨xx⟩ she could not tell, as to that; but she knew her own talk came from an angry heart. ("A Record," 86)*

13. An imagistic coherence exists between "I might as well go the whole hog" and "If you notice, most folks don't go to church only when they've got to; but a hog is different" (149). The action is seen as unrestrained, natural, sincere, and pleasurable. Perhaps Twain took some "hog" imagery away from the king because it was too good for him! See also Franklin Rogers's comments in the Twain chapter of *Occidental Ideographs*.

14. "*Full of principle*" seems to have been added at the end of a line because it is significantly higher than the normal line of writing.

15. In both books some local decision makers who urge death for the slave are finally convinced to drop the idea only because killing the slave destroys his monetary value.

9. Literacy, Copyright, and Books

A composite text of the author's speech at the opening of the Mark Twain library, Redding, Connecticut, October 18, 1908:

     . . . I like to talk. It would take more than the Redding air to make me keep still, and I like to instruct people. It is noble to be good, and it's nobler to teach others to be good, and less trouble. I am glad to help this library. We get our morals from books. I didn't get mine from books, but I do know that morals do come from books—theoretically at least.

Mark Twain Speaking, 630

I

Although Twain's attentions to the societal problems of slavery and the quest for freedom have been well understood, several less recognized concerns—literacy and copyright—also shaped the novel. Twain regarded the interrelated issues of literacy and copyright quite seriously, considering literacy in a personal, familial context, as well as from a national perspective. Twain knew that his audience was not as literate as, say, those who would read Henry James. Similarly, he realized the effects of copyright problems upon his personal finances, upon the reading preferences of his audience, and—most importantly—upon the values of American citizens. Indeed, the topics of slavery and freedom, conformity and individualism, hereditary and environmental determinism, literacy and copyright are interrelated, all of them powerful issues affecting the liberation of both Jim and Huck, as well as the nation.

    It is illuminating to regard the novel as the narrative of a newly literate Huck in conflict with a society that passes on its information and values through books. But most of these books, unfortunately, are unreliable or deceptive. Many people try to control or suppress Huck by using their greater literacy to exert situational dominance over him, and finally he is partially controlled by a boy who has read much literature about the adventures of European noblemen and heroes. Because European literature was not then protected by international copyright, those books sold in America very cheaply. *The Adventures of Baron von Trenck* sold for ten cents, while the similarly titled stories of *Tom Sawyer* or of *Huckleberry Finn* sold for $2.75. How much nationalistic pride or literary artistry would be necessary to overcome a 27 to 1 competitive price disadvantage? Twain's attitude toward the issue of international copyright changed radically between 1880 and 1886, and this change affects *Huck*. Although Twain at one early point thought that the lack of international copyright laws in America would lead to inexpensive European literature and would help America, he later viewed romanticized stories of nobility as corrupters of American youth.

In consequence, Twain's entire novel deals with the deceptive power of books, and the recently literate narrator often tries advice or "style" from bookish sources only to be disillusioned. Although the title, *Adventures of . . .* , probably carried favorable connotations when Twain began the novel, by the time of the story's completion the connotations for its author had become utterly negative. The title and the narrative both undergo dynamic reflexive change as the story undercuts its own authority. Moreover, although Jim is, after a cyclic return to captivity, finally liberated from slavery, Huck's battle with the influence of literacy has instead only a qualified outcome.

II

To create a context for this interpretation requires both extraordinary empathy from the readers of this critical study and a certain amount of information. Each reader of this theory, each person holding this book open to this page, has already won a struggle for literacy. Accordingly, empathy for losers or for non-contestants requires some imagination. Various studies reveal that illiterate people tend to be poorer and to suffer earlier mortality than their literate contemporaries. What little we know about Pap Finn and Huck's mother seems consistent with this knowledge. The attitudes of illiterates toward literacy may vary. Clearly Pap Finn feels threatened by Huck's ability to read and does not want Huck to remain in school. But Jim's attitude of deference to all knowledge that Tom or Huck relate from books seems more typical. In general, we know that many illiterate people attribute near-magical power to literacy, thinking it the key to making, preserving, and learning secrets. For example, most adults have watched a child who has memorized a story pretend to read it by reciting while the pages turn. Likewise, each individual's transition from an oral culture to a literate culture remains fascinating.[1] Huck has only recently made that transition and, consequently, for most of the book still has almost no skepticism about what he reads.

Because most people now learn to read at about four to six years of age, skilled readers have difficulty recalling the process of learning to read and write. But Huck learned at the somewhat later age of about twelve. Those of us who at such an age made the relatively easier step of learning an additional alphabet such as the Greek, Arabic, or Cyrillic or learning to read in another language can easily recall the combination of puzzlement and an awareness that our own fund of knowledge about the world was not, apparently, relevant to the new difficult task. Humility or deference to the teacher seemed appropriate, and many teachers continue to teach literacy to older students with a patronizing arrogance similar to Tom's attitude toward Huck. The condition of illiteracy or partial literacy creates a vulnerability. Conversely, literacy can be a weapon. For instance, the king and duke constantly try to exploit or swindle those less literate, a class which often but not always overlaps with those who are less intelligent. In Huck we have a character who possesses intelligence and whose literacy level changes during the time covered by the narration.

Full understanding of this context also requires some historical information. National census figures state that, in 1870, 11.5% of whites fourteen and older and 79.9% of Negroes were illiterate (*1776 Bicentennial Issue* 383). One may consider this tabulation as quite optimistic, probably overstating the ability to read, because in many locations it had been illegal to teach a Black person to read. But let us try to get back to an earlier era, Twain's fictional world, the period of 1835–1845. In the 1840 census, the male head of a family was simply asked how many illiterates were in his family. The national average was 22% (*Historical Statistics* I 364–65, 382). This figure is also probably conservative because no test was given; the census taker simply accepted the respondent's count at face value. And many people would consider a person literate if he—and more seldom she—could simply sign his or her name or make a distinctive mark. A second problem arises because the questioner and the respondent might not even include females or slaves in the category of people to be considered among the potentially literate. Another problem exists: would an illiterate child be considered in the category of those who should be counted? Furthermore, embarrassment, pride, or pretension could each affect the way the respondents replied. Moreover, a homeless person such as Pap Finn might not be contacted at all. Comparative information about other countries, with stable populations, stable borders, and higher expenditures for teachers per 10,000 citizens would lead us to believe that functional illiteracy in America would actually have been significantly higher than 22 percent.

Regional variations must also be considered. One statistical survey indicates that in 1850 the total number of public, school, Sunday School, church, and college libraries in the slave states was 722 compared to 14,902 in the free states, with a similarly lesser number of volumes. Another 1850 table of "Persons over 20 years of age who cannot Read or Write" reveals a much greater proportion of white illiterates in the slave states (Blake 836, 835). Except during periods of great immigration, rural illiteracy usually surpasses urban. In 1900, when the national average was 11 percent illiteracy, Arkansas claimed a 21 percent illiteracy rate, and Mississippi reached a 34 percent rate (*1776 Bicentennial* 190). It is reasonable to infer that in 1845 and in 1885 illiteracy in Missouri and Arkansas would be substantial. We must therefore note the incongruity of Tom indignantly asking Huck, while on the Phelps farm, if he had not read Baron von Trenck or "Chelleeny." Similarly, we can speculate whether Tom's notion of having Jim keep a journal about his imprisonment would be read differently by a citizenry which was in the 1880s already using literacy tests to prevent Black men from voting. Numerous explicit references to literacy, to the act of reading or of writing, constitute, I would suggest, a complex motif within the novel.

Of course, once Huck has exposure to the fundamentals, our concern shifts to the much more problematic topic of semi-literacy or quasi-literacy. This topic can be explored with information about the schools, about other countries, and about some of Twain's other works.

The schooling system that Clemens remembered, Twain recreated, and Huck would have attended—when he wished—relied upon parental fees. Data about that system are scarce, but we do know that at a later time, in 1870, when attendance was usually free, 57 percent of the youths between five and seventeen attended school. We suppose that many of the remaining 43 percent were youths who left school in order to work. The attendees faced a school year nominally requiring one hundred thirty-two days, but a child would actually be there, on the average, seventy-eight days (*Historical Statistics* I 376). Presumably attendance would have seasonal variations, with severe weather or family, farm, and job-related duties causing absences and preventing learning. In 1870, about 2 percent of the age group graduated from what we would consider a demanding high school curriculum. It seems reasonable to infer that in 1840–1845, when the educational system usually relied on fees, the role of education was considerably less than in 1870. As shall become clear, Twain inarguably recognized the importance of even primitive levels of literacy for the developing nation.

More definite information about semi-literacy can be gathered if we consider two countries which had more stable populations and which apparently spent more money for teachers and had more teachers per 10,000 population than Missouri in 1845. The records of tests done on French army recruits between 1881–1900 reveal that although illiteracy was fairly low (8% could neither read nor write and 2% could only read), 87 percent could read and write but had not reached the end of elementary school. Similarly, among Swiss Army recruits there were no illiterates, but only 48 percent were judged to have the ability to do "good reading with good accentuation and correct understanding of the piece read." Although the three intermediate, lower gradations made up 52 percent, there were no illiterates (Cipolla 11–13, 26–37). Since these conditions prevailed in confined, developed countries, one infers that in Missouri in 1845—and in America in 1885—when illiteracy was substantial, many more people would be caught in the prison of semi-literacy. Twain chose to explore the semi-literate condition, a subject matter that may have been unusually appropriate for many fellow citizens in his original audience.

Twain's sensitivity to such an issue appears in a comic gem, "English as She Is Taught" (1887). He claims to have received from a teacher a manuscript compilation of mistakes made by pupils, and, in a metafictional fashion, he wishes the readers to confirm his judgment that the compilation should be published. The list of definitions offered by students informs us that the word "Eucharist" refers to "one who plays euchre" and "plagiarist" refers to "a writer of plays." The examples represent a priceless gathering of the kinds of semi-literacy each generation of teachers discovers with its own indignation. Twain writes:

> There are several curious "compositions" in the little book, and we must make room for one. It is full of naivete, brutal truth, and unembarrassed directness, and is the funniest (genuine) boy's composition I think I have ever seen:
>
> ON GIRLS
> Girls are very stuckup and dignefied in their maner and be have your. They think more of dress than anything and like to play with dowls and rags. They cry if they see a cow in a far distance and are afraid of guns. They stay at home all the time and go to church on Sunday. They are al-ways sick. They

are al-ways funy and making fun of boy's hands and they say how dirty. They cant play marbels. I pity them poor things. They make fun of boys and then turn round and love them. I dont beleave they ever kiled a cat or anything. They look out every nite and say oh ant the moon lovely. Thir is one thing I have not told and that is they al-ways now their lessons bettern boys. (*Century*, 33: April 1887, 936)

The boy's essay sounds remarkably similar in its additive flow to how Huck talks. In this context, the funds of misinformation, confusion, and partial knowledge displayed by Tom to Huck and offered by Huck to Jim appear relevant. Throughout his career, for that matter, Twain had written with attention to naive or minimally literate, unsophisticated, dialect speakers.

Twain concludes this "essay" with an abrupt commentary, quoting a remark on the role of schools in ineffective education which certainly reveals that he saw the issue of literacy in nationalistic terms:

> From Mr. Edward Channing's recent article in "Science":
>
> The marked difference between the books now being produced by French, English, and American travelers, on the one hand, and German explorers, on the other, is too great to escape attention. The difference is due entirely to the fact that in school and university the German is taught, in the first place to see, and in the second place to understand what he does see. *Mark Twain* (*Century* 33, 936)

Channing's opinion echoes the values Twain himself proclaimed in, for example, prefatory material for *Innocents Abroad*, "to suggest to the reader how *he* would be likely to see Europe and the East if he looked at them with his own eyes instead of the eyes of those who traveled in those countries before him."

Biographical evidence reveals that Sam Clemens observed closely as his own children learned to read English, one at a somewhat later-than-normal age. In "A Record of Small Foolishnesses," the fond father wrote in loving detail about the events of 1880:

> about the 18th or 20th of Oct. 80, Bay (who has never been allowed to meddle with English alphabets or books lest she would neglect her German), collared an English juvenile-poem book sent her from London by Joseph the courier— & <u>now</u>, 10 or 12 days later (Oct. 30) she reads abstruse English works with an astounding facility! Nobody has given her an instant's assistance. Susie has learned to read English during these same 10 or 12 days, but she is 8 yrs old, & besides she can't read it as glibly as Bay. ("A Record," loose sheet labeled 20) *

The importance of this event to the author's mind is signaled by his unusual repetition in the journal and his further emphatic reflections upon the learning processes:

Oct. 1880 <u>Random Notes</u>
During the <u>ten days</u> of this month, Bay and Susie <u>taught</u> themselves to read English, with *out* help or instruction from anybody, and without knowing the alphabet, or making any attempt to <u>to spell</u> the words or divide them into syllables

Dec. 1880. They both read fluently, now, but they make no attempts at spelling; neither of them knows more than half the letters of the alphabet. They read wholly by the <u>look</u> of the word. Bay picks up any book that comes handy—seems to have no preferences.—the reason they have learned to read English and are so fond of it, is, I think, because they were long ago forbidden to meddle with English books till they could be far advanced in German. Forbidden fruits are most coveted, since Eve's time. ("A Record," 84)*

The children's independent, eager learning processes fascinated the author.

Another familial anecdote provides a context for knowledge about semi-literacy, an example of misunderstanding that seemed, to Clemens, worthy of preservation. Clara turned nine on June 9, 1883, the month when her father noted:

Clara picked up a book—"Daniel Boone, by John S. C. Abbott" and found on the fly-leaf ⟨this⟩ *a* comment of mine, in pencil; puzzled over it, couldn't quite make it out; her mother took it and read it to her, as follows: "A poor slovenly book; a mess of sappy drivel and bad grammar." Clara said, with entire seriousness (not comprehending the meaning but charmed with the sound of the words,) "O, that must be lovely!" and carried the book away and buried herself in it. ("A Record," 101)*

In this slight story we find a newly literate child's non-critical approval extended enthusiastically to "drivel." Although Clara could not comprehend the handwritten comment, in written or oral form, her honorific attitude toward the act of reading is optimistic and non-discriminative. At Quarry Farm Clara picked *Daniel Boone*, but in the Phelps farm section Twain carefully limited the detailed references about Tom's reading to foreign literature.

As an author primarily dependent upon a limited national audience of subscription book buyers, Twain of course had a professional and a financial interest in literacy. His attention to the quality and number of illustrations necessary to appeal to a mass audience indicates a keen sense of the ordinary reader's preference for visual aids.

Just as he was interested in the semi-literate, he was also fascinated by the credulous, those who believe what they read wholeheartedly or too easily. This issue ranges, of course, across his career, but it has a particular emphasis in the late 1870s and early 1880s. Many satiric and parodic pieces share what might be called a concern for "higher literacy," an ability to recognize conventional literary expectations and to toy with these conventions.

Those readers who believe readily in conventional literature will experience peculiar sensations, because Twain reveals a complex attitude toward literature and the issue of textuality itself. In addition to his famous satirical comments upon Cooper, Twain also exploits and mocks the expectations appropriate for conventional literature.

For example, in Twain's little volume of short works, *The Stolen White Elephant* (1882), the title story parodies detective fiction, and other stories show a similar literary focus. "A Curious Experience" seems like a Civil War spy story until the last three paragraphs. At that point, the narrator says:

> Let me throw in a word or two of explanation concerning that boy and his performances. It turned out that he was a ravenous devourer of dime novels and sensation-story papers—therefore, dark mysteries and gaudy heroisms were just in his line. Then he had read newspaper reports of the stealthy goings and comings of rebel spies in our midst, and of their lurid purposes and their two or three startling achievements, till his imagination was all aflame on that subject. (186)

The revelation of this "trick" at the end of the story is hardly artful. Other stories in the volume burlesque the literary interview and tales of lovers separated by great distance. In addition, random comments in the volume undercut conventional expectations about literature, as when a sailor complains, "If there's one thing that can make me madder than another, it's this sappy, damn maritime poetry" (54).

The most explicit piece about literature in the volume is "About Magnanimous-Incident Literature" (first printed in 1876, reprinted in 1882). The narrator poses as a believer in such literature, but he gives the disillusioning results. The story uses three anecdotes of generosity, each followed by disastrous conclusions; a few quotations make the points: a generous doctor, who had healed first one, than a daily doubling number of dogs, finally says:

> "I might as well acknowledge it, I have been fooled by the books; they only tell the pretty part of the story, and then stop. Fetch me the shotgun; this thing has gone along far enough. . . ." (133)
> "Beware of the books. They tell but half the story. . . ." (134)

A second hero finally laments, "Alas, the books deceived me; they do not tell the whole story" (136). The satire seems unmistakable and not terribly subtle.

Those reflexive concerns, prominent in works published in 1882, also run through several of the unpublished works closely associated in time with *Huck*. Twain's burlesque Hamlet project occupied part of 1881. And in March of 1883, a friend and would-be collaborator, Joseph T. Goodman, sent his version to Twain, saying, "Here is your 'Hamlet's Brother,' roughly blocked out" (M.T.P.)* Such literary burlesques intrigued Twain; he had a sophisticated knowledge of literary cliches and conventions, considering literature as a subject matter suitable for parodic treatment and burlesque duplication.

He worked on "1002ᵈ Arabian Night" during the summer of 1883. The prolixity of the narrator and her abuse of the conventions of elaborate phrasing in the Scheherazade story contrast with the sultan's impatient demands for the narrative, e.g., "Omit the rest of the catalogue" or "Put it in the appendix. Proceed, proceed!" Twain manages to include outrageous puns and concludes the tale by stating that the storyteller talked one thousand and ninety-five members of the royalty to death. Twain wanted to publish the work, informing Webster, "I think we'll publish '1002,' anonymously, in a 15 or 20 cent form, right after Huck" (Webster, 249).

The desire to indict literature as a deceptive way of knowing appears most explicitly in the intended sequel, when the boys "light out for the Territory" in "Huck Finn and Tom Sawyer among the Indians," which Walter Blair states Twain composed in 1884 (270). On July 6, 1884, Twain commanded Charley Webster:

> Send to me, right away, a book by *Lieut. Col. Dodge, USA*, called "25 Years on the Frontier"—or some such title—I don't remember just what. Maybe it is "25 Years Among the Indians," or maybe "25 Years in the Rocky Mountains." But the name of the *author* will guide you. I think he has written only the one book; & so any librarian can tell you the title of it.
>
> I want several other *personal narratives* of life & adventure out yonder on the Plains & in the Mountains, if you can run across them.—especially life *among the Indians*. Send what you can find. I mean to take Huck Finn out there.
> [*Crossed out:* Send me Washington Irving's]
> Yrs truly
> S L Clemens
>
> (Webster, 264–65)

In Dodge's *Thirty Three Years Among Our Wild Indians*, Twain would have found passages to confirm his theme such as:

Cooper and some other novelists knew nothing of Indian character and customs when they placed their heroines prisoners in their hands. I believe I am perfectly safe in the assertion that there is not a single wild tribe of Indians in all the wide territory of the United States which does not regard the person of the female captive as the inherent right of the captor; and I venture to assert further that, with the single exception of the lady captured by the Nez Percés, under Joseph, in Yellowstone Park, no woman has, in the last thirty years, been taken prisoner by any wild Indians who did not as soon after as practicable, become a victim to the brutality of every one of the party of her captors. (Dodge, 529)

After the boys have seen the murderous results of a sneak attack by Indians, Huck says:

"Tom, where did you learn about Injuns—how noble they was, and all that?"

He give me a look that showed me I had hit him hard, very hard, and so I wished I hadn't said the words. He turned away his head, and after about a minute he said "Cooper's novels," and didn't say anything more, and I didn't say anything more, and so that changed the subject. I see he didn't want to talk about it, and was feeling bad, so I just let it just rest there, not ever having any disposition to fret or worry any person. (Blair, ed., *Hannibal, Huck and Tom*, 109)

Thus Tom's credulity about literature and Huck's unillusioned pragmatism could have continued in the Territory, with American targets. Frequently in this period Twain attacks a belief in literary models or in perceiving the world as if it were shaped by fiction.

In addition, a related metafictional concern appears in both published and unpublished works of the *Huck* period and in works spanning Twain's career. Two short fictions, "The Story of the Bad Little Boy" (1865) and "The Story of the Good Little Boy" (1870), parody the Sunday School moralistic literature as well as they epitomize a thematic opposition. In *Innocents Abroad*, we recall that Twain concluded a "beautiful" and conventional description of Marseilles by joking: "[Copyright secured according to law.]," effectively warning of the tendency of guidebooks to plagiarize and mockingly shifting the rhapsodic tone. In *Roughing It*, we find a serial romance composed by different authors and an illegible Horace Greeley letter surrounded by five attempts to interpret it.

At least two endings of his other fictions have a metafictional twist. *The Gilded Age* includes an appendix explaining that Laura's father was not found, despite the conventions of novels. And the opening of *The American Claimant* declares:

> No weather will be found in this book. This is an attempt to pull a book through without weather. It being the first attempt of the kind in fictitious literature, it may prove a failure, but it seemed worth the while of some daredevil person to try it, and the author was in just the mood. (vii)

But Twain thoughtfully includes an Appendix, "Weather for use in this book" (230–31) which the reader may use to "help himself from time to time as he goes along." Similarly, in a note about the short story "Those Extraordinary Twins" and the novel *Pudd'nhead Wilson*, Twain informs the reader that he killed off extra characters by dropping them down a well and finally stopped because the well was getting full. This ability to belittle conventional expectations of the reader increasingly amused Twain. Several works, such as "A Medieval Romance" and an inset story about a lap-robe in *Following the Equator*, tease the reader's expectations by building up to a suspenseful conclusion and then refusing to conclude. Perhaps the most unconventional metafictional trickery occurs in *A Connecticut Yankee*, itself in part a distant burlesque of Sir Thomas Malory's *La Morte d'Arthur*, which includes two portions of a medieval newspaper (complete with numerous deliberate printing-house errors). One portion has the main column bordered by uneven typesetting which suggests the reader's peripheral vision of the texts beside the column.

Thus Twain's liberated attitude toward the conventions of fiction and of textuality itself enabled him to write highly imaginative, unconventional satires. The common literature of his day was, in fact, one of his subjects, and he turned his wit and uncommon common sense loose upon the material. The mere status of something simply being a text seemed to attract his satiric attention. Perhaps Clemens's early printing-house experiences contributed to his ability to regard literature as an object, a thing, a product, a certain number of lines of type rather than solely as a visual representation of words or ideas. We can speculate that some subscription purchasers of *Huck* read this well-illustrated book about a semi-literate boy's adventures with a sense of identification, while some more sophisticated readers might appreciate the parodic elements.

III

But Twain's thoughts about literacy were neither limited to familial and financial concerns nor restricted to the parodic and metafictional. As an author attempting to make a living by writing, Twain also had a keen interest in all matters of copyright, ranging from the financial to the philosophical. He quickly noticed fundamental injustices, especially involving theft of literary works by uncompensated reprintings. We may recall that in a letter cited in Chapter 1, Howells promised that Twain's rights would be protected by vigorous actions against reprinters. Moreover, it is useful to remember that Twain suggested facetiously in 1875 that all American property rights ought to be limited to forty-two years, proposing that Americans who own land, factories, or patents should thereby share the financial limitations put on authors. (See "Petition Concerning Copyright" in *Sketches New and Old*.) He realized the massive importance of copyright laws for our national literature and character.

Several major changes happened in the period surrounding 1880–1885. Although America did not have an International copyright agreement prior to 1891, most American publishers in the 1860s and early 1870s followed a system that Henry Holt called "trade courtesy." In this system, an American publisher would usually get a contract with a European author or publisher, pay fees to the author, and assume that other American houses would usually not print competing or pirated editions. But that system eventually broke down. Massive technological improvements led to the invention and production of high-speed, high-volume, more economical printing presses. And because these expensive presses only made money when running, such technology probably had a causative or contributory role. In a mythically Edenic America, there were many high speed printing presses in the Garden. As the Congressional hearings of 1886 revealed, American publishers could and did freely reprint European fiction, not paying any fees to authors or the copyright holders, and pricing the European books very cheaply. This free availability of foreign texts led publishers to reprint popular or mass-appeal books, which were a safe, cheap investment, capitalizing on an in-built cultural veneration for the European. In these circumstances, it was relatively uneconomic for a publisher to take a chance on an unproven or new American author who would, understandably, wish to be paid a fee for his or her book. The suppressive effect of this legal situation upon American literature could be—and was—incalculable.

Moreover, the lack of an International copyright could also work to harm popular American authors both abroad and at home. For example, although Twain gradually became adept at procuring British copyright for his early works, Canadian pirate publishers, such as Belford Brothers who had offices in Toronto and Chicago, could get one copy of the British edition of *Tom Sawyer* and then freely reprint the book in Canada and sell it in Canada and the United States.² Before and while the American Publishing Company edition of *Tom Sawyer* was available for $2.75, there were about eight Canadian editions selling in the U.S. for around 50 cents and 75 cents in paper covers and $1.00 in cloth covers. The Canadian pirates were underselling the creator's legitimate edition! Twain claimed that he lost approximately $5,000 U.S. annually because of this situation. The author's plight seemed likely to worsen. Because of his fame and because of the quality and popularity of his earlier books, the names "Twain" or "Clemens" on a book printed in Canada would make purchasers more willing to buy the book. It is as if the more famous an author becomes, the more probable and profitable piratical publication becomes; the more popular an author becomes, the more he gets robbed.

Although any individual might, in theory, favor "free trade," one can easily imagine how an author would feel if foreign competition had a great price advantage (as much as 27 to 1) and, moreover, nearby foreign manufacturers could also easily, legally, produce the American author's own creation and undersell the author's edition by about a 5-to-1 price differential.

In order to sympathize with Twain's situation as an author attempting to support himself and his family by writing, one need only conjecture what would happen nowadays to any American enterprise that demands originality, such as camera or computer design, or electronic appliance, steel, or scientific production, if a foreign manufacturer could steal the American invention and easily sell the products in the United States. If American retailers could sell European automobiles for 1/27th the price of American designs, while Canadian copies of the U.S. designs would simultaneously sell for about 1/3 of the U.S. builder's price, how long would the American design and manufacture enterprise last? Moreover, if the issue involves not mere machines but the shaping of national values, the formation of cultural norms, should an author be concerned? In Twain's time, the issue involved books about heroes—and also, as he came to realize, the values of the American reading audience.

As may easily be expected, the topic of International copyright occurs often in Twain's letters, appearing at least fifty times in the Howells-Twain correspondence, including thirty-seven times during the period of 1876–1885, while Twain was concerned with *Huck*. But we must move beyond mere statistical information to reveal how radically his notions changed. After learning numerous technicalities about British copyright law, Twain delayed the publication of *Tom* so that he could secure both British and American copyrights. Nevertheless, the lack of International copyright exposed him to Canadian piracy. As indicated, Belford Brothers of Toronto published and sold *Tom* in both Canada and the United States. Moreover, in December of 1876, almost as if calculated to add insult to injury, Belford Brothers inquired about what sums would be required to publish Twain's future *Atlantic* contributions, reminding him that "the law allows us to *pirate* them." Infuriated, Twain urged Howells to find some other magazine in Toronto or Montreal to give advance sheets to, thereby preventing or lessening the value of anticipated future brazen thefts (*Twain-Howells Letters*, Vol 1, 166–67).

Even though he had been victimized by the lack of U.S. participation in an International copyright treaty, Twain considered national literacy as a higher priority. In fact, on October 30, 1880, despite the personal financial injustice, Twain thought the lack of International copyright could work to America's benefit. This altruistic attitude would, however, ultimately change:

My Dear Howells:

Will the proposed treaty protect us (*& effectually*) against Canadian piracy? Because if it doesn't, there is not a single argument in favor of international copyright which a rational American Senate could entertain for a moment. My notions have mightily changed, lately. Under this recent & brand-new system of piracy in New York, this country is being flooded with the best of English literature at prices which make a package of water closet paper seem an "edition de luxe" in comparison. I can buy Macaulay's History, 3 vols., bound, for $1.25. Chambers's Cyclopedia, 15 vols., cloth, for $7.25. (we paid $60), & other English copyrights in proportion; I can buy a lot of the great copyright classics, in paper, at from 3 cents to 30 cents apiece. These things must find their way into the very kitchens & hovels of the country. A generation of this sort of thing ought to make this the most intelligent & the best-read nation in the world. International copyright must becloud this sun & bring on the former darkness and dime-novel reading.

Morally, this is all wrong—governmentally it is all right; for it is the *duty* of governments—& families—to be selfish & look out simply for their own. International copyright would benefit a few English authors, & a lot of American publishers, & be a profound detriment to 20,000,000 Americans; it would benefit a dozen American authors a few dollars a year, & there an end. The real advantages all go to English authors & American publishers.

And even if the treaty *will* kill Canadian piracy, & thus save me an average of $5,000 a year, I'm down on it anyway—& I'd like cussed well to write an article opposing the treaty. Dern England! Such is *my* sentiments.

Yrs Ever

Mark

(*Twain-Howells Letters*, Vol. 1, 334–36)

His concern for national literacy development, his desire that America become "the most intelligent and the best-read nation in the world," is both patriotic and touching. When he wrote this letter, however, Twain had thought that he had discovered his own private protection against the Canadian pirates. As of April 12, 1879, Sam Clemens believed that his use of the nom de plume "Mark Twain" protected even his uncopyrighted work as a trademark would.[3] According to Clemens's perceptions in October 1880, the weak link in the author's legal protection against theft was the Canadian situation. The Belford Brothers of Canada published in all more than twenty editions of Twain's books without paying royalties, almost always underselling the author's editions.

As part of his effort to secure Canadian copyright for *The Prince and the Pauper*, Twain traveled to Montreal in December 1881. On December 8th, he gave a speech to those who attended a banquet in his honor:

> To continue my explanation, I did not come to Canada to commit crime— this time—but to prevent it. I came here to place myself under the protection of the Canadian law and secure a copyright. I have complied with the require-ments of the law; I have followed the instructions of some of the best legal minds in the city, including my own, and so my errand is accomplished, at least so far as any exertions of mine can aid that accomplishment. This is rather a cumbersome way to fence and fortify one's property against the literary buccaneer, it is true; still, if it is effective, it is a great advance upon past conditions, and one to be correspondingly welcomed.
>
> It makes one hope and believe that a day will come when, in the eye of the law, literary property will be as sacred as whiskey, or any other of the necessar-ies of life. In this age of ours, if you steal another man's label to advertise your own brand of whiskey with, you will be heavily fined and otherwise punished for violating that trademark; if you steal the whiskey without the trademark, you go to jail; but if you could prove that the whiskey was literature, you can steal them both, and the law wouldn't say a word. It grieves me to think how far more profound and reverent a respect the law would have for literature if a body could only get drunk on it. Still the world moves; the interests of literature upon our continent are improving; let us be content and wait. (*Mark Twain Speaking*, ed. Fatout, 198)[4]

This speech must have received attention because Edward Eggleston al-ludes to the whiskey comparison in his article on copyright problems for the April 1882, issue of *Century* titled, "The Blessings of Piracy."

On September 21, 1882, in Elmira, New York, Clemens signed a Bill of Complaint against the Belford publishers of Toronto and Chicago. The suit was based on his trademark claim; he believed that, although his *novels* could be piratically printed and sold, the trade name, "Mark Twain," could not be stolen and used without his consent. On January 8, 1883, a negative decision was handed down in Chicago by Judge Henry Williams Blodgett. Blodgett ruled that a trademark could not substitute for a lack of copyright protection. The judge wrote, on page three of his decision, "It does not seem to me that an author or writer has any better or higher right in a *nom de plume*, or assumed name, than he has in his Christian or baptismal name . . ." (M.T.P.)* Twain received a copy of the opinion. Perhaps in an act of combative retribution, Twain's retentive mind demonstrated that the Judge also did not have an exclusive right to *his* name when, in the summer of 1883 while writing what would become the Wilks episode, the author decided that the thieving, sanctimonious king would begin the fraud by naming himself to the yokel: "No, my name's Blodgett—Elexander Blodgett—*Reverend* Elexander Blodgett, I spose I must say, as I'm one o' the Lord's poor servants" (206).

The issue of whether the United States should have a treaty on International copyright had, for Twain, at least three interrelated aspects. Obviously he would make a great deal more money and have much less need to travel if the U.S. simply adopted and enforced such a treaty. Moreover, although an author with Twain's sophistication, financial resources, and ability to travel could attempt to protect himself, most ordinary American authors, such as E. W. Howe, could not. In 1883, for example, an American author wishing to protect his or her copyright should arrange the following in rapid succession: register the title in the United States, publish the book with one set of plates in England, publish with another set of plates in America, and publish with a third set of plates in Canada within ten days of the British publication while "residing" in Canada. (Obviously "residence" and "domicile" could be more topics for wrangling lawyers and judges.) As many as three lawyers could be involved in these elaborate, and presumably quite costly, procedures. Only with such a procedure could an American author protect the "rights" in what he "writes" against "pirates" eager to steal his individually created "royalties."

A second aspect involved the effect upon the American reading public of the cheap, European literature that was widely pirated. The financial and philosophical "values" of the mass audience could be affected. Because European literature with its relatively higher status was cheaper to produce and to purchase, American readers would have to pay relatively more for American and less for European books. The prices would rise for European books only if an International copyright treaty became law; a higher price would be demanded for foreign books only if American publishers had to pay royalties to European authors and publishers. Consequently American publishers would only then be relatively more willing to publish American authors.

Twain had miscalculated the third aspect; it involved which European books the American audience would purchase. Although Twain picked Macaulay's *History* and similarly edifying books, the mass of other readers did not. With all due attention to the thematic continuity with the king and duke, at this point it is not too much to imagine that in the Phelps farm episode the fictional conflict shifts to present a dramatic opposition of American values versus European values, of the American literary profession and pragmatism versus European stratification. One could consider that in the Phelps section a new protagonist appears, a relatively defenseless youth; let us call him or her "American Literature." Two related questions can stand: What values shall American readers pick? How difficult is it for an American author to make a living by selling his or her books?

Let us imagine momentarily that we have walked into a bookstore in the 1880s, in order to contrast the list prices for several American and foreign books, recalling that the then less canonized *Adventures of Tom Sawyer* sold originally on a subscription basis for $2.75 and that *Huck* would list for $2.75–$4.25. Because this country did not have an International copyright agreement before 1891, American publishers were legally selling scores of European stories at very cheap rates. The literary names associated with two river boats may open the inquiry. Sir Walter Scott's *Ivanhoe*, for example, was available in a 1877 edition for ten cents, an 1881 edition for twenty cents, and an 1883 edition for fifteen cents. In addition to the seven multi-volume sets (priced from 75 cents to $3.50 per book), many works by Scott were available in thirty-nine editions priced at ten, twelve, fifteen, or twenty cents each. And Thomas Moore's *Lalla Rookh* could be purchased for twenty cents. (Some of these piratical firms relied upon aquatic names with positive sophisticated connotations for their cheap "Library" series: Seaside, Lakeside, and Riverside.) Because some piratical publishers produced at least one book each week in order to qualify for the cheaper periodical postage rates, the situation was unlikely to improve.

It is significant that Tom Sawyer, who controlled Huck through pirate and robber books in the first several chapters, has developed an exclusive preference for European literature by the middle of the Phelps episode. At one point he contemptuously says to Huck, "Why, hain't you ever read any books at all? Baron Trenck, nor Casanova, nor Benvenuto Chelleeny, ***nor***

Henri IV, nor none of them heroes?" (MS, 556). Baron von Trenck's two-volume story could be purchased in the 1880s for ten cents each; Cellini's story would have cost fifty cents. Anthologies of European literature, such as one that Alan Gribben informs us Twain owned, *Wonderful Escapes, revised from the French of F. Bernard with Original Chapters Added* (which included Von Trenck, Casanova, Cellini, and many others) ran $1.50. Tom's other readings, such as *Count of Monte Cristo* (20 cents) and Saintine's *Picciola* (50 cents), were also relatively inexpensive. Twain's contemptuous 1880 phrase about "dime novel reading" could by 1883 be applied to standard literature about European heroes.

But was the entire issue of a lack of International copyright only an issue of the 1880s? Would it be a blatant anachronism to place the problem back in time to the 1845 era, when Huck and Tom were being formed and deformed by their reading? No. Twain could have learned by reading "Two Letters on International Copyright, The Question Forty Years Ago" in the March 1882 *Century*. The portion reprints a letter from Harriet Martineau dated December 24, 1843, lamenting the loss to British authors caused by American reprinting, followed by P. A. Towne's January 1882 clear, vehement letter emphasizing the moral outrage of publishing "pirated" texts with impunity and insisting on the "universal recognition of the right of an author to the product of his labor." If Twain needed any encouragement to have the issue affect Tom and Huck in the fictional time of 1845, the two letters could remind Twain about the duration and, by implication, the scope and seriousness of the problem.[5]

Perhaps the printing of the Martineau letter prompted Twain to consider resuming work on Huck's story. And Twain's creative mind received another goad, a request which amounted to an insult! The American firm Funk and Wagnalls sent a letter to Twain's Hartford home on April 13, 1883. Thus, shortly before his summer of great creative achievement, Twain received what must have seemed a provocative, discourteous invitation. The firm's stationary proclaimed its publication of twelve books, six of which were religious. Moreover, the letterhead also boasted that the company printed *The Homiletic Monthly*, "read by nearly all the Clergy in America." The letter invited Twain to give a book to a projected series of works by twelve representative American authors. The books would be priced at twenty-five cents each, "the price of reprints of foreign books in the 'Libraries,'"* the low-cost series. But the proposed royalty terms were relatively meager, offering only two cents per copy sold in paper bindings and ten percent in cloth. If Twain even briefly entertained thoughts of joining this project, his partially completed Huck story might come to mind as a convenient candidate because the firm requested a book of about 80,000 words and a delivery date of January 1, 1884. But other parts of the letter absolutely would have offended Twain. This series was to include at least one author Twain did not respect, John Habberton. Furthermore, the letter was not even signed by one or both of the owners but by a functionary, "Funk and Wagnalls per B."* Overall this invitation almost seemed designed not to honor Twain, but to insult; certainly the invitation to join the series, and thereby to submerge his individuality, reveals the difficulty of the situation and the resulting shabby treatment of American authors. Twain wrote on the envelope, "Not answered" (M.T.P.)*; but, in a way, the entire Phelps episode represents his individual, creative, humorous, sarcastic, nationalistic answer to the situation.

The issue of International copyright occupied a good deal of Twain's time during 1883 and 1884. During his collaboration with W. D. Howells on an ultimately unsuccessful play, "Colonel Sellers as a Scientist," Twain inserted the following dialogue as a reporter named Suckers interviews the crazed pretender to a British earldom, Colonel Sellers:

> *Suckers: "Colonel Sellers, shall you favor the International Copyright Treaty in the House of Lords?"*
> *Colonel Sellers: "No sir! The American people demand cheap literature, and they shall have it if they have to steal it. Let the English authors look out for themselves.* (typescript p. 78, originally numbered A-15. Page numbers indicating an insertion are visible in M.T.P. typescript.)*

Twain received at least ten letters during the 1880s touching upon the topic of copyright protection, ranging from requests for advice from neophyte authors to newspaper clippings praising his cleverness in owning his own publishing house. Charles Dudley Warner wrote a long letter-essay in favor of International copyright to George P. Lathrop, had the letter printed, and sent a copy to Twain on January 12, 1884. Twain wrote on the envelope, "Concerning International Copyright" (M.T.P.).* A letter from George P. Lathrop to John Hayes (March 1, 1884) urges Hayes to get the Ohio delegation to support the bill favored by the American Copyright League. In the letter, Lathrop reveals that he had "declined Clemens's proposition to pay me a salary by combined effort" (M.T.P.).*

On January 28 and 29, 1886, Sam Clemens attended and testified at a Senate hearing on the problem. The testimony of Henry Holt established that prior to about 1875 "it was the rule for all American publishers to respect the contracts which any of them made with foreign authors, and not to print a rival edition to any book printed under such contract." But that system, called "trade courtesy," broke down with the "rapid appearance in the market, some ten or twelve years ago, of cheap rival editions of most successful books not protected by law." In the full transcript of the hearings one finds repeated images of "piracy," of America as "the Barbary coast of literature," and of "stolen fruit" underselling legitimate native products.

One other part of the emerging argument deserves particular attention. At one point James Russell Lowell testified in front of Clemens:

> . . . Of course, one can not generalize from a few instances which have come within his own knowledge or under his observation; but I know there are instances of people who have been overheard talking on the subject, as, for instance, in Boston, where they have book-stalls at the railway stations, and this is what has been observed: A person will come to the book-stall and take up a book of Howells's or Clemens's or some other author, and ask, "How much is this?" The reply is, "It is so much." Next to it will be a cheaper reprint of an English novel, very likely worthless, but he will buy that because it only costs 25 cents. (Testimony given on January 29, 1886. Report 622, Part 2, 48)

Twain certainly realized that he was being robbed of his "rights" by cheap Canadian reprints of his works: moreover, the same kind of legal loopholes were permitting American publishers to compete unfairly against his books by "pirating" European best sellers and "standards" without paying "royalties." This financial-ethical morass presumably underlies the authorial disgust behind an early passage:

> And he made every one of them tell him a tale every night; and he kept that up till he had hogged a thousand and one tales that way, and then he got out a copyright, and published them all in a book, and called it Domesday book— *which was a good name, and stated the case.* Of course most any publisher would do that, but you wouldn't think a king would. (MS, 200)

Thus some publishers could be placed in a category below "kings." And, intriguingly, the words he used satirically in the novel, "piracy" and "royalty," possessed secondary meanings relevant to literature. But Twain certainly saw much more than simply his own financial interests involved. The Congressional testimony included the devastatingly suppressive effect of cheap reprints of foreign works upon American authors. Why should an American publisher take a gamble on a book by an unknown American author, who might desire money, when esteemed European stories could be printed for only production costs?

How did Twain's contemporaries see the issue? Was Twain's interest only a selfish concern? Did others think of the situation as serious? Or did Twain distort his novel to include a minor issue? In 1886, the esteemed *Century* magazine printed forty-four open letters from American authors on International copyright, titling the section, "Plain Speech from American Authors" (XXXI, 627–34). The listing, in alphabetical order, includes most contemporary lights, including many of Twain's friends; his own essay is the longest. This highly selective but representative sampling indicates how his contemporaries assessed the problem, and one may infer that some would have read the concluding section of *Huck* with an almost automatic comprehension of analogies and meanings that would "escape" later readers. Lyman Abbott sets the context:

> We protect by our legislation every form of industry except that of the brain; the industry of the brain we subject to an unequal competition. The American author, in order to secure the publication of his book, must not only write a good one, but he must write one so much better than any that a foreign author can write, that the publisher can better afford to pay him for the privilege of publishing it than to publish his competitor's book for nothing. This system is dwarfing American literature, and would have done much to destroy it, if it had not been nurtured and kept alive by our popular periodicals.

Such a patriotic concern also appeared important to the president of Cornell University, C. K. Adams:

> Our present methods are disheartening to all authorship in America, and, consequently, we can never have an adequate national literature as long as foreign works are reprinted and sold in this country for next to nothing.

Interestingly, several authors saw an ethical similarity of oppression between prejudice, slavery, and the lack of authors' rights. Because Dr. Edward Eggleston was in Europe, the editors of *Century* reprinted part of his essay "The Blessings of Piracy" from their April 1882, issue:

> It is a disgrace that the law-makers of America will have to bear, that men of letters in this late age should have to persuade reluctant legislators to give, through an intricate diplomacy, a partial protection from pillage to the productions of brain-labor, that ought to stand on the common footing of all property. The nineteenth century is drawing toward its close while yet Jews in Russia and writers in America are alike excluded from the equality before the law accorded to other classes.

Similarly, Frederick Douglass thought:

Whatever by mind or by muscle, by thought or by labor, a man may have produced, whether it shall be useful or ornamental, instructive or amusing, whether book, plow, or picture, the said producer has in it a right of property superior to that of any other person at home or abroad.

And Frances Hodgson Burnett recognized that in "an age which recognizes in so many other ways the liberty of the individual," the lack of copyright protection "is but a remnant of those barbaric times when physical strength was the sole basis of right, and government only an organized power of oppression."

Several of Twain's acquaintances, such as Howells, George Washington Cable, Edmund Clarence Stedman, Brander Matthews, and Charles Dudley Warner, also offered statements about the complexity of this issue. Bill Nye thought about the issue in terms of the influence upon native values and literacy with compounding sarcasms:

> If foreign work is to be the cheapest here, and if that is to become the universal principle, what is to be the result? Is it not perfectly plain that as the literature of the age begins to show its effects upon those who read it, and as every one will naturally buy and read what he can get the cheapest throughout the civilized world, every one will read the works of foreign authors, and at last, as the reader partakes of this foreign literature and becomes more and more impregnated with it, will he not become at last a foreigner himself? That is the great question underlying International Copyright. It is a question whether we shall or shall not become not only a nation of foreigners, but a universe of foreigners. The only safe way, in order to remain a native, will be to refrain from learning to read. Of course there will be advantages connected with being foreigners here in America. We should have more political influence for one thing, and there would be other minor advantages, but not sufficient to counterbalance the disadvantages. (631–32)

Concern for the youth of the country seems paramount to John Boyle O'Reilly, who also touches on another familiar Twainian theme:

> For the sake of American writers and American readers the cheap pirated editions of foreign books should be stopped. No element is stronger than literature (*i.e.*, the novel and the drama) in the forming and cementing of a native social life. It is probable that ninety per cent. of the stories and plays offered the American people to-day are European in study or suggestion. Young people here are learning to make ideals of men and women and ways far removed from their own country. This has already gone so far that many American writers are induced to depict a bastard aristocracy here; and this in turn is becoming the ideal social order of a large class of American readers.
> This is not more lamentable than the wretched condition in which our

> professional *litterateurs* are left through the cheap reprints and translations of European books. While all kinds of trade and material interests are protected, the literary man, the most defenseless and surely one of the most precious possessions of the country, is literally robbed and disregarded. (632)

Although Twain emphasizes the false qualities of his "bastard" aristocrats, the king and duke, Tom does honor the European social order. If the Phelps episode does satirize Europeanized American readers, and if those who read *Huck* become thereafter impatient with books like *The Man in the Iron Mask*, then we could recognize another, quite unintended meaning within Hemingway's famous pronouncement that, "all modern American literature comes from one book by Mark Twain called *Huckleberry Finn*."

Charles G. Leland's conception of the issue apparently combined several intellectual complaints and also resembled Twain's:

> I am familiar with all the arguments which have been advanced in favor of refusing a copyright to foreign authors, and it seems to me that when they are not disgraceful in dishonesty, they are simply silly in their sophistry. We are struck by the infamous meanness of the *droit d'aubaine* by which a century ago all the personal effects of strangers dying in France were taken by the king. We, more ingenious, rob the author of his property on a far greater scale at a distance, without waiting for his death. There are few great nations which have not one crying infamy to disgrace them. England has the opium trade; we have had two. The first, slavery, we have abolished; the meaner and pettier outrage against the rights of a class we still retain. For all these wrongs there is retribution; and if inordinate national vanity did not blind us to the fact, we might see that our Nemesis is already overtaking us. It is not long since an American publisher wrote to me that there is a rapidly growing dislike in "the trade" to publish "literary" works by American authors, or anything, in fact, in which a large and certain sale could not be secured at little outlay. It is not the best intellectual training for a people to be confined to educational and technological books, or even magazines and newspapers, eked out by foreign pilferings. All of this, even if disseminated by millions at a cent a volume, will not make sound thinkers or cultivated minds. The average American believes, of course, that we "whip all creation" in poetry, philosophy, fiction, and art; but it is not true. Our position as respects these branches is creditable; in fact, it is remarkable considering the circumstances; but it is *very* far from being commensurate to our advance in what are foolishly called "practical" matters. And this backwardness is chiefly due to the absence of an International Copyright law. It was said of old that when the serpent devoured the brood of another, her own young died within her, and we are carrying out the simile in full. (631)

Again, the equivalence of America's two cases of "crying infamy," slavery and authors' rights, is related to their harmful effect upon the young.

Twain's own forthright, emphatic analysis in *Century* reveals how much his opinion had changed since 1880, how well he understood the issue, and how pungently and sarcastically he could phrase it. The 1886 statement also indicates how tightly interrelated were his ideas about American nationalism, American education, the formative effect of reading, the evil of novels, and the folly of inherited nobility. As it happens, Twain also includes a variant of his crucial, familiar phrase—"kings and dukes and earls." The passage certainly reveals what Huck was combating in the Phelps episode and how Tom had been victimized—poisoned and corrupted—by his reading:

> No one denies the foreign author's simple moral right to property in the product of his brain; so we may waive that feature and look at non-existent International Copyright from a combined business and statesmanship point of view, and consider whether the nation gains or loses by the present condition of the thing.
>
> As for the business aspect, a great argument of politicians is that our people get foreign books at a cheap rate. Most unfortunately for the country, that is true: we do get cheap alien books—and not of one kind only. We get all kinds—and they are distributed and devoured by the nation strictly in these proportions: an ounce of wholesome literature to a hundred tons of noxious. The ounce represents the little editions of the foreign masters in science, art, history, and philosophy required and consumed by our people; the hundred tons represent the vast editions of foreign novels consumed here—including the welcome semiannual inundation from Zola's sewer.
>
> Is this an advantage to us? It certainly is, if poison is an advantage to a person; or if to teach one thing at the hearthstone, the political hustings, and in a nation's press, and teach the opposite in the books the nation reads is profitable; or, in other words, if to hold up a national standard for admiration and emulation half of each day, and a foreign standard the other half, is profitable. The most effective way to train an impressible young mind and establish for all time its standards of fine and vulgar, right and wrong, and good and bad, is through the imagination; and the most insidious manipulator of the imagination is the felicitously written romance. The statistics of any public library will show that of every hundred books read by our people, about seventy are novels—and nine-tenths of them foreign ones. They fill the imagination with an unhealthy fascination for foreign life, with its dukes and earls and kings, its fuss and feathers, its graceful immoralities, its sugar-coated injustices and oppressions; and this fascination breeds a more or less pronounced dissatisfaction with our country and form of government, and contempt for our republican commonplaces and simplicities; it also breeds longings for something "better," which presently crop out in diseased shams and imitations of the ideal foreign spectacle: Hence the "dude." Thus we have this curious spectacle: American statesmen glorifying American nationality, teaching it, preaching it, urging it, building it up—with their mouths; and undermining it and pulling it down with their acts. This is to employ an Indian nurse to suckle your child, and expect it not to drink in the Indian nature with the

milk. It is to go Christian-missionarying with infidel tracts in your hands. Our average young person reads scarcely anything but novels; the citizenship and morals and predilections of the rising generation of America are largely under foreign training by foreign teachers. This condition of things is what the American statesman thinks it wise to protect and preserve—by refusing International Copyright, which would bring the national teacher to the front and push the foreign teacher to the rear. We do get cheap books through the absence of International Copyright; and any who will consider the matter thoughtfully will arrive at the conclusion that these cheap books are the costliest purchase that ever a nation made.[6]

Just as the king and duke embody the "shams and imitations," undoubtedly Tom, "an average young person," dramatizes such a poisoned imagination. Huck, because of his inferior, newer literacy, has a difficult struggle with the domination of European authorities and alien values. Significantly, in the Phelps episode, Tom does not imitate any named example of American fiction.[7] I suggest that Twain's way of fighting the danger of a "felicitously written romance" was to write a novel, set in America, which was simultaneously an adventure story and a self-qualifying parody of an adventure story. Furthermore, he wrote a book which is itself capable of self-transformation.

The Phelps section of the novel has been criticized for a variety of reasons. Critics have judged Tom to be tiresome, regarding him as if he were an "insidious manipulator." Critics also consider the behavior of the boys toward Jim's imprisonment demeaning. Moreover, the "Evasion" is regarded as too long. Many people object that Huck gives over control of the situation to Tom. Bernard DeVoto has accurately called the last section the "most chilling descent" (*Mark Twain at Work*, 92) and Leo Marx has said—brilliantly and persuasively—that the Phelps section "undercuts" the novel. But much of this anger, disgust, and disappointment should be focused not upon the author but upon his important target, the American tendency to revere European literature. In a way, Jim's liberation from the bonds of slavery can be paralleled with Twain's struggle to free the formation of Americans' imaginations from European bookish expectations.

IV

With knowledge about Twain's interests in literacy and copyright in mind, we can explore a new interpretation with special attention to the problem of the "failure" at the novel's end. *Adventures of Huckleberry Finn* presents a unified story of a minimally literate boy attempting to deal with a society which defines itself and exerts control through literacy and through books. Three framing incidents that occur outside the novel may be cited: in *Tom Sawyer*, Tom teaches Huck to sign his name; in "Huck Finn and Tom Sawyer Among the Indians," Huck pointedly asks Tom where he got his ideas about the nobility of Indians while the boys are staring at a massacre scene; and in *Tom Sawyer Abroad*, Huck and Jim debate Tom about the nature of a metaphor.

Most people have had the experience of being controlled or dominated by people who have read more books, or other books, or particular important books. Huck struggles to apply what he is told about reality from the books, and he learns that the books can be deceptive or unreliable. In this novel, which many Americans persist in considering somehow non-literary, the words "*book*" or "*books*" occur forty-nine times; in addition, many specific book titles receive mention. We encounter the Bible, *Pilgrim's Progress*, *Romeo and Juliet*, *Richard III*, *Hamlet*, *King Lear*, and various European histories or romances. Moreover, each of these titles is actually relevant to a part of *Huck*, which usually duplicates the action in a cruder, non-elevated fashion. The literary references simply become more outrageous in the Phelps farm episode as Tom Sawyer uses authors as authorities to gain power for his own authoritarian personality. He slavishly follows the authors, imposing his own authorial role, implicating Huck and himself in the reenslavement of Jim.

Huck's minimal literacy involves both his reading and his writing. The familiar opening, "You don't know about me without you have read a book by the name of 'The Adventures of Tom Sawyer,' but that ain't no matter. That book was made by Mr. Mark Twain, and he told the truth mainly, . . ." insists upon its own textuality, at the same time calculatedly, stridently pointing out the privileged status of books and yet calling into question their essential truthfulness, while usefully summarizing the earlier book. Thus the book begins by presenting itself as a self-conscious fiction, a story with a reflexive dimension.

Widow Douglas relies on the Bible to dominate Huck; Miss Watson employs the spelling book; Tom Sawyer uses, at the beginning, robber and pirate books; and later Huck can contrast Tom's bookish notions with real robbers on the *Walter Scott* and with the king posing as a pirate at the camp meeting. Huck's narrative actually spans the time of his initiation into semi-literacy:

> Well, three or four months run along, and it was well into the winter, now. I had been to school most of the time, and could spell, and read, and write just a little, and could say the multiplication table up to six times seven is thirty-five,

and I don't reckon I could ever get any further than that if I was to live forever. I don't take no stock in mathematics, any way. (34)

Even by this point readers can realize, with gratitude, that Huck's developing verbal skills surpass his mathematical ability.

When Pap Finn appears, he promptly questions Huck about this new ability to read—even before he asks about money. How did it feel to an author to write such a tirade against literacy? Pap threatens:

> "I'll take you down a peg before I get done with you. You're educated, too, they say; can read and write. You think you're better'n your father, now don't you, because he can't? I'll take it out of you. . . .
>
> "And looky here—you drop that school, you hear? I'll learn people to bring up a boy to put on airs over his own father and let on to be better 'n what *he* is. You lemme catch you fooling around that school again, you hear? Your mother couldn't read, and she couldn't write, nuther, before she died. None of the family couldn't, before *they* died. *I* can't; and here you're a-swelling yourself up like this. I ain't the man to stand it—you hear? Say—lemme hear you read."
>
> I took up a book and begun something about General Washington and the wars. When I'd read about half a minute, he fetched the book a whack with his hand and knocked it across the house. (40)

Pap uses primarily the words of an oral culture, "you hear?" He demands oral proof of Huck's ability, and the nationalistic symbolism of the passage Huck happens to read could not be more obvious. As it turns out, Pap Finn's murderers are literate enough to scrawl on the walls of the murder site what his more literate son calls "the ignorantest kind of words and pictures."

Huck's efforts to accommodate himself to the literate society comprise one significant *agon*, and his misperception of his failure to communicate creates tinges of discomfort. After Huck has "killed himself" to escape from his father, he floats down the river:

> I was pretty tired, and the first thing I knowed, I was asleep. When I woke up I didn't know where I was, for a minute. I set up and looked around, a little scared. Then I remembered. The river looked miles and miles across. The moon was so bright I could a counted the drift logs that went a slipping along, black and still, hundreds of yards out from shore. Everything was dead quiet, and it looked late, and *smelt* late. You know what I mean—I don't know the words to put it in. (58)

Despite such splendid control of sentence length and particular sensory details to convey confusion, the boy assumes that his synaesthetic description fails.

After getting books from the wreck of the *Walter Scott* and reading to

Jim, Huck feels awed by the literacy of the Grangerford home and devotes most of a paragraph to listing their titles. He samples the books, giving his semi-literate opinions, and even admits trying to imitate Emmeline Grangerford's poetry. At the episode's conclusion, a note in a Bible starts a sequence of killings.

When the king and duke appear, they also assert situational dominance based on "birth" and literacy, practicing distortions of Shakespeare and using a printing press to create a poster branding Jim as an escaped slave. Printed notices of their shows manipulate the townspeople, and old Boggs takes his last breath under the crushing weight of a large Bible. Later, during the Wilks episode, Huck swears falsely on a dictionary. After the lawyer tricks the duke into writing a letter revealing that he is not the genuine brother, tension increases. Toward the episode's conclusion, Huck's life could end if the dead man has the three letters "P-B-W" on his chest. And Huck does not even know that he wanders within an episode that parodies *King Lear*.

Because much critical complaint focuses upon the re-introduction of Tom Sawyer after the moral dignity of Huck's refusal to inform on Jim, our attention may turn to the passages which lead up to Tom's reappearance. Why did Twain permit Tom to return to the world of the novel? The transition can be examined, keeping equally present in our minds a sense of Twain's composing habits, his relatively aleatory plotting, and his consistent thematic concerns. After Huck learns that the king has sold Jim into slavery, he feels depressed and disillusioned. What can Huck do in this situation? Twain explored:

> Once I said *to myself* it would be a thousand times better for Jim to be a slave at home where his family was, as long as he'd got to be a slave, and so I'd better write a letter to Tom Sawyer and tell him to tell Miss Watson where he was. But I soon give up that notion, for two things. . . . (MS, 436–37)

The thought process characteristically begins with sympathy and sensitivity to Jim's situation. For these purposes Huck turned for help not directly to Miss Watson but to the boy in the town he admired, his companion in earlier adventures. Just as Miss Watson represented religion, Tom had earlier represented pirate and robber books. (At some level of Twain's mind, words such as "pirate" and "robber" might well have connected with the copyright issue.) In addition, Tom had read *Don Quixote* but had apparently understood only the "adventures," misreading totally the pervasive criticism of literary illusions. We should recall that in *Life on the Mississippi*, Chapter XLVI Twain wrote a harsh tirade against "the Sir

Walter Disease." In his categorical criticism of the shams, Twain mentions the "Northern or Southern literary periodical of forty or fifty years ago" (469), stating that the North has "thrown out that old inflated style," while to its great disadvantage, the South has clung to the Scott style. Twain concludes this cultural criticism by stating:

> A curious exemplification of the power of a single book for good or harm is shown in the effects wrought by Don Quixote and those wrought by Ivanhoe. The first swept the world's admiration for the mediaeval chivalry-silliness out of existence; and the other restored it. As far as our South is concerned, the good work done by Cervantes is pretty nearly a dead letter, so effectually has Scott's pernicious work undermined it. (470)

Given the circumstances in American publishing in 1882–83, Twain may have decided to re-open the battle. Should Twain create and introduce an entirely new character who represents American youth corrupted by European literature? Recalling Tom's name and his particular bossy style to the authorial mind probably allowed options to percolate. By summoning Tom Sawyer to the South, Twain could mock the coincidences of the adventure genre and could also comment reflexively upon his own regional background and growth as well as his own literary creations.

Twain had already used opportunities for satire on religion (Miss Watson and the Reverends Blodgett and Wilks); mild satire on literature (Tom) had been scattered throughout the novel. Perhaps on some lost holograph pages Huck wrote to Tom while Twain imaginatively explored the possibility of re-involving Tom in the action. Because the surviving MS pages 437–448C have many copy pages within the sequence and run, in total, about three pages more than the earlier version, we cannot now determine conclusively whether Huck once wrote to Tom.

But Tom at a distance would certainly cause several problems: the epistolary mode would receive another complication if Huck reports his writing and Tom's responses. Tom probably could not tell Miss Watson anything simply; instead he would have to elbow his way into the situation, exaggerating and grandstanding. The need to wait for replies would shackle Huck to one place for an indeterminate time. Intercepted or lost letters could provide plot complications but divert from the action. If Huck could read Tom's plans or advice in letters, he would either have to follow or to ignore the written words. The conflict or debate would lose dramatic tension in letter form. Moreover, any involvement of Tom at a distance would of necessity dilute or break Huck's point of view, one of the novel's strengths. The conflict could be better realized by having Tom on the scene, representing his values in person, scheming, strutting, bossing, condescending, lording his literacy over everyone. Huck's debate with himself and his decision to go to hell on MS, 441 et seq. may have occurred as a revision away from earlier pages in which Huck wrote directly to Tom.

When Twain wrote the death-in-life passage describing the Phelps farm, he probably had Tom's reappearance someplace in mind because the mood and description duplicate Huck's feelings in Chapter I just before Tom appears. Certainly Twain knew what turn his plot would take when Aunt Sally greets Huck by saying:

> "It's Tom!—ain't it?"
> I out with a "Yes'm," before I thought. (MS, 468)

But the identification had already served its purpose for Twain's mind because thereafter he could build suspense once he knew where he was going. For the printed version, however, Twain decided to conceal by having Aunt Sally say simply, "It's *you*, at last!—*ain't* it?" (279). The suspense builds as she identifies Huck to the children as "cousin Tom." Consequently, when the tension mounts to:

> "Who is it?"
> "It's Tom Sawyer!"
> By jingo, I most slumped through the floor. (MS, 484)

The surprised reader easily identifies with Huck's emotion. By plotting to such an outrageous coincidence, easily accepted in *Gil Blas* or the typical *Adventures of . . .* fiction, Twain could explore significant material with an established character. In psychological terms, Huck becomes the boy he most admires; for literary purposes, the book gains another—perhaps most important—target for satire.

This coincidence and transformation will permit Huck to explore an identity that comes with social acceptance; the Bad Little Boy with a sound heart can drop his outcast status and temporarily become integrated into society. In fact, Huck can soon become Tom under Tom's guidance. The doubling of deceivers of the Phelps family will include one boy who believes in literature and, in contrast, one boy whom we know to be enormously imaginative and inventively practical. The two boys represent an opposed pair of enemy-brothers, with the degree of literacy and the belief in literary authorities as the main differences between them. Tom comes to symbolize complicity without commitment to—or compassion for—Jim. Because Tom in the Phelps section has become totally transformed by the "felicitously written romances" he relies upon, his character seems irritating, aggravating, contemptible. He is, moreover, quite willing to impose gratuitous evil upon Jim and Huck. Tom's willingness to hurt or endanger people for the sheer thrill of it, for the sheer adventure of it, is a not-unlikely definition of pure evil. Tom represents an average American boy who has become a Europeanized victim of the cheap fiction. Unlike Jim, a physical slave of his color, Tom's enslavement is mental, literary. Twain presents Tom's personality by using repetition and comic exaggeration to provoke the reader's contempt and disgust. Huck comes to represent non-literary nativist common sense trammeled or shackled by Tom's literary precedents. Can Huck free himself of Tom's influence?

Could what Tom Sawyer would be able to do to Jim and Huck resemble in any way what the reprint houses were doing to America and American literature? Clearly both Tom and the reprinters imposed foreign values, while stealing both time and labor. Consequently, because of a generally unquestioned higher status attributed by Tom and the reprinters—and by too many American buyers—to European values, one free adult, Jim, could be reimprisoned—relegated to an entirely unjust inferior status—while the youthful Huck could be controlled or enslaved by Tom's reading. Moreover, the longer the parody can be strung out, the more effectively the American readers, young and old, can be reminded about how long, unrealistic, and tedious most of the targeted European books really are.

But potential problems exist; would a parody be regarded as a liberating revelation of the targets' conventions and limits or as a pointless or decadent imitation? Could a parody be used to destroy the targets and to break conventional expectations? Or would it be misunderstood? Can parody be used to question the arts of fictions and the acts of reading and writing?

In a later letter to Brander Matthews, Twain recorded his experience of reading Scott. His reactions seem to bear an uncanny resemblance to how critics have evaluated the Phelps episode:

> Brander, I lie here dying, slowly dying, under the blight of Sir Walter. I have read the first volume of *Rob Roy*, and as far as Chapter XIX of *Guy Mannering*, and I can no longer hold my head up nor take my nourishment. Lord, it's all so juvenile! so artificial, so shoddy; and such wax figures and skeletons and spectres. Interest? Why, it is impossible to feel an interest in these bloodless

shams, these milk-and-water humbugs. And oh, the poverty of the invention! Not poverty in inventing situations, but poverty in furnishing reasons for them. Sir Walter usually gives himself away when he arranges for a situation—elaborates, and elaborates, and elaborates, till if you live to get to it you don't believe in it when it happens. (Jensen, *Mark Twain's Comments*, 17)

The extensive "elaboration" of the Phelps farm section may have been appropriate to Twain's perceptions of the targeted European novels.

Twain probably did not realize at the time of this plot development that the chance to burlesque literary adventures could actually become a unifying, all-inclusive parodic theme. Upon reflection, we realize that both inherited nobility and conventional Christianity intrude their influence into Huck's world primarily by books read by Tom Sawyer and Miss Watson, with the king and duke providing a ludicrous contrapuntal accompaniment. Accordingly, the attempt to liberate Huck from deference to Tom and his European authorities constitutes a battle of national importance.

A brief struggle for control of the plot occurs early in the Phelps episode when Huck and Tom both create plans to free Jim. The values of another literary convention briefly shape the discovery process as Tom says:

"—I'm glad we found it out detective fashion; I wouldn't give shucks for any other way. Now you sail in and study out a plan to steal Jim, and I'll study out one, ⟨two⟩, *too*; and we'll take the one we like the best." (MS, 527)

At the stage of the first handwritten draft, the two plans could potentially have carried roughly equal importance. Twain's early version has the casual "sail in" for Huck and the correction/insertion of "*too*" to make his plan of approximately equal status. But by the time the novel was set in print, this section was modified to reflect the fact that Tom has already seized control and talks down to Huck, assuming Huck's intellectual inferiority:

"Now you work your mind and study out a plan to steal Jim, and I will study out one, too." (294)

The enthusiasm of "sail" no longer applies to Huck's mind. Instead Tom pictures Huck's mind as something to be worked (a slave? a beast? a machine?), and Tom shifts from the informality of "I'll" to the more formal, more commanding "I will." Because at this point Huck incorrectly venerates Tom's ability, Twain can develop that opinion, within Huck's own tonality, to make Huck's praise of Tom into a partial summary of Huck's book:

> What a head for just a boy to have! If I had Tom Sawyer's head, I wouldn't trade it off to be a duke, or mate of a steamboat. I went to thinking out a plan, but only just to be doing something: I knowed mighty well where the right plan would come from. (MS, 527–28)

The choice of Tom's thought processes over those of a duke can hardly be thought to be a favorable comparison, since the duke thought in a consistently exploitative way, with a streak of viciousness. But on reflection the comparison seems surprisingly apt. And Huck's experiences with wanting to be the mate of a steamboat had led to a dangerous situation in the *Walter Scott* episode. Twain inserted "***nor clown in a circus, nor nothing I can think of.***" The circus reference recalls the drunk/trick rider who represents both a comic version of the pathetic Boggs and an image of deception. Such a revision inclines the paragraph toward becoming a summary reference to earlier episodes on the river and on land. To cap the irony, Huck's final comparison, "***nor nothing I can think of,***" repeats the motif of his weakness in thinking. Huck feels inadequate compared to Tom because he mistakenly respects Tom's literary authorities. But this attitude will change by the end of the Phelps sequence.

Twain evidently thought of simply continuing the flight down the river, probably with Huck in control and with Tom along to act as a prankster. Huck announces his plan to:

> "shove off down the river on the raft, with Jim, hiding daytimes and running nights, just ⟨a⟩ as me and Jim used to do before. Wouldn't that plan work?"
>
> "Work? Why cert'nly it *would* work, ⟨li⟩ like rats a-fighting. But it's too blame' simple; there ain't nothing to it." (MS, 529)

As if to shift from similarity to identity, Twain revised the manuscript version "just as me and Jim used to do before" to read in print, "the way me and Jim used to do before." But Twain rejected this explicit plot possibility because, I think, he recognized that Tom's presence created the opportunity to write a nationalistic, realistic satire on European adventure literature. In addition, the escape motif could be continued; Huck had already succeeded in many escapes, but Tom's romantic techniques could now be put to the test.

We must be aware of the reflexive aspects of this writing, realizing that Twain's goals as a fictioneer at times coincide both with Huck's goals as a storyteller and with Tom's goals as organizer and complicator of the escape. On MS, 530–31, Twain wrote about Huck's conception of Tom's plans:

. . . He told me what it was, and I see in a minute it was worth fifteen of mine, for style, and *would* make Jim just as free a man as mine would, and maybe get us all ⟨killed⟩ ⟨*shot*⟩ *killed* besides. So I was satisfied, and said we would waltz in on it. I needn't tell what it was, here, because I knowed it wouldn't stay the way it was. I knowed he would be changing it around, every which way, and picturesquing it up, as we went along, and heaving in new bullinesses wherever he got a chance. And that is what he done.

By the time the passage was set in print, Twain had decided to omit "and picturesquing it up," perhaps because the words sound false for Huck's voice, or perhaps because the words convey too static a description of the changing plans. Or perhaps Twain wished to delay Huck's explicit sarcasm until later.

The elaboration and conflict of the escape plot become explicit in a manuscript passage. When the boys explore Jim's prison, Huck quickly, practically, decides:

> "Here's the ticket. This hole's big enough for Jim to get through, if we wrench off the board."
> Tom says:
> "It's as simple as tit-tat-toe, three-in-a-row, and as easy as playing hookey. I should <u>hope</u> we can find a way that's a little more complicated than <u>that</u>, Huck Finn."
> "Well, then," I says, "how'll it do to saw him out, the way I done before I was murdered, that time?"
> "That's more <u>like</u>," he says. "It's real mysterious, and troublesome, and good," he says; "but I bet we can find a way that's twice as long. . . ." (MS, 536–37)

Tom's tone indicates both contempt for Huck's practical plan and enthusiasm for more difficult ways. Clearly Twain was thinking of an explicit repetition of Huck's successful escape from his father's cabin-prison. As it developed, both escapes would involve the identical particular details of sawing a hole in a cabin wall which is hidden by a cloth. The contrast between Huck's clever planning of his effective escape and Tom's elaborate aping of literary escapes could embody satire against adventure literature. (It is amusing to note that Tom's approving phrasing "mysterious, and troublesome," and "twice as long" are similar to the reactions of critics evaluating the "evasion" sequence.) Moreover, an earlier frightening situation could now be duplicated in a comic mode, with the representative of the foreign literary tradition in charge, while Huck provides contrasting realistic commentary.

Tom faces problems, of course, making the escape into an "adventure." He says:

> "Blame it, this whole is ⟨ju⟩ just as it can be. It makes it so consounded difficult to get up a difficult plan. . . ." (MS, 552)

Twain in all likelihood composed quite rapidly at this point, as shown by omissions of fairly ordinary words. He revised in words so the corrected passage reads:

> "Blame it, this whole *thing* is just as *easy and awkward as* it can be. *And so* it makes it so ⟨consounded⟩ *rotten* difficult to get up a difficult plan. . . ."

We notice both the development of paradoxical pairing, such as "*easy and awkward*," and the shift from the milder "consounded" to "*rotten*." Shortly later Tom continues his complaint, and we may once more perhaps hear Twain commenting to himself about his own or the European novels:

> "Why, drat it, Huck, it's the stupidest, awkwardest fix I ever see: you got to invent <u>all</u> the difficulties." (MS, 553–54)

Twain canceled "awkwardest fix" in manuscript and substituted "*arrangement*," as Tom and Twain seem momentarily to merge as the creators of the difficulty. The resulting "stupidest *arrangement*" emphasizes only mental limitations.

The contrast between Tom's dependence upon European literary sources and Huck's individual realism appears most memorably in a conversation. When the boys discuss plans for Jim's escape from the cabin, Tom—true to his name—asserts a need for a saw and a preference for cutting, which Huck questions:

> "What do we want of a saw?"
> "What do we <u>want</u> of it? Hain't we got to saw the leg of Jim's bed off, so as to get the chain <u>loose</u>?"
> "Why, you just said a body could lift up the bedstead and slip the chain off."
> "Well, if that ain't just <u>like</u> you, Huck Finn. ⟨!⟩ You <u>can</u> get up the ⟨Sunday⟩ *infant*-schooliest ways of going at a thing. Why, hain't you ever read any books at all?—Baron Trenck, nor Casanova, nor Benvenuto Chelleeny, *nor Henri IV*, nor none of them heroes? Whoever heard of getting a prisoner loose in such an old-maidy way as that? No; the way all the best authorities does, is to saw. . . ." (MS, 555–57)

Constantly in the Phelps section Tom uses these inexpensive literary authorities to complicate and ultimately to ruin Jim's escape. Intriguingly, the insertion of another authority, an adventure story about King Henri IV, represents a brilliant, allusive synthesis of significant themes. *"Henri IV"* combines concerns about European escape literature, royalty, and religion. This king was, for religious reasons, virtually a prisoner of the French court. Ultimately he started the Bourbon lineage which would later be honored in the post Civil War American South. Henri's marriage led to the massacre of St. Bartholomew, but Henri ransomed his life by denying his beliefs; brought up as a Huguenot, he converted to Catholicism in 1572, reverted to Huguenot beliefs in 1576, and professed himself a Catholic again in 1593. The empathic reader has suffered with Huck as he makes complex moral decisions, and the reader may feel offended that Tom suppresses Huck by claiming the authority of a French king best known to popular history for his selfish, expedient solution to ethical difficulties, usually paraphrased as: "Paris is well worth a mass." Huck, whom no one would ransom, did make a successful escape of a type that no one publicized, has not read about any of Tom's various foreign authorities, and therefore can struggle to make difficult ethical choices free of literary influences. But, in the Phelps section, Tom's superior literacy tramples Huck. Twain deftly manages to present Tom's non-native sources while revealing his insensitive stupidity in asking such insinuating questions about Huck's reading ability and experience. Tom's tone conveys his surprise and indignation; of course, he has no compassion for Huck's lesser literacy.

Similarly, Tom's alien literary imagination wishes to duplicate and, cruelly, surpass past adventures. Tom spouts:

> "Well, some of the best authorities has done it. They couldn't get the chain off, so they just cut their hand off, and shoved. *And a leg would be better still.* But we got to let that go. There ain't necessity enough in this case; and *besides*, Jim's a nigger and wouldn't understand the reasons for it, and how it's the custom in Europe; ⟨anyway⟩; so we'll let it go." (MS, 560–61)

The addition of the leg amputation on one level simply exaggerates, but on another level Tom's enthusiastic imagination foreshadows the leg injury he himself will suffer in the escape. If Twain added *"And a leg would be better still"* after he had imagined or written of Tom's leg wound, the insertion would be valuable evidence of a commendable authorial meanness toward this educated, stupid child. Moreover, Tom, enslaved by European notions, states a racially based contempt for Jim's "understanding," although Jim is the person who will save Tom when the boy's leg is wounded.

Twain's ironic attitude toward Tom's fantastic plans was somewhat difficult to manage because his authorial criticism occasionally intruded. Twain has Tom say:

> But there's one thing—he can have a rope ladder; we can tear up our sheets and make him a rope ladder easy enough. ⟨If we can make it short enough.⟩ And we can send it to him in a pie; it's mostly done that way. And I've et worse pies. (MS, 561)

The crossed-out portion would have had Tom develop the idiocy of using a rope ladder in a one-story shanty, but the sentence could have been confusing in tone because Tom has absolutely no self-directed irony.

At one point Twain had noted to himself, "Teaches Jim to read and write—then uses dog messenger. Had taught him a little before" (Note C-5, *Huck*, 1988, 741), but apparently decided to keep Jim illiterate, able only to read "signs" in nature and in matters of luck. On manuscript pages 566–70, Tom and Huck argue about having the illiterate Jim write a journal on a shirt, use pens and ink, and write on tin plates. Repeatedly Huck realistically objects, "Journal your granny—Jim can't write," or "Can't nobody read his plates." At one point Tom explains that when Jim

> wants to send any little common ordinary mysterious message to let the world know where he's captivated, he can write it on the bottom of a tin plate with a fork and throw it out of the window. The Iron Mask always done that, ⟨"⟩ and it's a blame' good way, too." (MS, 568–69)

Apparently Tom, too, is "captivated" by these literary models. Originally Twain ended with the literary authority, but he decided to add Tom's emphatic approval to the sentence, thus increasing the contrast between the realistic, pragmatic Huck and the arrogant, derivative Tom.

Does the literacy motif affect how we should interpret Jim's situation and behavior in the Phelps section? His plight certainly resembles that of Blacks in the Reconstruction era. He was sold back into captivity by a pretender to hierarchical values. Jim's birth-determined status and his illiteracy combine to render him utterly powerless. Although he is actually a freedman, he thinks he is still a criminal, a fugitive slave, dependent upon a literate Europeanized child who heartlessly inflicts alien literary standards and procedures—while concealing Jim's legal freedom. Of course Jim, far from home and family, fearful of violence, behaves compliantly. In this situation, Jim's individualism will be suppressed until after Tom is shot. Only thereafter, in crisis, can Jim's individuality matter.

Later the boys have a similar argument about digging tools. Huck says:

> "Consound it, it's foolish, Tom."
> "It don't make no difference how foolish it looks, it's the <u>right</u> way—and it's the regular way. And there ain't no <u>other</u> way, that ever <u>I</u> heard of; and I've read all the books that gives any information about these things." (MS, 578–79)

Twain revised the manuscript "how foolish it looks" to "how foolish it *is*." Inexpensive European authorities have led Tom to imitate not only what appears foolish but what *is* foolish. Such a revision also lessens the possibility of any difference between appearance and reality. Twain's revision brands the corrupting influence of Tom's literary sources as silly in essence. (In the margin Twain jotted "Edmond Dantes.") Huck's original objection, "Consound it," perhaps bland in phrasing, became the slightly sharper term, "Confound it," in the printed version.

In general, Twain revised to increase Huck's explicit criticism of Tom's plans and to emphasize Tom's devotion to the literature. For example, Twain added, for the print version, Huck's extremely vehement objection to one of Tom's notions:

> I said, "Don't do nothing of the kind; it's one of the most jackass ideas I ever struck;" but he never paid no attention to me; went right on. It was his way when he'd got his plans set. (312)

Thus, late in the creative process, the author who had revised out "derned" and "dum'd" inserted "jackass." The importance of this addition must be emphasized; David Sloane states that "one of the most jackass ideas I ever struck" is "unusually strong language for a novel of the 1880's" (*Literary Comedian*, 142). Tom's self-assured, self-important arrogance overwhelms the mutual consideration and reciprocity of the earlier portion of the novel. Huck sounds independent and critical but, given his personality, he cannot totally control Tom's desire to imitate the books. And the next paragraph was also revised so that Jim receives directions primarily from Tom rather than from both boys. Such a revision makes Huck participate less in the "evasion."

The peculiar quality of this final section rests in large measure upon the combination of ingenious pranks and boyish cleverness (if one ignores

Jim's re-enslavement) with Twain's irony about the silliness. A passage on MS, 599–600 presents a typical example. After an evening meeting with Jim,

> we crawled out through the hole, and so home to bed, *with hands that looked like they'd been chawed by a dog.* Tom was *in* high spirits. He said it was the best fun he ever had in his life, and the most intellectual; and said if he *only* could see his way to it we would keep it up all the rest of our lives and leave Jim to our children to get out.

The adult Clemens/Twain was, indeed, enjoying childhood once more as he recreated, through fiction, an earlier era and enjoyed a moral effort to free a slave which was impossible then. Part of the novel's appeal may depend upon this unique combination of a rescue fantasy with an irresponsibility-idleness fantasy. In the printed version Twain changes Tom's praise to "the most intellectural" (312). The concrete inserted phrase, "*with hands that looked like they'd been chawed by a dog,*" makes Tom's claim of "most intellectural" sound absurd. The balance shifted slightly away from the concrete by the time the book reached print with the dropping of "*by a dog.*" Much of Twain's creative process reveals this sort of titration, balancing and rebalancing, of contrary impulses.

Twain was probably able to think simultaneously of his targets and of his own need for protection from the piratical publishers when he wrote one of his working notes. DeVoto has labeled this note as C-14, the last in the series:

> Publish this in England and Canada and Germany the day before the first number of it appears in Century or N.Y. Sun—that makes full copyright. (*Huck*, 1988, 750)

Thus even a work which addressed the copyright problem required, in the author's mind, careful timing of publication to meet different national requirements.

One may think of the conflict on the Phelps farm as involving an educated boy, Tom, who supports and slavishly imitates imported authority (Kohlberg's stage four), controlling a semi-literate boy who can nonetheless function at a higher level of moral reciprocity. Or one may think of the conflict as a struggle between a believer in literary illusions and a nonbeliever, the corrupted Europeanized American and the unsophisticated realistic American. With Tom's connivance, Jim is physically re-imprisoned; Tom takes Jim and Huck hostage to his delusions, enslaving them to his readings; Huck struggles ineffectively because he still has respect for Tom's authorities. Paradoxically, those who condemn the novel's ending would wish Huck somehow finally to assert control over Tom. Perhaps because most critics believe that "literature" is a higher, better form of knowledge, most critics are unhappy that Huck does not "win." If Twain knew enough to satirize Tom's reading of European fiction, why doesn't Twain permit Huck eventually to triumph over or control Tom? Perhaps because most critics frequently read "felicitously written" literature, the complications and qualifications of Twain's ending have been misunderstood.

V

This emphasis on books and literacy was carefully crafted. As indicated, Twain's longest insertion in the available manuscript material constitutes a complex, multi-stage creation which centers upon the role of books and "adventures." Twain composed the *Walter Scott* insertion, MS pages numbered 81-A-1 to 81-60, late in the writing process (print version Paragraph 12 of Chapter XII through to the end of Chapter XIV) but placed it early in the novel. If Twain had simply wished to locate books on the raft, he could easily have included a box of books in the loot taken from the floating house. Instead, it seems a tenable inference that Twain wished to develop at length Huck's early, unquestioningly favorable attitude toward Tom Sawyer-style adventures and values. This portion of the manuscript has great thematic importance, dealing with issues such as reading, nobility, heredity and training, cultural differences, and human equality. Of course, the *Walter Scott* insertion affects the way one should read the novel that follows.

The entire *Walter Scott* episode embodies Tom Sawyer's literary fantasies, but these piratical robbers, unlike those in Tom's books, are real. Of course, the dangerous sinking boat enshrines the name of the author Twain considered the epitome of destructive romantic fiction. (In *Life on the Mississippi*, Chapter XLVI, Twain had insisted that the South lost the Civil War because of Sir Walter Scott. We need only imagine how the Grangerford sons, if any survived, would behave in a Civil War charge to know the destructive effect of bookish notions about honor and chivalry.) Huck goes on the wreck, into danger, because, at that early point in the novel, Twain wanted him to value Tom Sawyer's illusions. Twain turned over a sheet and *revised into the insertion* Huck's explanation:

"I can't rest, Jim, till I give her a rummaging. Do you reckon Tom Sawyer would ever go by this thing? Not for pie, he wouldn't. He'd call it an adventure—that's what he'd call it; and he'd land on that wreck if it was his last act. And wouldn't he throw style into it?—wouldn't he spread himself, nor nothing? Why, you'd think it was Christopher Columbus discovering Kingdom-Come. I wish Tom Sawyer was here." (MS, 81-3 verso)

At this point in the novel, Twain has Huck link Tom and "*style*," approving both. The final comparison with "*Christopher Columbus discovering Kingdom-Come*" unites, interestingly, a European adventurer sanctioned by monarchy with a putative goal of religion, two satiric targets.

Furthermore, once Huck arrives on the boat, when discretion would call for a retreat, Huck says to himself, "*Tom Sawyer wouldn't back out now, and so I won't either*" (MS, 81-7). This passage Twain inserted interlinearly. In these cases, Twain emphasized a harsh contrast between Huck's veneration for Tom's values at the novel's beginning, preparing for a harsh contrast with Huck's more realistic opinion at the end (e.g., "it's one of the most jackass ideas I ever struck").

Huck's early attitude about Tom's literary delusions surfaces explicitly after Huck and Jim escape from the boat. During the next day they go through the loot and discuss the experience:

We laid off all the afternoon in the woods, talking, and reading the books, and having a general good time. I told Jim all about what happened inside the wreck, and at the ferry boat; and I said these kinds of things was adventures; but he said he didn't want no more adventures. (MS, 81-42)

When Twain revised the passage for print, the text changed to "and me reading the books," a modification which, in context, calls attention to Huck's situational dominance over Jim.

Huck's relationship with Jim seems to change once books are on board the raft. Huck apparently feels enthusiastic about adventures and uses the books. But the paragraph ends with Jim's wise statement about the danger of their circumstances, particularly his own danger of drowning or being caught. Huck admits: *"Well, he was right; ⟨fact is⟩ he was most always right; he had an uncommon level head, for a nigger."* (When Huck pays more attention to books and gives Jim information from books which causes debate and disagreement, Huck repeatedly refers to Jim in terms of his class, that of a "nigger," rather than respecting Jim's individuality as he had.) Earlier Huck had valued Jim's ability to interpret "signs" and later, as in the discussion about the origin of stars compared with the number of frog's eggs, their conversation seems less rancorous.

Manuscript page 81-43 ended half way down the page, with directions to go to the crucial segment mentioned earlier, originally numbered 1-17, but which was renumbered to fit into this sixty-page sequence. The segment, we remember, begins:

> *I read considerable to Jim about kings, and dukes, and earls and such, and how gaudy they dressed and how much style they put on, and ⟨how⟩ called each other your majesty, and your grace, and your lordship, and so on, 'stead of Mister; and Jim's eyes bugged out, and he was interested.* (MS, 81-44)

Obviously, Huck is taking the role of cultural explainer, informing Jim about the world of literature and nobility as Tom had and would. Equally obviously, the passage also prepares Jim to lend credence—or simply to accept intimidation and go along—when the two rascals take over the raft.[8]

The concluding portion of the manuscript insertion offers some of the best examples in Twain's writing of serious themes developed in a comic context. The conversation about kings leads smoothly into a discussion of "King Sollermun's" putative wisdom about splitting a child. The novel's concern about environmental determinism surfaces. Huck thinks that Jim misses the point of the story, but Jim replies:

> *"Blame de pint! I reckon I knows what I knows. En mine you, de real pint is down furder—it's down deeper. It lays in de way Sollermun was raised.* (MS, 81-52)

Jim manages to present a fairly plausible case that the king's supposed callousness developed from an over-supply of children. Again, Huck, unable to respond to Jim's argument, thinks not of Jim, his companion, but of Jim's category:

> *I never see such a nigger. If he got a notion in his head once, there warn't no getting it out again. He was the most down on Solomon of any nigger I ever see.* (MS, 81-53)

Since we may be reasonably certain that Huck does not usually scientifically survey people of color for their opinions about Solomon, we can conclude that Huck facilely evades the argument about unselfish love by mentally placing Jim in a subordinate category.

When the conversation shifts to the executed French king and *"his little boy the dolphin, that would a been king,"* Jim reacts sympathetically, parentally, to the information, hoping the child survived. Jim intuits that the dauphin would be lonely here and brings up America's lack of kings.

The comedy of a king who *"cain't git no situation"* in America reveals Jim's sympathy, his nationalistic practicality, and the realism created by his relatively narrow experience.

The ensuing debate about the French language similarly crystallizes a major concern.[9] Huck claims, *"I got some of their jabber out of a book"* (MS, 81-56). The topic of language facility appears repeatedly. Pap Finn was angry when he heard that there was "a free nigger" who was a "p'fessor in a college, and could talk all kinds of languages, and knowed everything" (49–50). Since the man could vote, Pap Finn decides to abstain from his drunken voting, in protest. Jim, in contrast, learns a slight amount and argues for universal humanness and natural communication within the species, transcending nationality. Jim knows nothing about cultural differences, and he accordingly assumes a man should "talk like a man." Since cultural differences are one of Huck's areas of ignorance, he loses the argument, concluding defensively in a portion that Twain revised into his insertion: "you can't learn a nigger to argue. *So I quit"* (MS, 81-60). Although the novel's least literate character proposes a rock-solid argument resembling a Socratic dialogue, once more a book-inspired debate leads Huck to treat Jim as only a racial stereotype.

This longest insertion has changed the way we should read the ending. The addition of Huck's early favorable attitudes about adventures and about books creates a dramatic contrast with his final attitudes. Huck is not liberated at the end of the Wilks episode; indeed at that point he still accepts the conventional hierarchy, giving an honored position to literacy, desiring to write to Tom about Jim. But by the end of the Phelps section, Huck will break free from his veneration for literary authority. In his progression from *"I wish Tom Sawyer was here,"* through to calling Tom's plans "one of the most jackass ideas I ever struck," Huck gains some but not total freedom from domination by literary authorities. Without the maligned Phelps episode, Huck—and perhaps other American youths—would remain enslaved to control by European literature. Of course, we cannot prove whether the Phelps episode influenced American literary history or the preferences of the American audiences, but it seems reasonable that those who have read the Phelps section and probably have been, in some way, irritated cannot easily remain patient with Scott or Dumas.

In addition, it must be noted that the reading of this entire novel has actually increased the reader's language facility, overcoming the initial shock of unfamiliarity with different American dialects. Readers of the novel must develop some openness, some comprehension of the different speech acts.[10] Not only must the reader gradually become aware of a different manner of speech, he or she must also become exposed and attentive to different points of view toward life, as embodied in the different speakers' dialects and voices. In this process there is growth, as there is in the realization of danger in self-deception, in "letting on."

The issue of Huck's own language facility unifies the book. We recall that Huck had earlier felt inadequate, "You know what I mean—I don't know the words to put it in." At the novel's conclusion, Huck again confronts the difficulty of literacy:

> . . . *and so* there ain't nothing more to write about, and I'm ⟨powerful⟩ ⟨*cussed*⟩ ⟨ *blame*⟩ *rotten* glad of it, because if I'd a knowed what a trouble it was to make a book I wouldn't a tackled it and ain't agoing to ⟨,⟩ any more. (MS, 786)

The series of cancellations preserve a touching struggle to find the right tone, moving from the forceful "powerful" through increasingly strong negatives to frame the final paradox. Huck's self-imposed silence, his refusal to continue the novelistic process can be understood as his rejection of even his own form of fabling.

Just as the beginning had called attention to its own textuality, the ending also presents itself as self-conscious writing, fiction with a reflexive dimension. This assessment of his own storytelling records another example of Huck's struggle with literacy, and he mistakenly feels defeated, overwhelmed by the difficulty of his battles. His intention to lapse into silence dramatizes, paradoxically, yet another misunderstanding; Huck, of course, cannot know that his narrative conveyed so much so precisely, nor that in a surprisingly sophisticated way the book forms its own qualifications, presenting evidence both of Huck's battle with literacy and of his transformation of an example of the adventure genre into an anti-adventure text. Twain reflexively respects critical readers who constantly remind themselves: this is an illusion; this is a book. Although Jim is freed, and although Huck has only a qualified victory, apparently generations of American readers have become freed of an uncritical veneration for "felicitously written" literature. Or at least they could have been freed. Some have been so unhappy with the ending of *Adventures of Huckleberry Finn* that they have blamed Twain. Apparently some who dislike the end have, because of a veneration for literature, confused the subject of the satire with the maker. They have been fooled. But those with more knowledge can appreciate why Twain focused the force of his ridicule as he did upon those who believe, uncritically, in literary authority.

Notes

1. *Literacy in Traditional Societies*, Jack Goody, ed., provides an interesting, stimulating survey. Carlo Cipolla's *Literacy and Development in the West* modestly and intelligently presents a great deal of information. Kevin Murphy's "Illiterate's Progress: The Descent into Literacy in *Huckleberry Finn*" presents a view consistent with my independent interpretation.

2. The following account of Twain's experiences and lawsuits draws upon the Mark Twain Papers and the dissertation by Herbert Feinstein, "Mark Twain's Lawsuits," University of California at Berkeley, 1968. The prices and numbers of editions can be found in *The American Catalogue Founded by F. Leypoldt*, 1876–1884.

3. Twain was relatively sophisticated where copyright issues were concerned. He had engaged a British piratical publisher, John Camden Hotten (d. March 1873), nicknamed by Twain "Hottentot," in a public debate; Hotten's successor as Twain's publisher, Andrew Chatto, was paying Twain royalties on a regular basis. See also Twain's letters to James R. Osgood about troubles with the Canadian situation covering the period October 1881 to January 1882 in Hill's *Mark Twain's Letters to His Publishers*, 141–52. Moreover, Twain took care to assure a British, a Canadian, and an American copyright for *Life on the Mississippi*. It seems likely that piratical Canadian publishers, disbelieving Twain's Canadian lawyer, indignantly checked the claims. (See letters to Twain from Chatto, May 29, 1883, and from Dawson Brothers, June 3, 1883, as well as a letter about Canadian and British copyright from S. H. Kent, July 10, 1883, in the Mark Twain Papers.)

4. The speech has two other remarks about the copyright situation. Apparently a diamond robbery had recently occurred. Twain reassured his audience that he was not the robber:

> These are mere assertions, I grant you, but they come from the lips of one who was never known to utter an untruth, except for practice, and who certainly would not so stultify the traditions of an upright life as to utter one now, in a strange land, and in such a presence as this, when there is nothing to be gained by it and he does not need any practice. I brought with me to this city a friend—a Boston publisher—but, alas, even this does not sufficiently explain these sinister mysteries; if I had brought a Toronto publisher along the case would have been different. But no, possibly not; the burglar took the diamond studs, but left the shirt; only a *reformed* Toronto publisher would have left the shirt.

Similarly, Twain claimed that he had seen Montreal's famous locations:

> I saw the Plains of Abraham, and the spot where the lamented Wolfe stood when he made the memorable remark that he would rather be the author of Gray's "Elegy" than take Quebec. But why did he say so rash a thing? It was because he supposed there was going to be international copyright. Otherwise there would be no money in it. (Fatout, ed., 157–59)

5. In fact, close examination reveals a peculiar collocation that could support a conjectural explanation about why Twain may have decided to include copyright problems in the fictional time. We know that Twain was following and praising Howells's *A Modern Instance* as it was appearing in serial form in *Century*, from December 1881 to October 1882. The March 1882 issue printed a review of *The Prince and the Pauper*, a novel with thematic similarities to *Huck* about nobility and low status as well as matching cases of mistaken identity involving a sensible, pragmatic, lower class "Tom" character. If Twain did read the review, he would, in all probability, have noticed on the facing page a title likely to pique his interest: "The Weak Point of Mormonism" (782). The majority of page 782 is devoted to Martineau's and Towne's two letters; each letter's vocabulary and point of view would appeal to Twain; the Towne letter, moreover, gave specific information about the then current topic of a possible separate Anglo-American copyright agreement. Perhaps that possibility might have led Twain to concentrate his satiric fire in the Phelps episode upon Continental literature, leaving British literature other than Walter Scott relatively unscathed. Twain's 1888 "American Authors and British Pirates" offers other reasons for not targeting England.

6. Twain's effective image of the Indian nurse passing on Indian values probably draws upon a similar image in a letter to Twain from R. W. Gilder (M.T.P., October 14, 1883).

7. Louis Budd has observed, in correspondence, that Twain knew of many American models he could have alluded to if he wished.

8. A note on C-4 reads: "Back yonder, Huck reads and tells about monarchies and kings, etc. So Jim stares when he learns the rank of these 2" (*Huck*, 1988, 740).

9. Two passages from "A Record of Small Foolishnesses" may be relevant to this section. Once, when Livy was talking about how peculiar the French looked to the Americans, Susy queried, "Mommy, don't you reckon we seem queer to them?"* (35). On a loose sheet Twain jotted, "Pooly vouz fran . . .".*

10. For an informative, stimulating treatment see David R. Sewell's *Mark Twain's Languages: Discourse, Dialogue and Linguistic Variety*, esp. Chapter 5.

The Question of Unity

Shall I tell the real reason why I have unintentionally succeeded in fooling so many people? It is because some of them only read a little of the squib I wrote and jumped to the conclusion that it was serious, and the rest did not read it at all, but heard of my agricultural venture at second-hand. . . . It is because, in some instances, the reader is a person who never tries to deceive anybody himself, and therefore is not expecting any one to wantonly practise a deception upon *him*; and in this case the only person dishonored is the man who wrote the burlesque. In other instances, the "nub" or moral of the burlesque—if its object be to enforce a truth—escapes notice in the superior glare of something in the body of the burlesque itself. And very often this "moral" is tagged on at the bottom, and the reader, not knowing that it is the key of the whole thing and the only important paragraph in the article, tranquilly turns up his nose at it and leaves it unread. One can deliver a satire with telling force through the insidious medium of a travesty, if he is careful not to overwhelm the satire with the extraneous interest of the travesty, and so bury it from the reader's sight and leave him a joked and defrauded victim, when the honest intent was to add to either his knowledge or his wisdom.

Mark Twain

10. Repetition, Cycles, and Structure

I

Is the ending of *Adventures of Huckleberry Finn* an artistic failure? Is the concluding section a flaw which damages the entire novel? Clearly this study suggests that although the Phelps portion may be widely misunderstood, it is not necessarily a thematic or an artistic failure. Indeed, the Phelps episode can arguably be seen as a patriotic, climactic defense of realistic, nativist, pragmatic individualism as opposed to foreign values. Moreover, the artistry of the Phelps section deserves careful, open-minded attention.

First, for heuristic purposes, let us construct a case for the theory that the novel ends badly, that the "flaws" damage the book fatally. Then we shall take a final look through the kaleidoscope at revisions which affect the novel's meaning and structure.

Perhaps the most famous criticism of the ending remains Hemingway's comment in *The Green Hills of Africa*:

> If you read it you must stop where the Nigger Jim is stolen from the boys. That is the real end. The rest is just cheating. (22)

The careful reader will certainly notice the error in Hemingway's recollected version that Jim is stolen "from the boys." Apparently Hemingway must have been one of many Americans who conflates all Tom and Huck stories and feels free to judge his own memorial fabrication. But the essential charge echoes through the years: that the end must be considered an evasion, a cheating.

Repeatedly perceptive critics have, understandably, been troubled by the novel's conclusion. The gifted Bernard DeVoto said about the ending, "In the whole reach of the English novel there is no more abrupt or more chilling descent" (*Mark Twain's America*, 92). We may note, in passing, that he uses as his relevant inclusive standard the British novels and that his vocabulary conveys hierarchical messages of heights and falls. Moreover, his judgment is essentially correct, but the "descent" could be in readers' comfort, not in artistry.

In essays designed to introduce popular editions of *Huck*, both Lionel Trilling and T. S. Eliot praise the book while recognizing difficulty with the end. Trilling states:

> In form and style *Huckleberry Finn* is an almost perfect work. Only one mistake has ever been charged against it, that it concludes with Tom Sawyer's elaborate, too elaborate, game of Jim's escape. Certainly this episode is too long—in the original draft it was much longer—and certainly it is a falling-off, as almost anything would have to be, from the incidents of the river. Yet it has a certain formal aptness—like, say, that of the Turkish initiation which brings Moliere's *Le Bourgeois Gentilhomme* to its close. It is a rather mechanical development of an idea, and yet some device is needed to permit Huck to return to his anonymity, to give up the role of hero, to fall into the background which he prefers, for he is modest in all things and could not well endure the attention and glamour which attend a hero at a book's end. For this purpose nothing could serve better than the mind of Tom Sawyer with its literary furnishing, its conscious romantic desire for experience and the hero's part, and its ingenious schematization of life to achieve that aim. (Trilling, ed., *Huckleberry Finn*, xv–xvi)

Trilling conveys—with repetition of the idea of a "fall" and with a simile to French literature—his severely qualified acceptance of the form. I agree with Trilling's sense that the ending is, indeed, appropriate, but for different reasons.

T. S. Eliot's analysis also recognizes readers' discomfort:

> Readers sometimes deplore the fact that the story descends to the level of *Tom Sawyer* from the moment that Tom himself re-appears. Such readers protest that the escapades invented by Tom, in the attempted "rescue" of Jim, are only a tedious development of themes with which we were already too familiar—even while admitting that the escapades themselves are very amusing, and some of the incidental observations memorable. But it is right that the mood of the end of the book should bring us back to that of the beginning. Or, if this was not the right ending for the book, what ending would have been right? (Eliot, ed., *Huckleberry Finn*, xiii)

Once more a hierarchical metaphor explains. But the words of praise, "very amusing" and "memorable," seem much less emphatic than "deplore," "descends," "protest," and "tedious." Eliot tries simple assertion and a hypothetical question in a relatively weak defense. I would contend that the comparison with the novel *Tom Sawyer* is utterly misleading because, although the character Tom reappears, the attitude toward Tom becomes contemptuous at the end of Huck's book. Eliot uses a formal justification, seeing the structure of the novel as cyclic and acknowledging thematic continuity. Again, I believe this perception to be acute and partial but would suggest both unfamiliar themes and an additional cyclic pattern.

Leo Marx took issue with both critics when he published in *The American Scholar* (1953) what has become one of the most influential essays on the novel, "Mr. Eliot, Mr. Trilling, and *Huckleberry Finn*." Marx asserts that the flawed ending episode cannot be a minor matter since it "comprises almost one-fifth of the text." He states that although "both critics see the problem as one of form," the content or meaning of the ending must also be considered. Marx brilliantly perceives that "the ending of *Huckleberry Finn* makes so many readers uneasy because they rightly sense that it jeopardizes the significance of the entire novel." Such a statement rings utterly true; the Phelps farm episode does indeed undercut "the significance of the entire novel." Marx makes a strong case for the novel having a flawed ending. "The most obvious thing wrong with the ending, then, is the flimsy contrivance by which Clemens frees Jim. In the end we not only discover that Jim has been a free man for two months, but that his freedom has been granted by old Miss Watson." Marx identifies Miss Watson as belonging with all the forces that Huck had previously opposed. The ending, consequently, seems to be a "vindication of persons and attitudes Huck and Jim had symbolically repudiated when they set forth downstream."

Marx also expresses discomfort with the "discordant farcical tone and the disintegration of the major characters." Huck reverts to a role subordinate to Tom, and Jim becomes a caricature or stereotype of a slave. Marx even suggests that the novel has "little or no formal unity independent of the joint purpose of Huck and Jim." A major amount of Marx's interpretation seems consistent with that proposed here, although, again, there are differences of emphasis. One part of Marx's approach with which I differ involves the degree of formal unity. He contends there is little; I would maintain that an extraordinary amount of repetition creates a formal unity in the misunderstood ending.

Additional criticisms of the ending can be made. The ending could be viewed as an "evasion" because Huck does not show great moral growth; instead he permits Tom to take over control of the situation. The atmosphere of mutuality certainly changes as Huck becomes an unwilling and unwitting accomplice in the tormenting of Jim. Furthermore, accusations can be made that in the Phelps section Twain wrote padding or filler, attempting to expand a slim volume so that buyers would feel, by the size of the book, that they had purchased their money's worth of words. Several of Twain's books, such as *Roughing It* and *Life on the Mississippi*, can be criticized for ending with long, padded sections. Twain definitely desired to write a book that would sell well for the subscription trade. But the volume did finally turn out to be so much longer than its companion volume, *The Adventures of Tom Sawyer*, that Webster suggested that Twain could shorten the novel by omitting the raftsmen section.

Repeatedly college students and other more mature readers express disappointment, confusion, and/or discomfort with the ending. Most college-age readers react, either timidly or angrily, with negative feelings about the Phelps section, even though they have been socialized to expect that *Huck* is "a great book." Typical complaints could be phrased: "The last section undercuts the power of the earlier narrative," or "That last section fools us and cheats us," or "How could Jim be 'freed' yet be 'not free'?" Moreover, because readers have a covert expectation that a masterpiece should be perfect, they usually respond with confusion and reluctance, often expressing great anger at Twain or at Tom, confirming Twain's judgment in the letter to Howells (July 5, 1875, *Twain Howells Letters*, Vol. 1, 92) that Tom would not be the right boy to trace to adulthood.

To construct a contrary case, to establish that in a complex way the ending is aesthetically and thematically appropriate, requires first that the dominant assumptions of most critics be examined, briefly, so that we may understand how some of these assumptions make it extraordinarily difficult to understand *Huck* fully. Some critics have a conscious or unconscious expectation that a novel about a youth, even a picaresque novel, will bear some resemblance to a *bildungsroman* or *kunstlerroman*. Accordingly, they assume that Huck will mature noticeably and are disappointed when his important but relatively non-commanding growth does not assure success. I would contend that Huck develops to have more independence from Tom at the end, but that his growth does not assure autonomy or success. Although Huck does go along with Tom's preposterous tormenting, Huck also becomes much more critical of Tom's notions than he had been at the beginning and middle of the novel, finally calling Tom's notion "the most jackass idea." But his maturation is not enough to overcome the power of Tom's literacy.

An equally important assumption involves the idea that a novel should have a unity of genre. Boldly stated, it is thought that a good adventure novel or *bildungsroman* should not end with a farcical or burlesque section;

a "good" adventure story should not question or qualify its own genre. Can an author who writes a reflexive criticism of literature be required to follow a unity of genre? If an author addresses metafictional concerns, may he shift genres?

Another assumption, perhaps most telling, is that Jim should be free at the end. The reading audience and the critics would be even more disappointed, saddened, indignant, or outraged if the novel ended realistically with Jim enslaved or tortured, mutilated or shot, hanged and perhaps burned. A curious literary sentimentalism wishes Jim to be freed by a clever boy, as if the evils of slavery, racial prejudice, and class discrimination were actually impotent. The readers and critics expect it possible in fiction—if nowhere else—for a fourteen-year-old naive, lower class lad to free a slave, to win for a minority person full dignity. This idea, both touching and baffling, measures the unreality of fiction. But Twain knew at least four things: the all-pervasive power of human evil, the difficulty of fighting it, and the necessary role of law and wills in establishing the possibility of freedom. Twain also knew that books, by and large, deceive; but most contemporary literary critics, who are often lodged in "English Departments," consider books a higher form of knowledge.

It must be obvious that although the ending of *Huck* is severely criticized, it nevertheless does solve several problems. Jim is decriminalized; his trip down the river was, apparently, just as free as Huck's. Tom's elaborate plans for the escape are made to seem even more ridiculous, more contemptible, because of his knowledge of their non-necessity. The king's action of selling Jim becomes even more despicable, because he has had the arrogance to sell not only a human being but a freed person. And Huck's early statement that he "don't take stock in dead people" is proven wrong. Moreover, if modern American readers were in the habit of reading much adventure-escape fiction about European nobility, they would find the ending literary burlesque, although in fictional form, just as amusing as "Fenimore Cooper's Literary Offenses."

Four questions may be kept in mind while evaluating the aesthetic and thematic importance of the ending. Does the "extraneous interest" of the travesty overwhelm the satire upon European literature and the criticism of Americans who are corrupted by reading cheap alien fiction? Three parallel issues arise: if American fiction can deal well with issues of individual conscience, finally reaching the anguished climax of "All right, then I'll go to hell," should American fiction be able to defend itself against alien values? Consequently, can American fiction criticize recurrent social evils?

Finally, could any known American social practice in the 1880s encourage Twain to conclude his novel with the perhaps outrageous idea of a Black man, who had been freed, being treated as a "prisoner"? Once the reader knows the relevant historical background, the Phelps section offers an enjoyable, powerful, comedic, artful conclusion with timeless cultural importance.

II

At the moment, many contemporary readers and critics experience the conclusion of *Adventures of Huckleberry Finn* with a pervasive sense of intense moral outrage. The intelligent readers' reactions of indignation and/or disappointment often express thoughts such as, "It is outrageously immoral for Tom Sawyer to participate, sanction, or permit the imprisonment of a person he knows to be free." Certainly Tom's compliance exploitatively re-enslaves a man he knows to be legally free so that he can boss around both Jim and Huck. In addition, it seems a fictional deceit for Twain to allow the readers to think of Jim as a fugitive slave, a criminal, when he is actually a freedman. Most critics judge the plot device of Jim's legal freedom but imprisoned status as a literary trick, a deception. Deception existed, but perhaps of an additional, different sort. What kind of "cheating" might have been happening?

Moreover, many readers and critics direct their moral outrage at Twain, thinking that they have been fooled, that the novel is unrealistic, that authorial deception and deceit have spoiled a good adventure story. Such emotions are genuine, appropriate reactions, but additional knowledge may redirect the emotions. The anger need not be directed only at Twain, but could instead be aimed at a Southern society that actually had re-imprisoned freed Black men in the 1870s and 1880s and treated them as slaves—or worse than slaves had been treated.

Just as some aspects of this novel draw upon the historical period of 1835–1850, some aspects may be deeply rooted in the period of 1875–1884, the time of composition, the era when the post-bellum Reconstruction was obviously failing (see Gollin and Gollin, and Schmitz articles). For example, by the 1880s the term "carpet bag" no longer referred, with neutral connotations, only to a common form of luggage; instead the term began to carry a heavy burden of extremely damaging connotations, referring to Northerners who profiteered from the South's post-war misery. We know that Twain revised his text to associate the strongly negative "carpet bag" with the king and duke and removed the term from association with Huck (see MS, 474, 475, 476, 487, and 497). And we recall that, indicatively, the social and legal climate was such that the 1875 Civil Rights Act would be declared unconstitutional in late 1883. Just as the copyright problem occurred in 1843 and in 1883, the problems of slavery and of individual freedom recurred in a way in the post-Civil War era. After the end of the Civil War and the creation of the Black Codes, some Northern newspapers and magazines regarded the conditions of the freed Blacks as an important topic. Although the problems were a familiar subject, "Studies in the South" (1882–83) and Shaler's "The Negro Problem" (1884) indicate continuing interest. In fact, alert readers of *The Atlantic Monthly* and *Century* might perceive, almost automatically, surprising analogies in the novel that might well "escape" later readers.

But it must be stressed that this reconceptualization, this interpretation of a latent, unrecognized, covert meaning, serves as a conjecture advanced in a speculative fashion. Was there any Reconstruction-era social system that involved the captivity, imprisonment, or re-enslavement of legally freed Black men, that made them work for white people, that made them follow white-determined rules and orders which they had not known, that permitted transfer of the control over the Black men for much less money than they had been worth as slaves? Moreover, did any such system use the vocabulary of the Phelps episode, including terms such as "prison," "prisoner," "chains," "shackles," "guards," and "escape"? Unfortunately, yes. Tom Sawyer's participation in Jim's captivity may represent figuratively the injustice done to countless Black freedmen under the convict-lease system. But the quality of evidence one would desire has not yet been found, and perhaps does not exist; authors and editors were more likely to write about copyright issues, while wardens, sheriffs, and illiterate prisoners were less likely to write about the convict-lease system. When exploring this theory, we deal not with exclusive, conclusive proof but with congruence and analogy. Consequently, some background information on this little-documented practice seems necessary and pertinent.[1] Just as the lack of international copyright led to the theft of an author's time and labor, the convict-lease system similarly harmed many Black men.

Some information may provide an initial context for Jim's status as a slave, as a fugitive, as a freed Black, and also as a possible symbol of Black prisoners who were leased as workers. In 1849–50, there were 87,422 slaves in Missouri, with 2,618 free persons of color. At that time in that state, there were 60 fugitive slaves, and 50 slaves received freedom by manumission. In the 1845 era, it was still legal in Missouri to free a slave in a last will and testament.

The thematic opposition of "Free" and "Slave" or "Freed" and "Prisoner" requires careful pondering, lest a reader suppose that "freeing" Jim could solve all his problems. A manumitted Black would certainly not enjoy genuine freedom in 1845. "Free Jim" would face a situation of restriction and isolation resembling that in "Free Joe and the Rest of the World." The likelihood of Jim earning enough money to purchase his wife and children is close to zero. Tom's statement that Jim is as "free as any cretur" can be read by those who know the actual historical situation of freedmen in Missouri or Arkansas as indicating how restricted most freed Blacks were. (See the groundbreaking articles by Berkove.) For example, anyone could contest the freed status of a Black such as Jim by claiming that he was not in Missouri when Miss Watson died. In the 1845–1850 era, Jim could very easily be re-enslaved in Arkansas. Moreover, as William Still's 1883 book, *The Underground Rail Road: A Record of Facts, Authentic Narratives, Letters,* *etc.*, which Twain annotated, explains, some thuggish whites would use fabricated "Runaway" notices in the 1845 era to kidnap and then sell freed Blacks into slavery. The duke's decision to write a description that fits Jim precisely probably reflects the actual practice Still explains that was used by some "slave hunters" who captured Blacks by writing and printing a runaway notice and then claiming that they were returning escaped slaves, although the people had been freed or had not ever been enslaved.

Jim's situation certainly worsened as he went downstream in the inescapable company of the king and duke, inevitably carried by the river's current into the more hostile deep South. In 1849–50 in Arkansas there were 47,100 slaves and only 608 "free colored." If a freedman stayed in Arkansas longer than 180 days, he could be imprisoned for a year; if he remained thereafter, he could be sold. In 1849–50, Arkansas had 21 fugitive slaves, but only one slave was given manumission.

The idea of "lighting out for the Territory" would make good sense. In 1846 the Wilmot Proviso, although not passed into law, had suggested a norm that there would be no slavery or involuntary servitude "except for crime, wherof the party shall first be duly convicted."[2] Later, oddly enough, the brief 1864 Thirteenth Amendment used phrasing similar to the Wilmot Proviso:

> Neither slavery nor involuntary servitude, except as a punishment for crime wherof the party shall have been duly convicted, shall exist within the United States, or any place subject to their jurisdiction.

Does the "except as a punishment" phrase refer only to involuntary servitude? Or does it also refer to slavery? Could a person who wished to "redeem" the South find in the Thirteenth Amendment an invitation to restore slavery by "duly" convicting Blacks? As will become apparent, in spite of the sacrifices of the Civil War and the Reconstruction, the process of criminal charges and convictions could lead legally to involuntary servitude or a punitive form of slavery after 1864.

Although all these figures are tentative and subject to large margins of error, it is significant that the 1850 Census indicated that in all the slave states there were 1,358 white and 323 colored in state prisons and penitentiaries. (But, of course, many slaves were worked or killed instead of being given over to a prison.) Later, in about 1882, six states (Tennessee, North and South Carolina, Georgia, Texas, and Missouri) had at least 7,228 state prisoners. I have not yet found figures for four states with very large convict-lease populations (Kentucky, Arkansas, Mississippi, and Louisiana). Local and county prisons would add to these counts. The vast majority of the prisoners were Black.

The post-Civil War South suffered many disruptions, including a shortage of cheap and no-cost labor. Depression, unemployment, and low cotton prices contributed to social and economic problems. Lawmakers, judges, and sheriffs combined forces to use the laws to create a greater controlled worker population, largely of Black freedmen. Several tactics were used including threatened eviction and labor-for-rent as well as written contracts with illiterate former slaves. "Contract-jumping" was a crime. Sometimes a white who needed labor would go to a local court, pick a good worker, and offer to "go his bond"; the Black would then have to work out his "fine" and "court costs." In addition, a complex network of credit advances, crop liens, contract obligations, and threatened charges of "fraud" or "breach of contract" if a laborer left a location could be used to control the freedmen in a condition resembling peonage.

But the most effective relevant device was the convict-lease system. Even though the convict-lease system had been used prior to the Civil War in the North, this system grew to dominate the post-War Southern penal process. Although undoubtedly some Black men did indeed behave in a criminal fashion, many laws were, in practice, used to conscript labor. "Vagrancy" statutes were commonly applied to unemployed freedmen, and poverty could lead to charges of "intent to steal." Florida used charges of being "idle" and "dissolute"; under the Louisiana laws and in Mississippi in 1880, a Black male who simply did not have a work contract for the next year could be arrested and convicted. Laws about gambling, drinking, gun taxes, or concealed weapons could be applied in a discriminatory fashion; "fisticuffs" was a particularly effective charge because two or more Black men could each get five years hard labor, and their mutual denials would, of course, be ignored as transparently self-serving. As the profitability of the convict-lease system became increasingly obvious, an incentive developed to prosecute and deal harshly with every factual or fictional legal infraction. "Fines" and "court costs" could be worked off with longer sentences. Blacks, of course, were not allowed to serve on juries. Most trials were conducted by local magistrates or justices of the peace. Although the Georgia laws specified a maximum ten-year sentence, many men received twenty years; across the South very few survived twelve years.

Convicts were leased out in all the Southern states except Missouri. The system, in practice, permitted the exercise of racial discrimination in both assignments and pardons; the author of "Studies in the South" commented upon the assignment of a white Louisiana gentleman murderer to civilized gardening duty where he could easily chat with the young ladies of the town; but the vast majority of Black men received "hard-time" assignments, such as mining, plantation, and railroad construction. Because its prisoners were leased out, Florida, in effect, closed its penitentiary. Efforts of Black South Carolina legislators to abolish the convict-lease system failed.

Because the prices involved vary widely from region to region as the supply of prisoners, the corruption, and the political exploitation increased, we probably cannot conclude that Jim's price is confirmation of this theory. Jim is worth at least $800–1000 as a slave, yet the king transfers his control, "sold out his chance," to Silas Phelps for $40, which seems slightly too high a price for convict labor. In Georgia in 1867, a convict would be leased for railroad construction labor for $25 a year, but by 1890, when the system had created a larger supply, the price for leasing a convict miner fell to only $11 a year.

But strong financial incentives supported the convict-lease system. It could be much more profitable than slavery, because the lessee had no capital investment and minimal health expenses, if any. In the pre-emancipation days, a slave-owner who lashed his slave lowered his slave's resale value because the scars and keloids might be seen at the resale and therefore serve as permanent evidence of past disobedience. But under the convict-lease system, flogging caused the lessee no such financial loss. The death rate could be high. In 1877–79 in South Carolina, one contractor averaged 45 percent mortality per year, but in other states the average annual mortality ranged between 16 and 25 percent (Novak 33). Mines were the most dangerous, with plantation and railroad labor more dangerous than manufacturing. The lessee usually did not have to account for or pay for those who escaped, died, or were killed. Both escape and mortality rates for the convict-lease system far surpassed the rates in Northern prisons.

The effect upon Black families would be, one imagines, destabilizing, devastating. Just as Jim's family and, later, Huck would not know what had happened to Jim when he is missing, friends and relatives were not always informed about a leased convict-prisoner. In the Reconstruction era, the Black family could not know whether the male had drowned, been injured or killed in the woods, had run off or been picked up by the authorities. Blacks had long ago become used to the actions of the "paddy rollers" or "pater-rollers," the surveillance gangs, usually of minimally-literate, armed white men on horseback, who would catch slaves who were off the plantation without a written "pass." It is easy to understand how, in the chaos after the war, the supposedly freed slaves might be confused by the similarity between the "paddy-rollers," the early Ku-Klux Klan night riders, and the patrolling deputies and sheriffs. In the early 1880s, an isolated, travelling, or friendless freed Black man, when confronted by armed whites, probably could not easily tell the difference between legitimate and illegitimate or abusive authorities.

The sheriff's forces would probably think that they were maintaining public order, acting with "authority," and preventing social trouble while supplying labor and making money. Freed Blacks might think that they had been harassed, captured, or kidnapped, and then they were usually moved to a new, unfamiliar location where they were brutally re-enslaved. The arresting skill of Joe Turner (brother of a Tennessee governor), who supplied large numbers of convicts for the lease system, would become legendary in Black folk knowledge. But most modern American readers, who have been trained to be indignant about the British press gangs which conscripted free Americans, know almost nothing about the convict-lease system and remain confident that slavery ended with the 1864 Emancipation Proclamation.

Did Americans then know about the system? Could Twain have learned of this injustice? He could have read a horrifying explanation about using chase dogs to track and a more fierce "catch dog" to kill escaping prisoner-laborers in the January 1883, *Atlantic* "Studies in the South" article entitled "The Survival of Slavery." But a much more knowledgeable and zealous personal informant existed. Twain met George Washington Cable in June of 1881 and subsequently visited him in New Orleans. The two men spent many days together during the period of 1883–1885, including a time when Cable was ill in Twain's home. Although we do not know what, if anything, Twain knew about the then-current Auburn or Elmira prison reforms, we do know that Cable was, initially, very concerned about the high rates of escape from the convict-lease system. Cable had become interested in asylum and prison reform in 1881 and was already quite knowledgeable and indignant about the horrible evils of the convict-lease system when he spoke in New Orleans, as reported in the *Times Picayune*, on January 9, 1883. He gave another lecture on the topic in New York on March 26, 1883, and later came to Hartford where he stayed with the Warners and visited Twain during April 2–5. Cable addressed the National Conference of Charities and Correction in Louisville on September 26. He read the proofs of his powerful essay, "The Convict-Lease System in the Southern States," on November 24, and this detailed, definitive essay appeared in the February 1884, *Century*. The same magazine would also soon publish Cable's relevant "The Freedman's Case in Equity." The second article included two pages Cable had originally put in the "Convict Lease" article but suppressed.

Cable's zealous attitude about prison reform and the convict-lease system is revealed in a letter to his wife in which he was contrasting the honors and deference given to him at the St. Botolph Club in Boston by people like Matthew Arnold, Thomas Wentworth Higginson, and Francis Parkman with his own sense of personal mission:

> Help me to remember that pleasing as all this is, it's not the *main thing*. No, no. I read the proof of my prisons article today. Ah! There's where I feel glad. When a Man feels that his sword has cleft Apollyon till he roars again. That's better than "Rabbi, Rabbi." (*George W. Cable: His Life and Letters*, 110)

(The reference to Apollyon alludes to Bunyan's *The Pilgrim's Progress*, Chapter XI, when Christian, in the Valley of Humiliation, has to fight the hideous monster Apollyon, the king of hell: "In this combat no man can imagine, unless he has seen and heard, as I did, what yelling and hideous roaring Apollyon made all the time of the fight; he spoke as a dragon:— and, on the other side, what sighs and groans burst from Christian's heart." [I, 74]) It is quite likely that Cable, with his great knowledge and strong convictions, would at some point have spoken about his current intellectual work and ethical project with his fellow Southerner, Twain.

This reconceptualization of the Phelps episode may be advanced in a conjectural fashion in order to be tested intellectually. In my opinion, this idea cannot be proven incontrovertibly but is a permissible interpretation, supplying an informative cultural context. The story of Jim's imprisonment, at a primary level, deals with the captivity of a runaway slave in about 1845. At a secondary level, Jim's imprisonment provides ample opportunity to mock the European adventure-escape fiction which Twain felt was then distorting national values. At a tertiary, perhaps distant, level, Tom's knowing compliance with the imprisonment of a freed Black may possibly serve as an analogy to the then current, legal but immoral exploitation of freedmen in the convict-lease system. But Twain's attitude was probably complex—affection and esteem for the Quarles/Phelps individuals, contempt for Tom's literary folly, and hatred of slavery and injustice.

Obviously a noticeable overlap of vocabulary exists that could apply to an escaped slave in 1845, a prisoner in a parody of European fiction, and perhaps to a convicted-leased freedman: "prison," "captive," "chains," "shackles," "guards," "authorities," "regulations," "digging," and "escape," to name a few. But this multivalence can be regarded not as confirmation but as mere consonance. Although the dominant reference of Twain's word "prisoner" is certainly the mocked European escape literature, in the Phelps episode the word occurs, in singular or plural forms, at least thirty times. Moreover, at the end of the episode the kindly Doctor observes that Jim "was all tired out, too, and I see plain enough that he had been worked main hard, lately" (357). We think of Jim within Tom's language system as a European prisoner, but perhaps Twain labels Jim doubly when Tom says, "Who ever heard of a state prisoner escaping with a hickry-bark ladder?" (303). An ideal reader might be able to read Tom's two statements that Jim is a "state prisoner" (303 and 324) while simultaneously hearing the folly of Tom's interest in European adventures and also hearing, with a flicker of doubt, a moment of uncertainty, the ignored reality of the convict-lease system as experienced by freedmen. It is one level of skill to hear first one interpretation, then another; but it requires an entirely different level of skill to hear, at the same time, certainty and uncertainty. Tom's desire to keep Jim a "prisoner" for many years could represent both the bookish romantic exaggeration and a glance at the actual excessive sentences. The novel's ending can hence be considered as simultaneously an exciting, improbable narrative, a playful and angry parodic attack upon "noble" European escape fiction, and perhaps as an oblique, serious commentary on the continuing deceptive imprisonment of legally freed Black men.

Several other bits of information may be relevant. At one point Twain had considered having Jim stand trial for Huck's murder, but this plot possibility would likely demand a return up river. Did Twain consider this option just because he loved trial scenes or because he wished Jim to be a "prisoner" for thematic reasons? Unknowable. It is perhaps worth mention that at the beginning of the Phelps episode Twain thought of the location, probably with the Quarles place in mind, as run by a "farmer" with a sawmill. But soon the place becomes primarily a "little one-horse cotton plantation" (277). In a notebook comment written after September 24, 1883 about things to add to *Huck*, Twain included "pater-rollers and slavery."

It is more significant to realize that Twain had once thought of the escape in comic terms, with a note on C-10 revealing plans:

> Steal guns and get away under a volley of blank cartridge. (*Huck*, 1988, 746)

But instead the final text treats the escape and chase seriously; Twain had insisted upon the potentially lethal nature of the escape with his revision of Huck's mocking statement that Tom's plan "was worth fifteen of mine, for style, and **would** make Jim just as free a man as mine would, and maybe get us all ⟨killed⟩ ⟨shot⟩ **killed** besides" (MS, 530–31). It may well be mere chance that in Cable's powerful essay he presents a tabulation for twenty-one Tennessee prisoners: "Found dead. Killed. Drowned. Not given. Blank. Blank. Blank. Killed. Blank. Shot. Killed. Blank. Blank. Killed. Killed. Blank. Blank. Blank. Killed. Blank. Blank." (Convict-Lease, 486).

Similarly, on C-10, Twain noted a possible comic comment by Huck on the escape:

> I fetched away a dog, part of the way—I had him by his teeth in my britches, behind.

But Twain decided not to use this amusing detail for the Phelps episode and instead chose to present the escape in a more serious tone. Perhaps the humor would be too great a contrast with a passage about the use of dogs to chase escapees from the convict-lease system which readers of that January 1883, *Atlantic* had seen, in the "Studies in the South" essay, "The Survival of Slavery":

> In Mississippi I found a republican official who hired prisoners from the authorities, and employed them in various kinds of labor. The convicts worked under guard, and occasionally some of them would try to escape. Most of them were negroes. When they ran away the employer and his guards chased them with dogs, using a pack of hounds to follow the scent. These will not

attack the fugitive, but they are accompanied by a powerful and ferocious "catch-dog," that will tear a man to pieces in a few minutes, if the flying wretch is unable to ascend a tree before the terrible brute is upon him. Just before I was in that neighborhood a runaway negro convict had played a shrewd trick which enabled him to make good his escape, for that time at least. Hearing the hounds upon his trail, he struck across the country for the railroad. When he reached it the dogs were in plain sight across the fields, and were rapidly gaining on him. Half a mile away he saw an express train approaching. He knew the dogs would follow the scent closely, so he ran to meet the train, which, but a moment after he stepped from the track, ran over the dogs, killing them all. (95)

It might therefore be unrealistic for Huck to be bitten by one of those hounds in a relatively harmless way. Instead the conclusion of the escape is done in a serious, riveting fashion. Because dogs are potentially formidable, inclusion of them in the fictional escape would require some trickery.[3]

In the final 100 pages of the manuscript there are only three places where Twain turned over the sheet and inserted a substantive addition. The only full-page reverse-side insertion occurs on 706 after the boys slip out of Jim's cabin, as MS, 705 states:

> Then there was a rush, and a bang, bang, bang*!* and the bullets fairly whizzed around us! We heard them sign out:
> "*Here they are!* They've broke for the river! after 'em boys! ⟨"⟩ *And turn loose the dogs!*"
> So here they come, full tilt. We could hear them, because they wore boots, and yelled, but we didn't wear no boots, and didn't yell. We was in the path to the mill; and when they got pretty close onto us, we dodged into the bush and let them go by, and then dropped in behind them ⟨; and when we⟩. OVER *They'd had all the dogs shut up, so they wouldn't scare off the robbers; but by this time somebody had let them loose, and here they come, making pow-wow enough for a million; but they was our dogs; so we stopped in our tracks till they catched up; and when they see it warn't nobody but us, ⟨they⟩ and no excitement to offer them, they only just said howdy, ⟨and boomed⟩ and tore right ahead towards the shouting and chattering; and then ⟨we picked up our heels and tore along after them till we⟩ we up steam again and whizzed along after them till we* OVER AGAIN was nearly to the mill, ⟨we⟩ *and then* struck up through the bush to where my canoe was tied, and hopped in and pulled for dear life towards the middle of the river, but didn't make no more noise than we was obliged to. Then we struck out, easy and comfortable, for the island where my raft was; and we could hear them yelling *and barking* at each other all up and down the bank, till we was so far away the sounds got dim and died out. And when we stepped onto the raft, I says:
> "Now, old Jim, you're a free man <u>again</u>, and I bet you you won't ever be a slave ⟨any⟩ *no* more." (MS, 705–7)

Although the addition of the dogs could certainly be thought of as merely an insertion of realistic detail into an exciting scene, one could suggest that Twain's imagination was intrigued by how the escapees could avoid harm from the dogs.

Twain's decision to keep the fictional escape non-comic is supported by other evidence, but again the evidence could apply to either an 1845 escape or a convict-lease prisoner escape. Once they are on the raft "Tom was the gladdest of all, because he had a bullet ⟨through the⟩ *in the* calf of his leg" (MS, 708). Two comments may suffice: the bullet remaining in the child would increase the likelihood of infection and a fatal result; this detail may weigh very slightly against the convict-lease analogy. Although Cable informs us that the convict-lease system had a distinct preference for shot-guns, J. C. Powell, a Florida warden, repeatedly refers in his 1891 memoirs to the effectiveness of rifles.

If Twain's purpose in the Phelps episode was only to write a comedic burlesque of European escape fiction, then his addition of dogs and a potentially mortal wound may seem a realistic but perhaps gratuitous shift into seriousness. Moreover, it may appear unlikely that Twain, who knew Cable very well, could write words such as "chain," "shackle," "escape," and "guard" with no awareness of any contemporary references for the words. Of course, it is possible for an artist to create a text with societal meanings he does not precisely intend or fully understand.

After the manuscript was completed, Twain added, for the printed version:

> and Tom give Jim forty dollars for being prisoner for us so patient, and doing it up so good. (365)

It should be observed that Twain did not write "Tom and I give Jim . . . ," which would have implicated Huck in the cash nexus. Similarly, Twain did not write, "Tom give Jim forty or eighty or twelve hundred dollars to buy his wife and children . . . ," which would have been more liberating. Nor did Twain write, "for being an escapee or an adventurer for us." Instead Tom is paying Jim, as a "prisoner," for his labor. An opponent of the theory could, however, object that it is confusingly unrealistic because in a convict-lease system (which could include subleasing), Tom's money should have gone to Silas Phelps or to the king, but not to Jim. Moreover, state leased-prisoners were most frequently handled in groups, with individual leases more usual at the local or county level.

Should a contemporary scholar/critic at least consider the possibility that the convict-lease system may be relevant to the novel's ending?

Although we may never know the full extent of Twain's inferable intentions or the full range of his novel's cultural meanings, readers concerned about Jim's freedom need to know that the convict-lease system existed and was used in the South to re-institute legalized slavery among freed Black men. Although we cannot prove inarguably that this analogy was intended, Twain could have known of the system; some textual details appear quite consistent with this interpretation, and the pattern of the evidence makes a case with only minor contradictions and with major analogies. At the very least we can decide that the re-enslavement of freedmen was, in 1849 or in 1883, quite realistic. Moreover, Tom's exploitative deceit may parallel the Southern resistance to Emancipation. Freedom had been granted, but Americans had twisted the shape of justice. The convict-lease system provides an important additional historical resonance for the novel's ending. In fact and in fiction, a Black person could be "freed," without really becoming "free."

If this reconceptualization of the ending of the Phelps episode seems plausible, it is misplaced indignation, misplaced outrage, that modern readers and critics focus blame for deception on Twain and do not consider his ingenuity as designer of Tom's role as a knowing re-enslaver of a freedman. For the book, and perhaps for Twain and the nation, the recurrence of slavery has massive thematic and structural importance.

Let this exploration close with a changed question: Does the extraneous interest of the travesty of European literature overwhelm the satire on a societal evil, the real willingness of whites, old and young, king and commoner, to re-enslave a freed Black man?

III

The overall interpretation advanced in this chapter recognizes elements of Trilling's, Eliot's, and Marx's views. I consider the novel to be cyclic in structure and aesthetically unified—to a surprising degree. I recognize, however, that Twain was simultaneously unifying his novel and reflexively undercutting his fiction. This interpretation agrees with those critics, such as Frank Baldanza, who see formal unity in the novel's ending; moreover, this approach incorporates thematic, familial, and historical dimensions.

To decide whether Twain's echoic imagination created formal unity, despite a shift in genre, requires a partial catalogue of the novel's repetitions and variations. In this rapid collocation of duplications, we may first consider connections within the novel, then between the Phelps episode and the rest of the novel, and, finally, within the Phelps episode.

An aesthetic perspective toward the deliberate use of repetition can be found in Twain's autobiographical dictation of August 31, 1906:

> For repetition is a mighty power in the domain of humor. If frequently used, nearly any precisely worded and unchanging formula will <u>eventually</u> compel laughter if it be gravely <u>and earnestly</u> repeated, at intervals, five or six times. (M.T.P.)

Although *Huck* does not include quite so many repetitions of items, the point remains that much of the repetition is humorous in tone. Accordingly, the ending should in general be read with rapidity and comedic lightness, directing the humor primarily at Tom and at those Americans who are poisoned or corrupted by foreign novels; Twain's American audience can laugh at Tom's Europeanization; moreover, the trivialization of earlier important themes reflects badly not on Twain but on Tom and on those devoted to European literary values. That Tom knew that Jim was already freed just makes his efforts more silly, more immoral, more exploitative, more offensive, more outrageously contemptible.

The very act of doubling, which Blair calls "motif with variations" and Baldanza names "repetition with variation," calls attention to the partial, fictional nature of each occurrence. Within the novel's world, examples of repetition cannot be avoided. For instance, parallel delusional signings involve the boys' pirate club and Pap Finn's reformation. In Huck's conversation with the judge and with his father, a dollar changes hands, although there is a great contrast in courtesy toward the boy. An equal contrast exists between Pap's addictive, disgusting, frightening, lethal drunkenness and Jim's deliberate, situational drunkenness to combat the snake bite. Other repetitions exist: in his conversation with Mrs. Judith Loftus about Jim, Huck blurts out and stops, "Why he—" (85), and Tom later stops himself from revealing Jim's freedom by saying, "What! Why Jim is—" (285). Lynching threatens Pap Finn, Colonel Sherburn, the king and duke and Huck, and finally Jim. Jim declares that he would attempt to steal his children, but actually some children later try to steal Jim. And although Jim had run away to avoid being sold down river, he is later forced to continue down river and is, unknowingly, sold into illegal imprisonment.

Numerous instances of disguising and false naming occur. Transvestitism occurs twice for Huck and once for the king, when he dresses as Juliet. Twain includes an honest show, the circus, and a series of dishonest shows by the king and duke. The Shakespearean references include *Romeo and Juliet*, *Richard III*, Hamlet's soliloquy, and *King Lear*.

Familial situations recur; both Miss Boggs and Mary Jane Wilks are bereaved. Emotional contrast happens when Jim relates a touching story about his daughter's deafness shortly before the duke shams deafness. Moreover, Jim's emotions about the break up of his family take another real form when the Wilks slaves are sold in different directions.

The king's deceitfulness enables him to take numerous unifying functions. The king, in actuality, provides a shabby incarnation of the pirates and robbers in Tom's early reading. Further, the king's imposture as a reformed pirate echoes Pap Finn's brief reformation, and twice the king poses as a sanctimonious minister.

Huck's eyes water when he prepares to leave Buck Grangerford's body and when he thinks about Mary Jane Wilks. Huck twice deceptively controls other people's actions by invoking diseases, smallpox and the pluribus unum mumps. Twice Huck gets trapped in a dangerous situation and overhears thieves planning, once on the *Walter Scott* and once in the Wilks home. Huck twice runs to the raft hoping to escape from the king and duke, but each time the effort fails.

Just as the king pumps the rural lad for information at the beginning of the Wilks episode, so also Huck quizzes a country lad at the beginning of the Phelps section. Similarly, just as the king gets dressed up to begin his impersonation of Rev. Wilks, Huck gets well dressed to approach the Phelps farm.

The fooling of a sharp country woman has several manifestations. The deception of Mrs. Judith Loftus echoes in our minds as first Huck and then Tom deceive Aunt Sally Phelps. And both Aunt Sally and Aunt Polly summon Huck from his hiding place by the bed.

In a highly significant repetition, the precise detail of escape from captivity by sawing and digging out of a cabin with the exit hidden by a blanket occurs twice. Huck made a practical, successful escape from his father's cabin, with deceptive clues; later Tom engineers an impractical, unsuccessful escape, with deceptive clues. At one point, Twain noted a direction to himself on C-12: "Cut Jim out of cabin the back way" and, probably after it was done, scrawled a cancelling line through that section (*Huck*, 1988, 748). Even the idea of Jim's voluntary participation in captivity recurs. As he had earlier acted the sick Arab, Jim dutifully pretends that the

Phelps shanty can hold him. In the Wilks episode two men pretend to be relatives in order to steal for selfish purposes, with much of the action parodic of *King Lear*; in the Phelps episode two boys pretend to be relatives in order to steal (one with unselfish motives and one with egotistical motives), with much of the action parodic of European heroic literature. In each case a real relative appears and an authoritative Doctor contributes to the resolution. The serious theme of escape from social boundaries extends to an absurd degree because the escape would be easy were it not for the difficulties of the literary conventions which Tom feels compelled to duplicate.

The final section on the Phelps farm provides many opportunities for balancing in the book by summoning up or recalling a past (usually frightening) situation and repeating it in a comic mode. Psychologically terrifying events are recreated in a more manageable fashion. One obvious example involves snakes. We recall that, in Chapter VI, Huck's father had alcohol-inspired hallucinations about snakes crawling on him and biting him in the cabin and later, in Chapter X, Huck had planned to play a trick on Jim by putting a dead rattler in the blanket; Jim is bitten by the mate of the snake, suffers terribly, and cures himself, but Huck never acknowledges his causative role in the accident. In the Phelps section, Tom wishes Jim to have a rattlesnake in his prison. When Jim objects strongly, Tom informs him:

> "Why, Jim, you wouldn't be afraid of it, after a little. You could tame it."
>
> "Tame it!"
>
> "Yes—easy enough. Every animal is grateful for kindness and petting, and they wouldn't <u>think</u> of hurting a person that pets them. Any book will tell you that. You try—that's all I ask; just try for two or three days. Why you can get him so, in a little while, that he will love you; and will let you wrap him round your neck and put his head in your mouth." (MS, 652–53)

In the manuscript, Twain inserted after "he will love you" the explicit repetition *"and sleep with you; and won't stay away from you a minute;"* as if to underline the duplication. And into Jim's subsequent reply Twain revised the sentence: *"En mo' en dat, I doan' <u>want</u> him to sleep wid me"* (MS, 653). Jim's previous experience with a rattler in his sleeping place contradicts Tom's romanticized bookish notions; the connection becomes absolutely unmistakable by the insertion of these two references to sleeping with snakes.

Another example of repetition occurs in the use of sentimental music.

Tom recommends that Jim, in evenings and mornings, "play The Last Link is Broken—that's the thing that'll ⟨fetch⟩ *scoop* a rat, quicker'n anything else" (MS, 659). Huck had heard the tune in a more serious, emotional context at the home of Emmeline Grangerford.

Several other duplications also involve minor details. The illegitimate advertisement for Jim created by the duke recurs in a socially sanctioned fashion as Silas Phelps advertises for Jim's owner in the New Orleans and St. Louis papers. Just as the king had posed as a minister, kept Jim in captivity, sold the Wilkses' slaves, and later reimprisoned Jim, the genuine "preacher," Silas Phelps, despite his reading about the apostle Silas and imprisonment, also keeps Jim in captivity and expects to receive money for him. The boys' original escapade in Chapter II involved playing a trick on the sleeping Jim, and a sleeping slave in Chapter XXXIX receives the trick letter. Moreover, the letter about the plot, from an "Unknown Friend," sounds the same note of false repentance and reformation used so effectively by the pirate-king at the camp meeting.

There are also, of course, duplications even within the Phelps episode. The comic frightening of the slave by the hounds who appear from under Jim's bed reappears in the more serious anxiety of the farmers as they await the robbers:

> They couldn't a been worse scared if they'd a tried. If a door banged, aunt Sally jumped, and said "ouch!" (MS, 684)

Twain canceled "they'd a tried" and turned over the manuscript page to write that the whites were as frightened as if *"the place had a been full of ghosts laying for them behind everything and under the beds and shivering through the air."* Momentarily, comically, the farmers resemble the slave who had been terrified by "witches" in Jim's cabin.

Although the majority of the Phelps section duplications present a frightening event in a comic mode, there is also a simple, significant repetition of a terrifying chase. Of course, survival in a chaotic night fire-fight of this sort is utterly random. On manuscript pages 704, 704 1/2 (recto and verso) and 705 we find a rewritten version of the escape. The most frightening moment of the chase occurs on MS, 705:

> Then there was a rush, and a bang, bang, bang! and the bullets fairly whizzed around us! We heard them sing out:
> "*Here they are!* They've broke for the river! after 'em boys! ⟨"⟩ *And turn loose the dogs!*"

The scene partially echoes and recreates a frightening and moving daylight scene, Huck's observation of the end of the Shepherdson/Grangerford feud:

> All of a sudden, bang! bang! bang! goes three or four guns—the men had slipped around through the woods and come in from behind without their horses! The boys jumped for the river—both of them hurt—and as they swum down the current the men run along the bank shooting at them and singing out, "Kill them, kill them!" It made me so sick I most fell out of the tree. I ain't agoing to tell *all* that happened—it would make me sick again if I was to do that. I wished I hadn't ever come ashore that night, to see such things. I ain't ever going to get shut of them—lots of times I dream about them. (154)

This situation recurs when the targets flee to the river, with the addition of Jim as another fleeing person. The point of view changes from Huck's earlier tree-level observation to include his own involvement as a target; the consequences are lessened to include only one wound, in Tom's leg.

As indicated, Twain had toyed with the possibility of presenting the flight from the shooting farmers in a comic light. Huck could have said:

> I fetched away a dog, part of the way—I had him by his teeth in my britches, behind. (Note C-10, *Huck*, 1988, 746)

Such a comic statement would have certainly lightened the tone. Similarly, at one point Twain imagined that the escape could have been shaped without serious consequences:

> Steal guns and get away under a volley of blank cartridges. (Note C-10, *Huck*, 1988, 746)

But Twain's decision not to develop or to suppress these possibilities kept the Phelps farm escape similar to the death of Buck Grangerford.

It seems fair to say that the novel has at least some formal unity, some doubling or repetition of earlier events. Indeed, the ending may even be seen as a too-schematic recapitulation of earlier parts of the novel. In all likelihood, if the novel's ending related that Tom and Huck freed Jim and that Jim or some doctor in a distant town cured Tom before the trio set off for the territory, many critics and readers would like the novel better and would not criticize the Phelps episode. In other words, if the escape resembled the literary models, many readers would like the book better. It is, in fact, revelatory that Hemingway, with his reliance on "codes," would be so offended by his memory of his faulty reconstruction of the ending.

The continuity with *Huck* resides, I would suggest, in the repetition of the details; the variation in the later part of the Phelps section lies in the change to explicitly anti-literary and serious tones. But Twain apparently wished to create a story in which bookish delusions have consequences.

IV

This brief catalogue of repetitions has not yet fully explained the most significant insertion, a repetition which provides both thematic and structural unity. After the chase and after Jim is recaptured, there is a scene in "Chapter the last" of Huck and Jim in Tom's sick room. Twain added this highly important short revision late in the process; it does not appear in the manuscript or manuscript revision but was added for the printed version:

> . . . and Tom give Jim forty dollars for being prisoner for us so patient, and doing it up so good, and Jim was pleased most to death, and busted out, and says:
> "*Dah*, now, Huck, what I tell you?—what I tell you up dah on Jackson islan'? I *tole* you I got a hairy breas', en what's de sign un it; en I *tole* you I ben rich wunst, en gwineter to be rich *agin*; en it's come true; 'en heah she *is! Dah*, now! doan' talk to *me*—signs is *signs*, mine I tell you; en I knowed jis' 's well 'at I 'uz gwineter be rich agin as I's a stannin' heah dis minute!" (365)

Although, theoretically, it is conceivable that Twain may have added this section for no reason whatever, the reference, in the second paragraph, to another section of the novel (Chapter VIII) leads one to infer that the addition was not simply a chance occurrence. The illiterate Jim's ability to read and interpret "signs" is triumphantly re-validated. On the most obvious level the second paragraph fulfills one of Jim's prophecies, satisfying reader expectations and providing a sense of closure and completion while creating an apparently happy tone, since Jim once more is "rich."

Yet another relevance for the insertion indicates the novel's covert structure and meaning. The first specific detail of the addition demands close critical attention. Why "forty dollars"? This question may best be answered by considering the other uses of forty dollars in the novel. We remember that the two men who were searching for escaped slaves on the river each give Huck twenty dollar gold pieces and that later the king gets the same amount for Jim.

The placing of these financial dealings reveals one important way in which the author structured the novel. Twain created in *Adventures of*

Huckleberry Finn three parallel sequential patterns of action, a triple lattice structure. Each pattern involves first the meeting of Huck with someone who thinks him dead, the formation (or renewal) of a partnership to free the slave which ends in failure, and finally, the exchange of forty dollars. This triptych-like repetition involves different settings and characters in Huck's effort to free the slave: first, the simple flight through a natural world on the Mississippi; second, the predominantly picaresque adventures and deceptions of the king and duke; and, finally, the burlesque romanticism—and perhaps the country's "cheating" through the prisoner-lease reenslavement—of Tom's plot on the Phelps farm. These patternings of events and the ultimate impossibility of *winning* the slave's freedom gradually become more explicit as the novel progresses.

The first element of these patterns can be perceived by simply juxtaposing three similar passages. The first occurs when Huck searches for the other occupant of Jackson's Island:

> So I took my gun and slipped off towards where I had run across that camp fire, stopping every minute or two to listen. But I hadn't no luck, somehow; I couldn't seem to find the place. But by-and-by, sure enough, I catched a glimpse of fire, away through the trees. I went for it, cautious and slow. By-and-by I was close enough to have a look, and there laid a man on the ground. It most give me the fan-tods. He had a blanket around his head, and his head was nearly in the fire. I set there behind a clump of bushes, in about six foot of him, and kept my eyes on him steady. It was getting gray daylight, now. Pretty soon he gapped, and stretched himself, and hove off the blanket, and it was Miss Watson's Jim! I bet I was glad to see him. I says:
> "Hello, Jim!" and skipped out.
> He bounced up and stared at me wild. Then he drops down on his knees, and puts his hands together and says:
> "Doan' hurt me—don't! I hain't ever done no harm to a ghos'. I awluz liked dead people, en done all I could for 'em. You go en git in de river agin, whah you b'longs, en doan' do nuffn to Ole Jim, 'at 'uz awluz yo' fren'."
> Well, I warn't long making him understand I warn't dead. I was ever so glad to see Jim. I warn't lonesome, now. (66–67)

This meeting is echoed after Huck and Jim have been separated by the fog. Huck, after having great difficulty finding the raft, finally discovers Jim sleeping:

> Then I see another speck, and chased that; then another, and this time I was right. It was the raft.
> When I got to it Jim was setting there with his head down between his

knees, asleep, with his right arm hanging over the steering oar. The other oar was smashed off, and the raft was littered up with leaves and branches and dirt. So she'd had a rough time.

I made fast and laid down under Jim's nose on the raft, and begun to gap, and stretch my fists out against Jim, and says:

"Hello, Jim, have I been asleep? Why didn't you stir me up?"

"Goodness gracious, is dat you, Huck? En you ain' dead—you ain' drownded—you's back agin? It's too good for true, honey, it's too good for true. Lemme look at you, chile, lemme feel o' you. No, you ain' dead! you's back agin, 'live en soun', jis de same ole Huck—de same ole Huck, thanks to goodness!" (119)

The relationship between these two passages may seem simply a chance similarity, but the third such confrontation, which occurs toward the beginning of the Phelps farm sequence, demonstrates the unity of the author's artistic imagination by recapitulating elements from the previous scenes, combining the terror of a ghost, the possibility of trickery, and the tactile proof of Huck's vitality:

So I started for town, in the wagon, and when I was half-way I see a wagon coming, and sure enough it was Tom Sawyer, and I stopped and waited till he come along. I says "Hold on!" and it stopped alongside, and his mouth opened up like a trunk, and staid so; and he swallowed two or three times like a person that's got a dry throat, and then says:

"I hain't ever done you no harm. You know that. So then, what you want to come back and ha'nt *me* for?"

I says:

"I hain't come back—I hain't been *gone*."

When he heard my voice, it righted him up some, but he warn't quite satisfied yet. He says:

"Don't you play nothing on me, because I wouldn't on you. Honest injun, now, you ain't a ghost?"

"Honest injun, I ain't," I says.

"Well—I—I—well, that ought to settle it, of course; but I can't somehow seem to understand it, no way. Looky here, warn't you ever murdered *at all?*"

"No, I warn't ever murdered at all—I played it on them. You come in here and feel of me if you don't believe me."

So he done it; and it satisfied him; and he was that glad to see me again, he didn't know what to do. And he wanted to know all about it right off; because it was a grand adventure, and mysterious, and so it hit him where he lived. (284–85)

And in each case the reunion leads to the formation or renewal of a cooperative effort to free Jim which eventually fails in an appropriate way.

In the first case Huck and Jim agree to float a raft down the river to Cairo only to have the fog, nature's obstacle, conceal their goal; once beyond Cairo they plan to get a canoe to go upriver only to pick up the king and duke, whose last roguish deception is to return Jim to captivity; and, finally, Huck and Tom plan to steal Jim out of slavery and imprisonment on the Phelps farm only to confront, ultimately, the reality of a child with a bullet in his leg.

Twain signals the failure of each attempt to free the slave by the exchange of forty dollars. We remember that after the fog, when the raft is apparently below Cairo, Huck paddles the canoe toward shore, thinking of turning Jim in, and instead protects him from the two men hunting runaway slaves. These men, who believe that Huck's family has smallpox, salve their consciences by directing Huck to go downriver and giving him forty dollars. The first and second rehearsals of the dominant pattern overlap slightly; after the fog Jim rediscovers Huck, beginning the second sequence (Chapter XV), and in the next chapter Huck gets the money, ending the first sequence.

The end of the second sequence happens when the duke and the king in their final violation of another human conspire to use the poster to sell Jim into a fabricated escaped slave status for forty dollars. Twain emphasizes the exact amount by mentioning it three times. The boy Huck meets on the road says, "It was an old feller—a stranger—and he sold out his chance in him for forty dollars, becuz he's got to go up the river and can't wait. Think o' that, now! You bet I'd wait, if *it* was seven year" (MS, 434). This is followed by Huck's meditation upon the event:

> I went ⟨in the wood⟩ to the raft, and set down in the wigwam to think. But I couldn't come to nothing. I thought, *till I wore* my head sore, but I couldn't see no way out of the trouble. After all this long journey, and after all ⟨the⟩ we'd done for them scoundrels, here was it all come *to* nothing, everything all busted up and ruined, because they could have the heart ⟨to be mean enough⟩ to serve Jim such a trick as that, and make him a slave again all his life, and amongst strangers, *too,* for forty dirty dollars. (MS, 435–36)

And the duke, later in the same chapter, informs Huck that the "old fool had made a trade and got forty dollars" (MS, 451–52). The king's sale of Jim represents the attitude of those privileged people (the slave hunters, king, duke, and Tom) who believe that they can sell or control even those Blacks who do not "belong" to them. Such an emphasis upon the specific amount augments the force of concrete detail to enhance the meaning and to reveal the frequency of such an attitude.

We find that the consistency and integrity of Twain's artistic imagination select the same amount as he adds to the published version of "Chapter the last" the passage which punctuates the third pattern:

> . . . and Tom give Jim forty dollars for being prisoner for us so patient, and doing it up so good. . . . (365)

The pattern was completed; the chosen "brick" which could serve as a structural keystone was locked into place. Any residual random thought that the $40 might be a chance, impulsive, meaningless insertion should be balanced against the knowledge that on note C-1 Twain wrote "$40 from men—95" and on C-3 "$40 for Jim—who says "told you I'd be rich agin" (*Huck*, 1988, 737, 739). Since this final payment is both conscience money in substitution for a moral obligation and payment received for an illegal enslavement, the insertion recapitulates the comparable parts of the previous patterns.[4]

With this conception of the book's structure in mind, we can realize that the demonstrated dramatized theme is the impossibility of winning the slave's permanent freedom. Each attempt ends with Huck and Jim facing a controlling, defeating reality: fog, greed, a bullet. The first cycle fails because of nature, the second because of human avarice, the third because of literary illusions and, if the convict-lease interpretation is accepted, racist deceit. The arc of Twain's imagination, the pattern his artistry repeatedly dramatized, is implicitly as dark, as pessimistic, as his later works are explicitly. But the very form of the work suggests an opposing meaning. The repetition of the pattern, and of others we have observed, indicates that although the struggle to win freedom appears ultimately unsuccessful, the attempt continues, cyclically, heroically, comically. Freedom only exists in the pursuit of freedom. Freedom is not a condition, but an activity, an action. The repetition of this paradoxical moral insight—that the attempt to gain freedom fails and begins again—reveals why the book renders, rends, and haunts the American consciousness.

Why is the explicit attack on literature as a way of knowing last? The attack on literature unifies the criticisms of nobility and religion—the abuses of throne and pulpit, of birth or belief—because these deceptions usually make their claims and justify their status through the codified authority passed on by means of literacy and literature.

With these conceptions of the novel's structure and meaning in mind, we may understand more fully the aesthetic achievement of the final paragraph. On a basic level, the last paragraph helps create a frame for the novel by returning to the present tense of the first paragraph and by emphasizing the implicit pessimism we have observed by repeating the use of a neck pendant. In Chapter II, Jim's nickel symbolized his credulous superstition; in the final portion, Tom's choice to wear the bullet that wounded him as a decorative necklace reveals that *his* visions of bookish romanticism remain uncorrected by experience, his attitudes unmodified by reality. Although Huck has changed, Tom still believes in "adventures":

> Tom's most well, now, and got his bullet around his neck on a watch-guard for a watch, ***and is always seeing what time it is, and so*** there ain't nothing more to write about, . . . (MS, 786)

Twain threw in the revision interlineally, emphasizing that Tom still, characteristically, wishes to be conspicuous.

Moreover, Huck's final assessment of the situation brilliantly concludes earlier motifs. Repeatedly in the novel, when his unillusioned wisdom had detected sham in religion, people, or literature, Huck had confided something like, "But I never said nothing." The conclusion transforms this motif into a comment upon the entire novel and the novelistic act, with obvious relevance to Huck's anxiety about his literacy. The book's subjects include its own reading and writing. The narrator who began, "You don't know about me, without you read a book. . ." concludes:

> . . . ***and so*** there ain't nothing more to write about, and I'm ⟨powerful⟩ ⟨***cussed***⟩ ⟨***blame***⟩ ***rotten*** glad of it, because if I'd a knowed what a trouble it was to make a book I wouldn't a tackled it and ain't agoing to ⟨,⟩ any more. But I reckon I got to light out for the Territory ahead of the rest, because ⟨they're⟩ ***aunt Sally she's*** going to adopt me and sivilize me and I can't stand it, I been there before. (MS, 786–87)

The process of writing may have—for the narrator and the readers—temporarily regained freedom, but Huck feels he must stop writing. He has recapitulated his experience, and he has, on one level, used up his experience.

The implicit darkness of the passage is clarified when we re-consider the genetic development of the word choice, the compression of the contradiction. Twain had first written "and I'm powerful glad of it" only to change "powerful" to "***cussed***"; the emotional intensity seems roughly the same, but the attitude has changed radically. The next change to "***blame***" maintains the same intensity and negative tone, while being perhaps more appropriate to Huck's own vocabulary. Then Twain re-canceled all the previous versions and inserted "*rotten*." In this process of sharpening the oxymoron from "powerful glad" through to "*rotten* glad" we can observe the artist creating the paradoxical complexity appropriate to this novel. And the printed version adds the life like, emphatic double negative, "aint't agoing to no more."

The identity of the people attempting to change Huck shifts from the general "they" to this specific Southern woman, "*aunt Sally*," as civilizing force; consequently, his situation at the end duplicates his situation at the beginning with a shift to the South.

The final expansion of an earlier motif involves, of course, the decision "to light out for the Territory" to escape being "sivilized." In all likelihood, the continuation, "Huck Finn and Tom Sawyer Among the Indians," would have developed the deceptive, destructive effect of American books in the Territory. But beyond expanding from the attempt to gain the slave's freedom to the pursuit of a young white male's individual freedom in this peculiar time-space we call America, the decision to "light out" also frames the book by recuperatively repeating on a larger scale Huck's action at the end of the first chapter when he left the Widow Douglas's house.

Twain also increased the emphasis of "I been there before" by changing it in print from a comma phrase to a complete independent sentence. Such a change is, for Twain, a relatively rare revisionary act.[5] The entire novel presents a complex, coherent, recursive structure of parallel patterns which embody a perceptive moral insight of the first order, dramatizing that for Huck freedom exists, if at all, only in the process of seeking freedom.

In manuscript the text ends with double underlined, "The End, yours truly Huck Finn." and the printed version is "THE END. YOURS TRULY, HUCK FINN." Each version presents, appropriately enough, a double conclusion, a reciprocal qualification. "The End" seems fitting as an ending for a novel, but Twain also uses the conventional form employed for ending a letter. Utilizing the combination, of course, calls into question the book's identity as either a novel or as perhaps the longest American letter. Why would Twain end the book as a letter? The transformation of a novel into a letter again upsets expectations about genre. Is there anything more than the chance to continue the illusion of Huck's speaking or writing voice? The signature transforms the general "you" of the beginning to second person singular, addressing you, the individual who reads the letter. The novel becomes a letter which includes other letters.

The treatment of letters in the book provides increased insight about Twain's attitudes and about how we can interpret the conclusion. In conventional fiction and in the epistolary fiction genre, letters frequently function as explanatory devices or for smoothing of plot and motivation. In this book, however, the note in the Grangerford episode led to the renewal of the feud and multiple deaths. Letters in the Wilks episode attempted to convey the truth, but ultimately failed to expose the king and duke. Huck's jotting to Mary Jane, which would have led her to the money, proved to be unnecessary. Huck's note to Miss Watson represents a moment of moral crisis, as he judges whether it is better to turn Jim in or to leave him in a Southern prison, significantly holding his breath and the paper (the spirit and the letter) before deciding to tear up the note. Because the letters of Aunt Polly to Aunt Sally Phelps disappear, they fail to communicate. The "nonnymous letters" frighten and deceive the Phelps family and ultimately lead to the shooting of a boy. Twain, as a man of letters, knew the difficulty of communication, the textual and contextual complications of letters, the unexpected outcomes, the deceptive and destructive power of fabrication. Further, his sense of distrust extended even to letters in his own fiction, convenient plot devices but ultimately deceptive.

The double conclusion epitomizes the repetition and duplicity of this novel in an autotelic reductive act. Momentarily, kaleidoscopically, the genres change, and the reader's expectations are again modified. This shift calls attention to the artificiality and artifice of the literary conventions. Although Huck may feel frustrated or worn by the difficulty of writing and by his conflicts with literate society, the reader's perceptions are expanded. This ending presents art of a high order which reflects upon itself.

Twain simultaneously polished his craft, improving his art, and qualified his fiction, transforming his novel when he wrote and revised *Adventures of Huckleberry Finn*. The process of transformation even applies to the title which should initially be interpreted with favorable connotations for the word *Adventures* but which finally conveys completely negative connotations which criticize both the adventure genre and fiction. Twain, with daunting parodic skill and independence, has created an enactive, self-qualifying work of literature which instead of inadvertently enslaving the reader to "felicitously written" literary illusions genuinely liberates the reader from an uncritical veneration of books. As a result of Twain's creative mind, his reading, writing, re-reading, and rewriting have given generations of Americans a complex, continuously rewarding masterpiece.

Notes

1. The following account draws upon information given by Foner, Blake, Cable, Tourgee, Ayers, Novak, and Rawick's edition, *The American Slave: A Composite Autobiography*. I have found only one personal narrative—from a guard's point of view; J. C. Powell's story covers the years 1876–1890 in the Florida prisoner-lease system. I am especially indebted in my investigations to Alfred Bendixen for helpful suggestions.

2. Attitudes among Blacks toward "the Territory" may be somewhat similar in the 1850 and 1883 eras. During Reconstruction, those freedmen who wished to leave the South for the Territory were called "Exodists," although it was actually provocative for those freed Black tenant farmers or contract-laborers even to speak about leaving within the landowner's hearing. Biblical language provided honorific terms for opposing sides; just as Blacks who desired better conditions were "Exodists," whites who worked toward the restoration of slavery-style white domination were called "Redeemers."

3. Peter Beidler has recently discovered that Twain bought a 1823 book by Faux which included a description of training a dog to attack a slave.

4. One may well ask, "Why forty dollars?" Because the money usually is involved in some form of deception or betrayal, one would have supposed that Twain's familiarity with the Bible would have led him to use some amount like "thirty pieces of silver." But the Biblical associations for "forty" usually involve periods of testing or temptation. A biographical association may also be mentioned because here we may be at some depth in Clemens/Twain's mind. Dixon Wecter informs us that:

> In the winter of 1841–42 Judge Clemens tried to do a little Negro trading himself, in the course of a long and financially unprofitable trip first into the Deep South and then back to the old homestead in Kentucky. "I still have *Charley*," he wrote to "Dear Jane and the Children," aboard a steamboat near Memphis, on January 5, 1842, "the highest price I had affixed for him in New Orleans was $50, and in Vicksburg $40. After performing the journey to Tennessee I expect to sell him for whatever he will bring where I take water again, viz. at Louisville or Nashville." Charley was apparently a slave whom he had picked up in Missouri, with the hope that he would fetch a better price along the lower Mississippi. Coming across this letter in the family papers half a century later, Mark Twain commented wryly upon his father's mention of Charley as if the man had been "an ox—and somebody else's ox. It makes a body homesick for Charley, even after fifty years. Thank God I have no recollection of him as house servant of ours; that is to say, playmate of mine, for I was playmate to all the niggers, preferring their society to that of the elect, I being a person of low-down tastes from the start, notwithstanding my high birth, and ever ready to forsake the communion of high souls if I could strike anything nearer my grade." Charley's fate is unknown, but a promissory note

given Judge Clemens by one Abner Phillips "for value received this 24th day of January 1842" suggests that he may have sold the slave for ten barrels of tar to be delivered in Missouri on or before the next Christmas. (Wecter, *Sam Clemens of Hannibal*, 74–75)

Thus it is within the realm of possibility that at some deep psychological level this novel may have been influenced by memories of the father's action leading to the son's imaginative effort to free the slave and redemptively erase a family shame.

In offering Jim, a freedman, "forty dollars for being prisoner for us so patient," Tom has created his own one-sided contract-labor device, perhaps resembling the convict-lease system, to exploit a fugitive/criminal just as whites exploited countless freedmen.

In offering Jim "forty dollars," Tom gives not "forty acres and a mule," but a simple cash nexus. Tom denies Jim's humanity and takes an action that puts him in structural resemblance to the two slave hunters and the king.

5. Probably the phrase, "I been there before," had an additional private yet triumphant meaning for Twain. In 1882 Howells had written for *Century* a four-page praise of Twain which built toward the phrase "been there" in the context of shared national experiences and values. The passage, although long, deserves attention for the reverberation, for the way the phrasing resonates, adding a dimension to Twain's decision to put the significant claim in Huck's voice. Howells states:

> . . . I mean to say of him that as Shakspere, according to Mr. Lowell's saying, was the first to make poetry all poetical, Mark Twain was the first to make humor all humorous. He has not only added more in bulk to the style of harmless pleasures than any other humorist; but more in the spirit that is easily and wholly enjoyable. There is nothing lost in literary attitude, in labored dictionary funning, in affected quaintness, in dreary dramatization, in artificial "dialect"; Mark Twain's humor is as simple in form and as direct as the statesmanship of Lincoln or the generalship of Grant.
>
> When I think how purely and wholly American it is, I am a little puzzled at its universal acceptance. We are doubtless the most thoroughly homogeneous people that ever existed as a great nation. There is such a parity in the experiences of Americans that Mark Twain or Artemus Ward appeals as unerringly to the consciousness of our fifty millions as Goldoni appealed to that of his hundred thousand Venetians. In one phrase, we have somehow all "been there"; in fact, generally, and in sympathy almost certainly, we have been there. In another generation or two, perhaps, it will be wholly different; but as yet the average American is the man who has risen; he has known poverty, and privation, and low conditions; he has very often known squalor; and now, in his prosperity, he regards the past with a sort of large, pitying amusement; he is not the least ashamed of it; he does not feel that it characterizes him any more than the future does. Our humor springs from this multiform American experience of life, and securely addresses itself—in reminiscence, in phrase, in its whole material—to the intelligence bred of like experience. It is not of a class for a class; it does not employ itself with the absurdities of a tailor as a

tailor; its conventions, if it has any, are all new, and of American make. When it mentions hash we smile because we have each somehow known the cheap boarding-house or restaurant; when it alludes to putting up stoves in the fall, each of us feels the grime and rust of the pipes on his hands; the introduction of the lightning-rod man, or the book-agent, establishes our brotherhood with the humorist at once. But how is it with the vast English-speaking world outside of these States, to which hash, and stove-pipes, and lightning-rod men and book-agents are as strange as lords and ladies, dungeon-keeps and battle-ments are to us? Why, in fine, should an English chief-justice keep Mark Twain's books always at hand? Why should Darwin have gone to them for rest and refreshment at midnight when spent with scientific research?

I suppose that Mark Twain transcends all other American humorists in the universal qualities. (*Century*, 1882, 781–82)

The novel's closing claim, in a separate sentence, "I been there before," sounds not in Twain's voice but in Huck's, stating for us as readers what we have also perceived, a shared world of American conflicts, evolving values, social problems, individual solutions, and cyclical endurance.

Appendix

Twain made four interesting decisions which are relatively distinct from the narrative compositional process. These decisions have less to do with the story but more to do with how the anticipated audience of subscription pruchasers would perceive the story. Yet these presentational decisions also affect the story's meaning.

I

On July 24, 1884, Twain jotted a note to Charles Webster, who was supervising the publication process:

> Dear Charley:
>   Can you alter the title page so as to say, "Time, forty to fifty years ago," instead of "Time, forty years ago." If the printing isn't begun, you can make the alteration, of course—so do it; but if it *has* begun, never mind, let it go.

On one level, it is obvious that this additional temporal distancing roughly corresponds to the extended time of composition (1875–1884). The casual attitude, "forty to fifty" and "but if it *has* begun, never mind, let it go," implies that Twain was nearing or had already reached a stage of psychological separation or decathexis from the work.

As it happens, the phrase "forty to fifty years ago" echoes phrasing he had used in *Life on the Mississippi* (1883) for the temporal placement of a relevant target, "the Sir Walter [Scott] disease." Twain explains, in Chapter 46, that it was Scott who "created rank and caste down there, and also reverence for rank and caste, and pride and pleasure in them. Enough is laid on slavery, without fathering upon it these creations and contributions of Sir Walter." His attack in *Life on the Mississippi* on the older and still current literary style—which he considers as anti-democratic as slavery—reveals his nationalistic concerns:

> One may observe, by one or two signs, how deeply that influence penetrated, and how strongly it holds. If one take[s] up a Northern or Southern

literary periodical of forty or fifty years ago, he will find it filled with wordy, windy, flowery "eloquence," romanticism, sentimentality—all imitated from Sir Walter, and sufficiently badly done, too—innocent travesties of his style and methods, in fact. This sort of literature being the fashion in both sections of the country, there was opportunity for the fairest competition; and as a consequence, the South was able to show as many well-known literary names, proportioned to population, as the North could.

But a change has come, and there is no opportunity now for a fair competition between North and South. For the North has thrown out that old inflated style, whereas the Southern writer still clings to it—clings to it and has a restricted market for his wares, as a consequence. There is as much literary talent in the South, now, as ever there was, of course; but its work can gain but slight currency under present conditions; the authors write for the past, not the present; they use obsolete forms, and a dead language. But when a Southerner of genius writes modern English, his book goes upon crutches no longer, but upon wings; and they carry it swiftly all about America and England, and through the great English reprint publishing houses of Germany—as witness the experience of Mr. Cable and Uncle Remus, two of the very few Southern writers who do not write in the southern style. Instead of three or four widely-known literary names, the South ought to have a dozen or two—and will have them when Sir Walter's time is out.

A curious exemplification of the power of a single book for good or harm is shown in the effects wrought by Don Quixote and those wrought by Ivanhoe. The first swept the world's admiration for the mediaeval chivalry-silliness out of existence; and the other restored it. As far as our South is concerned, the good work done by Cervantes is pretty nearly a dead letter, so effectually has Scott's pernicious work undermined it. (469–70)

Twain's decision to change *Huck*'s title page correlates with the satiric target, emphasized in this interpretation; moreover several issues, including the nationalistic emphasis and the concern with reprint publishing, are once more seen in close conjunction. The author who inserted the *Walter Scott* episode in *Huck* and who wrote of Tom Sawyer's escapades on the Phelps farm would probably be pleased if he could learn that American literature, both Northern and Southern, has now largely transcended "the Sir Walter disease."

II

Twain composed two prefatory squibs which assert, through humor, claims of artless entertainment and craftsmanlike authenticity. This claim is strategic because to deny meaning is to assert play rather than work, the nostalgia for childhood rather than the world of adulthood. The first surviving version of the NOTICE can be found in the Buffalo MS. A:

Persons attempting to find a Motive in this ⟨book⟩ *narrative* will be prosecuted. Persons attempting to find a Plot in ⟨this book⟩ *it* will be shot.*

Significantly, for the finished version Twain added a middle element, a
comment about "a moral"; in addition, the final version has the three
elements presented not as separate sentences, but as a unit, with three
parallel warnings.

NOTICE.

Persons attempting to find a motive in this narrative will be prosecuted;
persons attempting to find a moral in it will be banished; persons attempting
to find a plot in it will be shot.

BY ORDER OF THE AUTHOR
Per G. G., CHIEF OF ORDNANCE.

The book is posted, so to speak, as a section of land might be; a part of the
American literary landscape is reserved, absolved from the burden of meaning. The tone is peremptory, self-protective, and whimsical; we can enter
Twain's complex world only on his terms. Readers may also consider that
this notice also attempts to conceal the disturbing knowledge Twain discovered in the process of his writing.

To paraphrase, to attempt the dangerous act of decoding Twain:
Anyone who would understand the book partially and attribute its creation
only to a selfish competitive financial motive will receive Twain's favorite
solution, a lawsuit; or, anyone attempting to find a motive may end up in a
prison; anyone attempting to find a moral about European values controlling American values or about the recurrences of slavery and the difficulty of
freedom will be forced to leave the country, as Twain himself later would
be; anyone believing that the entire narrative structure only leads up to the
plot device of Tom being shot should receive the same punishment given to
that credulous, corrupted fool. Of course, this notice is given by the author
with the aid of an intermediary with a military title with religious origins.
Perhaps Twain's NOTICE is a self-protective bit of hermeneutic cryptogra-
phy.

III

The second prefatory notice is a bit more obviously meaningful:

EXPLANATORY.

In this book a number of dialects are used, to wit: the Missouri negro
dialect; the extremest form of the backwoods South-Western dialect; the

ordinary "Pike-County" dialect; and four modified varieties of this last. The shadings have not been done in a hap-hazard fashion, or by guess-work; but pains-takingly, and with the trustworthy guidance and support of personal familiarity with these several forms of speech.

I make this explanation for the reason that without it many readers would suppose that all these characters were trying to talk alike and not succeeding.

THE AUTHOR.

The first paragraph sounds like an introduction to a linguistic study and is, moreover, fairly accurate. As we have observed, an immense amount of time and effort went into numerous revisions which were primarily dialectal in nature. For example, the king's "can" Twain frequently changed to "k'n," and he often modified "help" to "he'p." Similarly, Twain usually shifted Jim's word "was" to "wuz" or "'uz" and evidently did not want his laborious efforts in this area to go unnoticed.

But Twain would not let the rather serious statement of the first paragraph stand alone. The second paragraph offers a masterful comic blend of elevated diction and wordy phrasing combined with self-deprecation by THE AUTHOR who knows that his audience could easily misunderstand and might mock an incompetent. The resulting authorial voice is helpful but self-critical, eager to be understood yet comic; the supreme authority is the author's personal familiarity, his experience. The combination of these two prefatory pieces is a fairly sophisticated beginning which, by denying any conventional starting point, attempts to create an immunity from criticism.

IV

Twain's well-known decision to drop the raftsmen episode, with all its local color, had several aesthetic effects. In this section Huck had overheard the men speaking "about what a king had to do, and how much he got," an obvious comedic announcement of a recurrent theme from a quite pragmatic, workmanlike point of view. The raftsmen episode also included a tall tale about a dead child's search for his murderous father, a story which inverts Huck's chance finding of his dead father on the river. In addition, Twain's agreement to delete the raftsmen portion took out a quite effective storm scene, another lynch threat, and another threat to paint a person. Moreover, two of Huck's aliases are dropped. Overall, this enjoyable episode certainly could have contributed aesthetically to the novel by repetition of incidents and motifs. The deletion is aesthetically regrettable, but other factors may have weighed more heavily on Twain's mind.

The decision to cut the raftsmen portion grew out of Twain's concern that the advertising material used by canvassers to sell *Huck* should not include writing he had already used in *Life on the Mississippi*. His letter to Charles Webster of April 14, 1884 closed:

> Be particular and don't get any of that *old* matter into your canvassing book—(the *raft* episode). (Hill, ed., *Letters to His Publishers*, 173)

A week later Webster's letter to Twain suggested dropping the raftsmen from the novel in order to bring *Huck*'s size closer to that of *Tom*, using the same phrasing Twain had used:

> the book is so *much* larger than Tom Sawyer would i[t] not be better to omit that old Mississippi matter? I think it would improve it. I have read it through & think it a *splendid* book. (*Huck*, 1988, 446)

If the decision was based solely on financial considerations, then a case could certainly be made for restoration. But perhaps the repeated phrasing "that old [Mississippi] matter" indicates that the issue in Twain's and Webster's minds centered on reprinting. Twain's active, combative mind could easily anticipate a hostile reviewer, perhaps with connections to a satirized reprint publisher, writing a snappy criticism of *Huck* along the lines of "Twain criticizes those who reprint, but nevertheless reprints himself for his own great profit."

Twain's reply, dated April 22, reveals his feeling of disconnection from the novel while indicating that he gave at least some consideration to the relation between the raftsmen episode and the remainder of the novel:

> Yes, I think the raft chapter can be left wholly out, by heaving in a paragraph to ⟨say that Huck visited the raft⟩ say Huck visited the raft to find out how far it might be to Cairo, but got no satisfaction. Even *this* is not necessary unless that raft-visit is referred to later in the book. I think it is, but am not certain. . . . (*Huck*, 1988, 446)

His cancellation and repetition in running sequence, with the minor change of dropping "that," indicates that his mind was ruminative, attentive, precise at the moment of his authorization of the cut. The decision seems regrettable in aesthetic terms, but understandable for financial or thematic reasons.

Bibliography of Works Consulted

Readers who wish a general introduction to Mark Twain will find the following books to be helpful. Dixon Wecter presented, in 1952, a widely read study of Clemens' boyhood, *Sam Clemens of Hannibal*, and this material is obviously in many ways the raw material of *Huck*. Justin Kaplan's prize-winning *Mr. Clemens and Mark Twain* picks up the biography at the age of thirty-one. Hamlin Hill's *Mark Twain: God's Fool* deserves special mention for the significant reevaluation of the writer's personality.

In 1885, James Frazer Gluck requested a manuscript from Mark Twain for the Young Men's Association Library in Buffalo, where Sam Clemens had once been a member. Although Gluck desired and expected the manuscript of *Life on the Mississippi*, Twain sent, in two separate packages, the manuscript of *Huck*. The first 665 pages were lost but recently were rediscovered. The known portion of the manuscript has received careful, respectful attention from DeLancey Ferguson in his 1938 essay, "Huck Finn Aborning," and in his 1943 book, *Mark Twain, Man and Legend*. In 1942, Bernard DeVoto explored the then known manuscript in *Mark Twain At Work* in the chapter "Noon and Dark: *Huckleberry Finn*." Walter Blair's definitive 1958 essay, "When Was *Huckleberry Finn* Written?" and his 1960 book, *Mark Twain and Huck Finn* remain very useful. Similarly, in 1959 Sydney J. Krause's "Twain's Method and Theory of Composition" presented an accurate interpretation, using a tabular format. Henry Nash Smith's 1958 edition reprints revision information from manuscript, galley proof, and lecture script sources, with interpretation.

Any list of the most helpful book-length interpretations of Twain's writing would have to include Henry Nash Smith's *Mark Twain: The Development of a Writer*, and James M. Cox's *Mark Twain: The Fate of Humor*. Forrest Robinson's recent *In Bad Faith* deals subtly and trenchantly with *Tom Sawyer*, *Huck*, and some other works.

Book-length treatments of *Huck* include Blair's valuable study, George C. Carrington's ground-breaking *The Dramatic Unity of Huckleberry Finn*, and Michael Egan's *Mark Twain's Huckleberry Finn: Race, Class and Society*. Harold Beaver's *Huckleberry Finn* and David E. E. Sloane's *Adventures of Huckleberry Finn: American Comic Vision* each provide intelligent and stimulating interpretations.

The most comprehensive bibliography about Sam Clemens/Mark Twain and about *Adventures of Huckleberry Finn* must be Thomas Asa Tenney's *Mark Twain: A Reference Guide*. Other valuable bibliographies are available in Blair's book, *Mark Twain and Huck Finn*, in numerous casebooks, in the Spring 1968 special issue of *Modern Fiction Studies*, and in *One Hundred Years of Huckleberry Finn: The Book, His*

Book, and American Culture, a volume edited by Robert Sattelmeyer and J. Donald Crowley to celebrate the novel's centennial. Yearly additional bibliographies may be found in *American Literary Realism, American Literary Scholarship*, and *The Mark Twain Circular*. Journals frequently devote sections or special issues to Twain, such as the recent *South Central Review* for the Winter of 1988.

The following books, documents, and essays have been most helpful in developing this study.

The American Catalogue Founded by F. Leypoldt 1876–1884. New York: Bowker, 1885.
Armstrong, Paul B. "The Conflict of Interpretation and the Limits of Pluralism." *PMLA* 98:3 (1983): 341–52.
Ayers, Edward L. *Vengeance and Justice: Crime and Punishment in the 19th-Century American South*. New York: Oxford University Press, 1984.
Baetzhold, Howard. *Mark Twain and John Bull: The British Connection*. Bloomington: Indiana University Press, 1970.
Baldanza, Frank. *Mark Twain: An Introduction and Interpretation*. New York: Barnes and Noble, 1961.
———. "The Structure of *Huckleberry Finn*." *American Literature* 27(1955): 347–55.
Beaver, Harold. *Huckleberry Finn*. London: Allen and Unwin, 1987.
Berkove, Lawrence I. "The Poor Players of *Huckleberry Finn*." *Papers of the Michigan Academy of Science, Arts, and Letters* 53(1968): 291–310.
———. 'The Free Man of Color' in *The Grandissemes* and Works by Harris and Mark Twain," *Southern Quarterly* 18, 4 (summer 1980): 60–73.
Blair, Walter. *Mark Twain and Huck Finn*. 1960. Berkeley: University of California Press, 1962.
———. *Native American Humor*. 1937. San Francisco: Chandler, 1960.
———. "When was *Huckleberry Finn* Written?" *American Literature* 30 (1958): 1–25.
Blair, Walter, and Hamlin Hill. *American Humor: From Poor Richard to Doonesbury*. New York: Oxford, 1978.
Blake, W.O. *The History of Slavery and the Slave Trade*. Columbus, Ohio: Miller, 1857.
Blakemore, Steven. "Huck Finn's Written Word." *American Literary Realism* 20, 2 (Winter, 1988): 21–29.
Branch, Edgar Marquess. *The Literary Apprenticeship of Mark Twain*. New York: Russell, 1966.
Brown, Richard D. and Stephen G. Rabe, eds. *Slavery in American Society*. Lexington, MA: D. C. Heath, 1976.
Bunyan, John. *The Works of John Bunyan*. 2 vol. Philadelphia: Clarke, 1836.
Cable Bikle, Lucy Leffingwell, ed. *George W. Cable: His Life and Letters*. New York: Russell, 1967.
Cardwell, Guy A. *Twins of Genius*. East Lansing: Michigan State College Press, 1953.
Carkeet, David. "The Dialects in *Huckleberry Finn*." *American Literature* 51 (1979): 315–32.
Carrington, George C. *The Dramatic Unity of Huckleberry Finn*. Columbus: Ohio State University Press, 1976.
Cassara, Ernest. *Universalism in America: A Documentary History*. Boston: Beacon, 1971.

Cipolla, Carlo. *Literacy and Development in the West*. Baltimore: Johns Hopkins University Press, 1969.

Clemens, Susy. *Papa: An Intimate Biography of Mark Twain*. Charles Neider, Ed. Garden City, NY: Doubleday, 1985.

Covici, Pascal. *Mark Twain's Humor: The Image of a World*. Dallas, TX: Southern Methodist University Press, 1962.

Cox, James M. *Mark Twain: The Fate of Humor*. Princeton, NJ: Princeton University Press, 1966.

Cummings, Sherwood. *Mark Twain and Science: Adventures of a Mind*. Baton Rouge: Louisiana University Press, 1989.

DeVoto, Bernard. *Mark Twain's America*. Boston: Little, Brown, 1932.

———. *Mark Twain at Work*. Cambridge, MA: Harvard University Press, 1942.

Dodge, Colonel Richard I. *Thirty Three Years Among Our Wild Indians*. Intro. General William T. Sherman. Hartford, CN: Worthington, 1882.

Egan, Michael. *Mark Twain's Huckleberry Finn: Race, Class and Society*. London: Published for Sussex University Press by Chatto, 1977.

Eliot, T. S., ed. *The Adventures of Huckleberry Finn*. London: Cresset, 1950.

Ensor, Allison. "The Contributions of Charles Webster and Albert Bigelow Paine to *Huckleberry Finn*." *American Literature* 40 (May, 1968): 222–27.

Faux, William. *Memorable Days in America Being a Journal of a Tour to The United States*. London: Simpkin and Marshall, 1823.

Feinstein, Herbert. "Mark Twain's Lawsuits." Dissertation, University of California, Berkeley, 1968.

Ferguson, DeLancey. "Huck Finn Aborning." *Colophon* n.s.3 (Spring, 1938): 171–80.

———. *Mark Twain, Man and Legend*. Indianapolis: Bobbs-Merrill, 1943.

Fiedler, Leslie. "Come Back to the Raft Ag'in, Huck Honey!" *Partisan Review* 15 (June, 1948): 664–71.

Fischer, Victor. "Huck Finn Reviewed: The Reception of *Huckleberry Finn* in the United States, 1885–1897." *American Literary Realism, 1870–1910* 16 (Spring 1983): 1–57.

Foner, Eric. *A Short History of Reconstruction*. New York: Harper and Row, 1990.

Fuller, Horace W. *Noted French Trials: Impostors and Adventurers*. Boston: Soule and Bugbee, 1882.

Genovese, Eugene D. *The Political Economy of Slavery*. New York: Vintage, 1967.

Gerber, John C. "Practical Editions: Mark Twain's *The Adventures of Tom Sawyer* and *Adventures of Huckleberry Finn*." *Proof* 2 (1972): 285–92.

Gollin, Richard and Rita Gollin. "*Huckleberry Finn* and the Time of the Evasion." *Modern Language Studies* 9 (1979):5–15.

Goody, Jack, ed. *Literacy in Traditional Societies*. Cambridge: Cambridge University Press, 1968.

Government Publication. *1776 Bicentennial Issue 1976 Pocket Data Book, USA 1976*. Washington: U.S. Bureau of the Census, 1976.

———. Congressional Testimony. 50th Congress, First Session, Report 622, 622A.

———. *Historical Statistics of the United States: Colonial Times to 1970*. Washington: U.S. Government Printing Office, 1975.

Gribben, Alan. *Mark Twain's Library: A Reconstruction*. 2 vols. Boston: Hall, 1980.

Harris, Susan K. *Mark Twain's Escape from Time*. Columbia: University of Missouri Press, 1982.

Heath, William. "Tears and Flapdoodle: Sentimentality in *Huckleberry Finn*." *South Carolina Review* 19 (1986, Fall): 60–79.

Hemingway, Ernest. *The Green Hills of Africa*. New York: Scribners, 1935.

Hill, Hamlin. *Mark Twain: God's Fool*. New York: Harper, 1973.

———, ed. *Mark Twain's Letters to His Publishers 1867–1894*. Berkeley: University of California Press, 1967.

Holland, Laurence B. "A 'Raft of Trouble': Word and Deed in *Huckleberry Finn*." *Glyph 5* (1979): 69–87.

Howells, William Dean. *My Mark Twain*. 1910. Baton Rouge: Louisiana State University Press, 1967.

Hudon, Edward G. "Mark Twain and the Copyright Dilemma." *American Bar Association Journal* 52 (1966): 56–60.

Jensen, Franklin L. *Mark Twain's Comments on Books and Authors*. Emporia, KA: Emporia State Research Studies, 1964. XII, 4.

Kaplan, Justin. *Mr. Clemens and Mark Twain*. New York: Simon and Schuster, 1966.

Kohlberg, Lawrence. "Moral Stages and Moralization: The Cognitive-Developmental Approach." in *Moral Development and Behavior*. Ed. Thomas Lickona. New York: Holt, 1976.

———. "The Cognitive-Developmental Approach to Moral Education." *Phi Delta Kappan* (June 1975): 670–78. See also reply by Richard S. Peters, 679.

Kohlberg, Lawrence, and Donald Elfenbein. "Development of Moral Reasoning and Attitudes Toward Capital Punishment." *American Journal of Orthopsychiatry* (Summer 1975).

Krause, Sydney J. "Twain's Method and Theory of Composition." *Modern Philology* 56 (1959): 167–77.

Lecky, W. E. H. *History of the Rise and Influence of the Spirit of Rationalism*. 2 vols. The Quarry Farm copy was originally owned by Susan Crane and has Twain's marginal annotations in Vol I.

Lynn, Kenneth. *Mark Twain and Southwestern Humor*. Boston: Little, Brown, 1959.

McKay, Janet Holmgren. "'Tears and Flapdoodle': Point of View and Style in *The Adventures of Huckleberry Finn*." *Style* 10 (1976): 41–50.

Marx, Leo. "Mr. Eliot, Mr. Trilling, and *Huckleberry Finn*." *American Scholar* 22(1953): 423–40.

Miller, J. Hillis. "Three Problems of Fictional Form: First-Person Narrative in *David Copperfield* and *Huckleberry Finn*." In *Experience in the Novel*. Ed. Roy Harvey Pearce. New York: Columbia University Press, 1968, 21–48.

Mitchell, Lee Clark. "'De Nigger in you': Race or Training in *Pudd'nhead Wilson*." *Nineteenth Century Literature* 42 (1987): 295–312.

Murphy, Kevin. "Illiterate's Progress: The Descent into Literacy in *Huckleberry Finn*." *Texas Studies in Language and Literature* 26, 363–87.

Novak, Daniel A. *The Wheel of Servitude: Black Forced Labor After Slavery*. Lexington: University of Kentucky Press, 1978.

Paine, Albert Bigelow. *Mark Twain: A Biography, The Personal and Literary Life of Samuel Langhorne Clemens*. 3 vols. New York: Harper, 1912.

Parker, Hershel. *Flawed Texts and Verbal Icons*. Evanston, IL: Northwestern University Press, 1984.

Pettit, Arthur G. *Mark Twain and the South*. Lexington: University of Kentucky Press, 1973.

Phillips, Ulrich Bonnell. *American Negro Slavery*. Gloucester, MA: Peter Smith, 1979.

Poirier, Richard. *A World Elsewhere: The Place of Style in American Literature*. New York: Oxford University Press, 1966. Esp. Chapter IV, 144–207.

Powell, J. C. *The American Siberia*. Gainesville: University of Florida Press, 1976. This book was originally printed by H. J. Smith and Co. in 1891.

Quirk, Tom. "'Learning a Nigger to Argue': Quitting *Huckleberry Finn*." *American Literary Realism* 20, 1 (Fall 1987) 18–33.

———. "Nobility out of Tatters: The Writing of *Huckleberry Finn*." In *Writing the American Classics*. Ed. James Barbour and Tom Quirk. Chapel Hill: University of North Carolina Press, 1990.

R, B. J. "Features of American Slavery." *Sewanee Review* (1893): 474–90.

Rawick, George P., ed. *The American Slave: A Composite Autobiography*. 19 vols. Westport, CT: Greenwood Press, 1972–1979.

Reichert, John. *Making Sense of Literature*. Chicago: University of Chicago Press, 1977. Esp. 191–203.

Robinson, Forrest G. *In Bad Faith: The Dynamics of Deception in Mark Twain's America*. Cambridge, MA: Harvard University Press, 1986.

———. "The Characterization of Jim in *Huckleberry Finn*." *Nineteenth Century Literature* 43: 361–91.

Rogers, Franklin R. *Mark Twain's Burlesque Patterns*. Dallas, TX: Southern Methodist University Press, 1960.

———. *Occidental Ideographs: Image, Sequence, and Literary History*. Lewisburg, PA: Bucknell University Press, forthcoming.

Roper, Gordon. "Mark Twain and His Canadian Publishers." *American Book Collector* X (June 1960): 13–29.

Rose, Willie Lee. *Slavery and Freedom*. Ed. William W. Freehling. New York: Oxford University Press, 1982.

Rourke, Constance. *Native American Humor*. New York: Harcourt, 1931.

Rozwenc, Edwin L. ed. *Reconstruction in the South*. Lexington, MA: D. C. Heath, 1972.

Rubin, Jr., Louis D. *George W. Cable: The Life and Times of a Southern Heretic*. New York: Western, Pegasus Series, 1969.

Salsbury, Edith Colgate, ed. *Susy and Mark Twain: Family Dialogue*. New York: Harper, 1965.

Sattelmeyer, Robert and J. Donald Crowley, eds. *One Hundred Years of Huckleberry Finn: The Boy, His Book, and American Culture*. Columbia: University of Missouri Press, 1985.

Schmitz, Neil. *Of Huck and Alice*. Minneapolis: University of Minnesota Press, 1983.

———. "The Paradox of Liberation in *Huckleberry Finn*." *Texas Studies in Language and Literature* 13 (1971): 125–36.

———. "Twain, *Huckleberry Finn* and the Reconstruction." *American Studies* 12 (1971): 59–67.

Scott, Arthur L. "*The Century Magazine* Edits *Huckleberry Finn*, 1884–1885." *American Literature* 17 (November 1955): 356–62.

Sewell, David R. *Mark Twain's Languages: Discourse, Dialogue and Linguistic Variety*. Berkeley: University of California Press, 1987.

Shaler, Norman S. "The Negro Problem." *Atlantic* 54 (November, 1884): 696–709.

Sloane, David E. E. *Adventures of Huckleberry Finn: American Comic Vision*. Boston: Twayne, 1988.

———. *Mark Twain as Literary Comedian*. Baton Rouge: Louisiana State University Press, 1979.

Smith, Henry Nash. *Democracy and the Novel: Popular Resistance to Classic American Writers*. New York: Oxford University Press, 1978.

———. *Mark Twain: The Development of a Writer*. Cambridge, MA: Harvard University Press, 1962.

———, ed. *Mark Twain: A Collection of Critical Essays*. Englewood Cliffs, NJ: Prentice-Hall, 1963.

Spengemann, William L. *Mark Twain and the Backwoods Angel: The Matter of Innocence in the Works of Samuel L. Clemens*. Kent, OH: Kent State University Press, 1966.

South Central Review: The Journal of the South Central Modern Language Association (Special Editor James D. Wilson). 5 (Winter 1988).

Still, William. *The Underground Rail Road. A Record of Facts, Authentic Narratives, Letters, etc., Narrating the Hardships, Hair-breadth Escapes and Death Struggles of the Slaves in their efforts for Freedom*. Philadelphia: William Still, 1883.

Tanner, Tony. *The Reign of Wonder: Naivety and Reality in American Literature*. Cambridge: Cambridge University Press, 1965.

Tanselle, G. Thomas. *A Rationale of Textual Criticism*. Philadelphia: University of Pennsylvania Press, 1989.

———. *Selected Studies in Bibliography*. Charlottesville: University Press of Virginia, 1979.

———. *Textual Criticism Since Greg: A Chronicle 1950–1985*. Charlottesville: University Press of Virginia, 1987.

Tenney, Thomas Asa. *Mark Twain: A Reference Guide*. Boston: Hall, 1977.

Thomas, Brook. *Cross-examinations of Law and Literature: Cooper, Hawthorne, Stowe, and Melville*. Cambridge: Cambridge University Press, 1987.

Trilling, Lionel, ed. *The Adventures of Huckleberry Finn*. New York: Rinehart, 1948.

Tourgee, Albion W. *A Fool's Errand and The Invisible Empire*. New York: Fords, Howard, and Hulbert, 1880.

Turner, Arlin. *Mark Twain and George W. Cable: The Record of a Literary Friendship*. East Lansing: Michigan State University Press, 1960.

Twain, Mark. *A Connecticut Yankee in King Arthur's Court*. New York: Webster, 1889.

———. "Adventures of Huckleberry Finn." This manuscript is in the Buffalo and Erie County Library, Buffalo, NY. It is also available on microfilm.

———. *Adventures of Huckleberry Finn: A Facsimile of the Manuscript*. Intro. Louis

Budd. Afterword William H. Loos. 2 vols. Detroit: Bruccoli Clark, Gale, 1983. This set offers a photo-facsimile of the manuscript.

———. *Adventures of Huckleberry Finn*. New York: Charles L. Webster and Co., 1885.

———. *The Art of Huckleberry Finn*. Ed. Hamlin Hill and Walter Blair. San Francisco: Chandler, 1962. This volume offers a photo-facsimile of the first American edition.

———. *Adventures of Huckleberry Finn*. The Works of Mark Twain. Vol 8. Ed. Walter Blair and Victor Fischer. Berkeley: University of California Press, 1988.

———. *Adventures of Huckleberry Finn*. Ed. Henry Nash Smith. Boston: Houghton, 1958.

———. *Huck Finn and Tom Sawyer Among the Indians and Other Unfinished Stories*. Berkeley: University of California Press, Mark Twain Project, 1988.

———. *Life on the Mississippi*. Boston: Osgood, 1883.

———. *Mark Twain Speaking*. Ed. Paul Fatout. Iowa City: University of Iowa Press, 1976.

———. *Mark Twain's Hannibal, Huck and Tom*. Ed. Walter Blair. The Mark Twain Papers. Berkeley: University of California Press, 1969.

———. *Mark Twain's Letters, 1853–1866*. Ed. Edgar Marquess Branch, Michael B. Frank, Kenneth M. Sanderson. The Mark Twain Papers, under the General Editorship of Robert H. Hirst. Berkeley: University of California Press, 1988.

———. *Mark Twain's Notebooks and Journals*. Ed. F. Anderson, 3 vols. Berkeley, CA: University of California Press.

———. The Mark Twain Papers in the Bancroft Library of the University of California at Berkeley, under the curatorship of Robert H. Hirst, contains primary and secondary research materials of immense importance to scholars.

———. *Mark Twain's Sketches, New and Old*. Hartford, CT: American Publishing, 1887. Originally published in 1875.

———. *Pudd'nhead Wilson and Those Extraordinary Twins*. New York: Harper, 1906.

———. "A Record of Small Foolishnesses of Susy and 'Bay' Clemens (Infants)." Unpublished journal. University of Virginia Collection.

———. Reply on Methods of Composition in *The Art of Authorship*. Ed. George Bainton. New York: Appleton, 1890: 85–88.

———. *The Stolen White Elephant*. Boston: Osgood, 1882.

Twain, Mark and William Dean Howells. *Mark Twain-Howells Letters: The Correspondence of Samuel L. Clemens and William D. Howells, 1872–1910*. Ed. Henry Nash Smith and William M. Gibson, with the assistance of Frederick Anderson. 2 vols. Cambridge, MA: Harvard University Press, 1960.

Vogelback, Arthur L. "The Publication and Reception of *Huckleberry Finn* in America." *American Literature* 11 (November 1939): 260–72.

von Frank, Albert J. "Huck Finn and the Flight from Maturity." *Studies in American Fiction* 7: 1–15.

Wecter, Dixon. *Sam Clemens of Hannibal*. Boston: Houghton, 1952.

Wexman, Virginia. "The Role of Structure in *Tom Sawyer* and *Huckleberry Finn*." *American Literary Realism* 6 (1973): 1–11.

Index

This book has been set in Linotron Galliard. Galliard was designed for Mergenthaler in 1978 by Matthew Carter. Galliard retains many of the features of a sixteenth century typeface cut by Robert Granjon but has some modifications which gives it a more contemporary look.

Printed on acid-free paper.